HIGH

STORIES OF SURVIVAL
FROM EVEREST AND K2

H I G H

STORIES OF SURVIVAL FROM EVEREST AND K2

EDITED BY CLINT WILLIS

(adrenaline)

**Balliett & Fitzgerald Inc./
Thunder's Mouth Press**

New York

First Edition

Compilation copyright © 1999 by Clint Willis
Introductions copyright © 1999 by Clint Willis

An Adrenaline Book

Published by
Balliett & Fitzgerald Inc.
66 West Broadway, Suite 602
New York, NY 10007
and
Thunder's Mouth Press
841 Broadway, 4th Floor
New York, NY 10003

Book design: Sue Canavan

frontispiece photo: North Face of Everest from the Rongbuk base
camp © Ed Webster

Manufactured in the United States of America

ISBN: 1-56025-200-6

Library of Congress Cataloging-in-Publication Data

High : stories of survival from Everest and K2 / edited by Clint Willis.
     p.   cm. -- (Extreme adventure)
   ISBN 1-56025-200-6
    1. Mountaineering expeditions—Everest, Mount (Nepal and China)
  2. Mountaineering accidents—Everest, Mount (Nepal and China)
  3. Mountaineering expeditions—Pakistan—K2 (Mountain)
  4. Mountaineering accidents—Pakistan—K2 (Mountain)   I. Willis,
Clint.   II. Title: Stories of Survival from Everest and K2.
III. Series.
GV199.44.E85H54   1999
796.52'2'0954914—dc21   98-44857
                                                  CIP

For
Harold Brodkey, who loved the Catskills

and

Neill Jeffrey, who loved the Blue Ridge

c o n t e n t s

p h o t o g r a p h s

introduction

Everest and K2 serve many purposes these days. Advertisers invoke their names to evoke danger, hardship, courage, size, difficulty, ambition, whatever. Journalists have tried to transform the two mountains into celebrities. Travel companies have tried to reduce them to tourist destinations. Climbers have used both mountains as garbage dumps, and exploited them to build resumes and reputations. The list of first Everest ascents is seemingly endless—from first Australian ascent to first ascent by a Japanese woman over forty. We've done our best to make these mountains boring.

It won't work.

The writers whose work is anthologized here have been to the mountains and brought back the truth, which in reality is never boring. Matt Dickinson tells us what it's like for an amateur to climb a swaying aluminum ladder high on Everest's North Col route; we understand something of his fear. Jim Haberl waits for the sunrise over China to slow the wind from the summit of K2 and warm his extremities; we are convinced he is cold. Chris Bonington watches through a telescope as his friends Peter Boardman and Joe Tasker creep along Everest's Northeast Ridge in 1982; we see them, as he does, for the last time. Doug Scott with his mate Dougal Haston summits Everest after climbing the horrendously difficult Southwest Face, and later writes of the moment: *All the world lay before us*—and it lies before us, too.

Like other titles in the Adrenaline Books series, this one includes only work that can stand on its merit as prose. The collection spans the years 1933 to 1996, but doesn't try to offer a coherent history of climbing on the two mountains. A scheme to arrange the selections in chronological order and include writing about all the most historically significant (whatever that pretends to mean) expeditions broke down. I threw out anything that was even slightly tedious and arranged what remained on the same deeply serious principal: Make it fun to read. If you want history, try Walt Unsworth's fat and meticulous *Everest* (1989) and Jim Curran's less comprehensive *K2: The Savage Mountain* (1995).

That said, it might help the reader of this anthology to know something of what men and women have undertaken on each mountain. Everest's history for our purposes begins on the north side of the mountain, in Tibet. (Nepal, which encompasses Everest's south side, was closed to foreigners until 1949.) The 1921 British reconnaissance saw George Leigh Mallory and Guy Henry Bullock discover an approach to the North Col, the key to early attempts on the peak. The British returned to the north side in 1922, when seven Sherpas were killed in an avalanche, and again in 1924. The third trip saw two more deaths, of Englishmen this time: Mallory and Andrew Irvine disappeared on a summit attempt after being sighted at 8,500 meters on Everest's Northeast Ridge.

The thirties saw four more British expeditions, including the 1933 attempt chronicled in Frank Smythe's *Camp Six*. Smythe describes his shot at the summit, beginning on page 259 of this collection. World War II put a stop to further efforts on Everest, and Tibet closed its borders in 1950. Fortunately, Nepal opened to visitors the same year. That made possible a series of expeditions to the mountain's south side, which presented its own formidable obstacles. The British made two attempts from the south at the start of the fifties, finding a way through the difficult and dangerous Khumbu icefall. Then the Swiss had a couple of cracks at the mountain in 1952—and very nearly got up it. The following year New Zealander Edmund Hillary and Sherpa Tenzing Norgay climbed the mountain by the now-standard South Col route as part of a British expedition.

The decade after Hillary and Tenzing topped out on Everest saw a half-dozen attempts by parties from various countries, including a successful expedition by the Swiss in 1956. They followed the British route, which still seemed challenging enough even to the world's elite climbers. But that elite soon began to look for harder ways up the peak.

The 1963 American expedition included the first traverse of Everest (by Willi Unsoeld and Tom Hornbein). By the late sixties climbers had their eyes on the Southwest Face, which rejected a flurry of attempts before succumbing to the Second British Southwest Face Expedition in 1975. The expedition, led by climbing impresario Chris Bonington, put two of the era's famous hardmen on the summit. Doug Scott and Dougal Haston described their climb and its aftermath in Bonington's 1976 book, *Everest the Hard Way* (page 61). The next year the Joint British and Royal Nepalese Army Expedition climbed the mountain via the South Col route. British climber Brummie Stokes had to spend a night in the open on his descent from the summit; his description of the consequences starts on page 253.

The crowds at base camp thickened in the late seventies. Italian Tyrolean Reinhold Messner and Austrian Peter Habeler made the most significant ascent of that period, climbing the South Col route without oxygen in 1978. Their feat stunned the mountaineering community. More important, the climb eliminated the perception that bottled oxygen—and huge teams of climbers and porters to carry it—were crucial to success on the world's highest mountains. The eventual result was a new age of relatively lightweight, "alpine-style" expeditions in the Himalaya. Messner in 1980 became the first person to climb the entire mountain alone; taking a route on the North side, he made that climb without oxygen, too.

Climbers continued to try still harder routes on the peak. The lightweight 1982 British Northeast Ridge Expedition ended when Peter Boardman and Joe Tasker failed to return from their summit attempt. Chris Bonington led that expedition as well (page 105). The following year, Boardman's widow, Hilary, and Tasker's girlfriend, Maria Coffey, visited the mountain (page 127). Meanwhile the 1982 Canadian Everest Expedition gave up its attempt on the South Pillar after three Sherpas and a cameraman were killed in the icefall. Six climbers quit, and those remaining changed their objective to the South Col route. Alan Burgess wrote of the team's response to the tragedy in *Everest Canada: The Ultimate Challenge* (page 117). A 1988 expedition made an alpine-style ascent of the fearsome Eastern, or Kangshung, Face. Even purist Reinhold Messner praised the climb for its impeccable style—no oxygen or Sherpas were used on the difficult and dangerous route. Ed Webster's forthcoming book, *Snow in the Kingdom: My Storm Years on Everest*, includes an account of the expedition (page 229).

The era of guided climbs on Everest was ushered in by the 1983 American South Col Expedition. Amateur adventurers Dick Bass and Frank Wells, as part of their effort to climb the "Seven Summits" (the highest peak on each continent), hired experienced high-altitude climbers to help them get up Everest. They failed, but Bass returned to summit in 1985 at age 55. Hundreds of climbers, many of them guided amateurs, had reached the top of Everest by the spring of 1996, when 11 climbers died on the mountain, including three guides and two clients from a pair of commercial expeditions. Filmmaker and amateur climber Matt Dickinson, attempting the peak from the north, just missed the storm that killed eight of the season's victims; still, his account (page 11) of going for the top helps to show how hard Everest is to climb under the best of conditions. Jon Krakauer's best-selling book about the 1996 disaster, *Into Thin Air*, helped fuel a surge of public interest in climbing and Everest. It probably attracted more climbers to the mountain than it deterred. Expeditions, many of them run by commercial guides for clients with varying degrees of experience, continue to throng Everest's slopes.

While Everest was largely a British mountain before its first ascent, K2 seemed to belong to American climbers during the middle years of this century. British, Italian and other European travelers had explored the region around K2, located in northern Pakistan near the center of the Karakoram Range. Luigi Amedeo di Savoia, duke of the Abruzzi, made the most notable early attempt on the mountain. His 1909 expedition reached a height of 6,250 meters on what eventually proved to be the scene of most future K2 climbs, the Southeast Ridge—now known as the Abruzzi Ridge.

The next serious attempt on the peak came in 1938, when an American expedition led by Charles Houston put up seven camps on the Abruzzi before turning back at 7,925 meters. Houston's book about the trip, written with Robert Bates, offers a textbook example of a happy expedition; a chapter from *Five Miles High* starts on page 147. The following year, German-born Fritz Wiessner led a second American attempt on the ridge, nearly reaching the mountain's summit; then poor communications led to a series of mistakes that ended with the deaths of three Sherpas and an American. David Roberts' essay about Wiessner and his ill-fated expedition begins on page 293. Houston led another team to the peak in 1953, but a team member's illness forced a harrowing retreat. Bates' description of the epic descent (page 279), is from a second book he and Houston wrote togther. And that was it for the Americans' determined bid to be first on top of K2: The following year, an Italian party made the ascent. Walter Bonatti, one of Italy's great mountaineers, made a crucial contribution to the success of the party as its youngest member. His account of his efforts (page 83) comes from his book *On the Heights*.

The Italians' 1954 ascent of K2 was followed by a single 1960 attempt—and then nothing for fifteen years. In 1961 the Pakistanis closed the Central Karakoram, which included K2, to expeditions. Among their reasons was friction with neighboring India. Eventually, political tensions eased, and in 1975 the Americans again tried the mountain. That trip, led by Jim Whittaker (who in 1963 had become the first American to summit Everest), reached only 6,700 meters on a new route and was plagued by conflict between team members. Galen Rowell's *In the Throne Room of the Mountain Gods* (page 163) was among the first tell-all expedition accounts. The second ascent of K2 did not come until 1977, when one Pakistani and six Japanese climbers reached the top as part of a fifty-two-member expedition that employed 1,500 porters. The Americans finally climbed the mountain in 1978, with four members reaching the summit. One of them was Rick Ridgeway, who tells how the four fared in their struggle to descend (page 187).

Reinhold Messner made K2's fourth ascent the following year, and by the start of 1986 ten expeditions had reached the summit. That summer another nine expeditions attempted the mountain, getting twenty-seven climbers to the top. Many of them failed to return, however: K2 claimed thirteen lives that season in a series of tragedies Jon

Krakauer and Greg Child recounted in a 1987 *Outside* article. Their article was the basis for Krakauer's piece on page 215.

Since then, more climbers have stood on K2's summit, and more have died on the mountain—most famously England's Alison Hargreaves. She lost her life in a 1995 storm that presaged the 1996 Everest disaster. Jim Haberl's account of climbing K2 with fellow Canadian Dan Culver in 1993 offers a glimpse at the motives of some modern high-altitude climbers and the risks they confront (page 45).

Once, mountaineers were asked why they climbed. Today they more often are asked who was to blame for the latest casualty or disaster on a famous mountain. Did commercial guides like Rob Hall and Scott Fischer overextend themselves and their clients on Everest in 1996? Were their clients foolish to try the mountain at all? Alison Hargreaves climbed higher on a day when weather conditions seemed iffy to some other climbers on K2. Was she selfish to risk leaving her children motherless? Much recent writing about climbing—and there has been a lot of it—is by journalists or climbers concerned with assigning or fending off blame.

It makes sense to bear witness and to analyze events; to hunt for mistakes so that we can try to avoid repeating them. And there are times when seeking to lay blame is part of seeking the truth. But some of the public charges and countercharges seem to carry two assumptions. One: It's possible to do everything right in the mountains. Two: If you do everything right, no one will get hurt.

But even the best, most conservative climbers make mistakes. And big mountains like Everest and K2 would be dangerous even if climbers were perfect. Sometimes, the biggest mistake is going there.

Those of us who choose not to accept that set of conditions don't visit the Death Zone. We go to the Tetons or the White Mountains or we take the kids to the rock gym. We manage base camp. We stay low. We read the stories. When the stories are good, it's enough—or almost.

—Clint Willis

from The Other Side of Everest
by Matt Dickinson

Matt Dickinson went to Everest in 1996 to film a British expedition on the North side of the mountain. Dickinson, who had almost no climbing experience, eventually set out for the top with professional mountaineer and guide Alan Hinkes and three Sherpas. The five men climbed soon after the storm that Jon Krakauer described in his 1997 book Into Thin Air. *Dickinson's account shows how alone every climber is in the Death Zone.*

Sunset must have been an incredible sight, but all I saw of it was a glimmer of red light reflected in the metal of an oxygen cylinder outside the tent. I was determined to conserve every single scrap of energy and getting out of the tent to take a still photograph was not a priority no matter how splendid it was.

Our main discussion was about the oxygen. With three members of our own team now definitely out of the equation, there was the possibility that we could take an extra cylinder each for the summit push. The pro was that we would be able to set the cylinders on a higher flow with the obvious advantages that would bring. The con was the weight, an extra six kilogrammes—a very serious consideration given the physical demands of what lay ahead. We talked round the issues and decided we would postpone a decision until we packed to leave in a few hours time. (In fact when it came to it Al decided he would take an extra cylinder and I decided against it.)

By 8 p.m., we were into the third round of melting snow, when footsteps approached from outside. A figure crouched down at the entrance to the tent, red-eyed and desperate. It was the Hungarian climber who, with Reinhard Wlasich, the Austrian, had been attempting the North Face without oxygen.

His first words were in French but when he saw our blank faces he changed to English.

'I need some . . . have you a way to help . . . some oxygen and some gas . . . please.' His speech was slurred and barely understandable. He sounded like he was suffering from the onset of high-altitude sickness.

'Take it easy and calm down a bit. Now what's the problem?' Al made some space for him to kneel in the front of the tent.

'My friend is dying. I want you to try and help me rescue him. We're in that tent over there.' He pointed out into the night.

'You're talking about Reinhard?'

'Yes. Reinhard. He's dying. If we don't get him down the mountain he'll be dead. You have to help me.'

'What about the Norwegian doctor—Morton. Has he seen him?'

'He did. This afternoon.'

'And what did he say?'

'He has oedema—on the lungs and cerebral.'

'Is he conscious?'

'He's in a coma.'

'Well, if he's in a coma he *is* going to die. There's no way anyone can get him off the mountain. Have you got oxygen?'

'It's finished. Can I take a bottle?'

'You can take as much as you need. Have you got a regulator?'

'Yes. But if we go now we can rescue him.'

'How?' Al was icy calm.

'I don't know. We can carry him. I have to do something!' The Hungarian was distraught, and beginning to vent his frustration as anger on us.

'There's nothing we can do. No matter how many people we had up here, we still couldn't get him down to five. Think about the rocks, how are you going to lower him down?'

The Hungarian went quiet. In his heart he knew that Al was right. Even if Reinhard had been conscious, a rescue would have been impossible. The fact that he was in a coma was as good as a death sentence here at 8,300 metres.

'How much longer do you think he will live?'

'I don't know. He's hardly breathing.'

Al and I exchanged a glance. The same thought occurred to both of us at the same time: the Hungarian, determined to stay with his fellow climber right to the bitter end, was even now putting his own life in danger.

'Listen. Your friend is definitely going to die. You have to get off the mountain or you'll die too. Do you understand?' Al was speaking forcefully now, driving the news as hard as he could into the Hungarian's confused mind. He went quiet once more as this sank in.

'You'll be dead by tomorrow night if you stay here. So take two oxygen bottles now, get through the night, and come back at first light to take another bottle to get you back down to five. OK?'

The Hungarian nodded slowly.

'You're doing as much as you can by staying with him. But he can't be rescued. If you stay here now you'll be putting other lives in danger. Are you still fit enough to get down tomorrow on your own?'

'Yes.' His reply was barely audible.

He picked up the two oxygen bottles and walked off into the night, the very picture of a broken man. I wondered what kind of hell he was returning to: within a few hours Reinhard would be dead by his side.

'You know the strangest thing?' A chilling memory had come back to me.

'What?'

'When you and Barney decided to turn Brian back on the ridge you saw Reinhard and his mate carrying on and said he might die.'

'That's true. I could see by the speed they were moving that they were heading for trouble.'

Then another memory hit me—a recollection of a discussion I had with Al before leaving for Kathmandu.

'And do you remember the conversation we had when you came round for the meal?' Al had visited us in Hertfordshire a few weeks before the expedition left. 'You predicted this would happen. You said we'd get to camp six and find someone in exactly that state. In fact I think you specified it would be an Eastern European.'

'Yeah, I do remember.'

'Don't you think that's bizarre?'

Al thought for a moment. 'Not really. There's so many disorganised teams on Everest these days you're more likely than not to find someone in trouble here.'

And with that we resumed the cooking and the subject was closed. But in my mind the extraordinary conversation we had just had with the Hungarian was churning away. Why didn't I feel more compassion for him? Why hadn't we at least offered to go and check on Reinhard just in case he had miraculously recovered?

The truth was that the mountain had dehumanised me and hardened my emotional response. The news about Reinhard's impending death had neither surprised me nor shocked me. Instead it seemed normal. This is camp six—8,300 metres, my mind was telling me, this is where people *do* die if something goes wrong. Reinhard was beyond help. We all were. To be prepared to go this high, we had all willingly made an unwritten pact with the mountain that says: 'I'm putting myself in a position where I know I can die.' Given that level of personal commitment, perhaps it is not surprising that luxuries like pity and compassion are often left behind at base camp along with other unnecessary baggage. If we had brought those emotions with us, perhaps we would be needing them now—for ourselves?

I was beginning to understand what the Death Zone really means.

At 11:20 p.m. Al drifted off into a light sleep, his rhythmic breathing muffled by the oxygen mask. At midnight, summit day would begin.

Even though my body craved it, for me there was no question of sleep.

I was like a child lying wide-eyed in bed on Christmas Eve. Expectation ran like an adrenalin shot through my body. I pulled the frozen fabric of the down sleeping bag as tight as I could around my head and lay perfectly still.

Staring into the dark confines of the tent, super-sensitive to the ghosts of wind playing around us, I found myself entering a state of Zen-like calm. During the long-haired phase of my teens, fuelled by a dangerous overconsumption of Carlos Castaneda and Aldous Huxley, I had often tried to meditate my way into an altered state of consciousness. How I had tried!

In a candlelit bedroom, filled with the aromatic smoke of joss-sticks and the trance-inducing pentatonic synthesizer chords of the psychedelic band 'Gong', I sat in a half-lotus position and waited to lock on to the astral plane. But no matter how long I spent in the ticket queue, my journey to Ixtlan never began. Perhaps Hemel Hempstead is not the best starting place when you're heading for Nirvana.

Now, zipped into that tiny plastic capsule 8,300 metres above the rest of the world I slipped effortlessly into a state of euphoric trance. The cramped Quasar mountain tent suddenly took on the dimensions of a cathedral, its domed roof becoming a series of soaring arches suspended hundreds of feet in the air. The soothing hiss of the oxygen feeding into my mask took on a musical quality, like pan-pipes, and the wind became a whispering voice murmuring encouraging words for the day to come.

The music faded and was replaced by the thudding beat of blood-rush echoing in the back of my skull. The fantasy changed. I imagined myself diving into the sea and letting my lungs fill with water.

Then I snapped back to consciousness with a horrible gasp, gulping frantically for air. That was why the music had faded: the oxygen cylinder was out of air. Confused and disorientated, I had trouble finding my headtorch and then struggled to unscrew the frozen regulator valve on the dead tank.

The interior of the tent was now encrusted with a thin hoar frost of frozen vapour. With every movement, irritating showers of tiny crystals fell, freezing any exposed skin.

Replacing the valve on to a fresh oxygen bottle, I set the gauge on one litre a minute and slumped exhausted back into the sleeping bag. Now the waking trance was anything but euphoric; the sweet dreams went distinctly sour. I suddenly remembered that not ten metres from our tent the Austrian, Reinhard, was dying, beyond help.

Camp six, which had seemed such a welcome refuge when we'd arrived some hours before, now became a place of overwhelming fear and anxiety. The fact that there was nothing we could do for Reinhard put everything into perspective; the mountain was in control. Altitude, with all its deadly effects, was snuffing the life out of a strong, healthy mountaineer, as if he were a sickly child. In the face of this invisible force, our own enterprise felt fragile and doomed to fail.

For the remaining twenty minutes before midnight I lay in a state of cold fear, praying that the weather would hold, that my body would be capable of meeting the challenge ahead, and—most important of all— that I would not make a mistake. My lack of confidence in my own mountaineering abilities had dogged me from the start of the expedition. Now the fear of a trip, of a sudden fall, of fumbling a piece of protection as I'd done with the figure-of-eight on the Col; those were mistakes which I had got away with in the early stages of the climb. On summit day, even the slightest mistake would be a potential killer.

Mallory and Irvine probably died that way . . .

Midnight. Al's digital watch bleeped a feeble alarm and I could hear muffled shouts from the Sherpas' tent. Al roused himself from sleep and we set about the tiresome task of lighting the gas cookers.

The cigarette lighters were now even more reluctant to ignite than at camp five. It took forty or fifty strokes with my thumb to coax a flame out of the frozen gas. By the time I succeeded, blood was flowing freely from the cracked skin.

The gas cooker burned fiercely for a few seconds then spluttered out.

'Bastard!' I was beginning to loathe the cookers.

Al patiently took over with the cigarette lighter and managed to relight it. This had been a regular pattern since camp five. The intense cold and thin air made the propane burners extremely fickle. They frequently flared out for no apparent reason, filling the tent with nause-ating gas until they could be relit.

Once warmed up, the gas seemed to flow better, and after ten min-utes of frustration, we had both cookers happily burning. Al busied himself cutting up blocks of snow into pieces small enough to fit into the pans while I tried to make some order out of my side of the tent.

Al, canny as ever, had bagged himself the flatter, uphill sleeping plat-form, leaving me to compete for space with the pile of equipment. Thanks to the precarious angle, leaning sharply down the snowfield, the interior, and my side in particular, had become a jumbled mess.

Used oxygen cylinders, food rations and climbing equipment formed a chaotic heap on the downward slope. The side wall of the tent was sagging alarmingly under the weight of the gear, and I imag-ined that the slightest tear could split the fabric like the belly of a whale, emptying the contents and me on to the ice slide outside, where a one-way trip down the North Face would rapidly ensue.

I tried to rearrange the heavier objects at the foot of the tent where they would be out of the way. Then I set about extracting the vital pieces of gear which would be needed for the day ahead: the lithium batteries for the video camera, the red wind suit, the outer shells of my plastic boots. Highlighted by the beam of the headtorch I saw the food packets which each of us had prepared with such optimism back at base camp seven weeks before.

Written in blue marker pen were the names of the owners: Tore, Simon, Sundeep, Barney, Brian . . . I ripped open Brian's pack and extracted the precious sachet of muesli. My appetite had become super-selective and this was one of the few foods I could face.

It took over an hour to melt the compacted snow down to boiling water. We shared a pack of pistachio nuts and drank mugs of tea and Bournvita before loading the pans with more snow for another melt-down . . . our drinking supply for the climb.

Gagged by the oxygen masks, we had little urge to talk, but con-centrated on the vital task of forcing as much food and liquid down as we could.

Al's long years of Himalayan expeditions had taught him the enviable knack of pissing into a pee bottle whilst lying on his side. Lacking the confidence to risk a sleeping bag full of urine by getting this wrong, I relied on the surer but less energy-efficient technique of crouching on my knees to perform the act.

The minutes ticked by, and with them came another dreaded bodily demand.

'I need a crap.'

'Me too.' Al was in the same state.

The prospect of putting on the boots and going out into the freezing night wind was extremely depressing. Just the thought was exhausting and demoralising.

'Better do it,' Al advised. 'Nothing else for it. No point in taking any excess baggage up. Besides, if you're shitting yourself now, imagine what you'll be like on the second step.'

As an avid consumer of Himalayan climbing books, I had always been mystified by the high-altitude mountaineer's obsession with bodily functions. What, I had wondered, was the problem?

It took nearly fifteen minutes to prepare ourselves to exit the tent. Taking our oxygen cylinders with us was not a realistic option. Moving carefully to avoid the cookers, I crawled out of the front of the tent. Doing so, I nudged an empty cylinder which had been propped outside. It fell on to the ice slope and accelerated away quickly. There was a clanking sound as it hit rocks once—twice—and then cartwheeled out of sight down the North Face to land on the glacier some six thousand feet below.

Mistake.

Stumbling across the ice slope, I realised that what I was doing was extremely stupid. I should have crampons and an ice-axe. One slip and I would follow the oxygen cylinder down the Face. With a shudder I remembered that this was exactly how one of the Taiwanese climbers had fallen on the southern side just days before.

I found a narrow ledge and managed to pull down the down suit and thermal underclothes. Calf and thigh muscles protesting, I squatted for what seemed like an eternity, puffing and panting for air. A few metres away, Al was doing the same. There is no such thing as embarrassment at 8,300 metres.

At the Col and above I found myself experiencing acute pain when going to the toilet. This time was by far the worst, bringing tears to my eyes. My whole system was completely dried up, and it felt like I was splitting inside.

'I'm having a baby here, Al.'

An answering grunt came in reply.

With the pain came blood—quite a substantial amount. I closed my mind to the implications of this, putting it down to that well-known climbers affliction, piles, even though I was pretty sure I didn't have them.

Collapsing back into the tent I strapped on the oxygen mask and gulped hungrily at the clean-tasting air. In the warmth of the sleeping bags I thrust my hands under my armpits to defrost, another surprisingly painful process.

Al came in. 'You all right?'

'Fine,' I replied, not wanting to let on how I really felt. Close to vomiting, with a skull-splitting headache, I now knew why a visit to the toilet above 8,000 metres inspires such dread amongst mountaineers.

Al added some more snow blocks to the pans of water and then curled up in his bag to try and regain some precious warmth. I could just make out his muffled words:

'My feet are frozen.'

Outside, I could hear the three Sherpas preparing their equipment. Gyaltsen made his way across the snowfield and shouted into the tent.

'Two o'clock. You ready?'

'We need another brew,' At replied. 'Let's leave in half an hour.'

The two other Sherpas, Lhakpa and Mingma, came across to join Gyaltsen outside our tent. They began to sort out the oxygen cylinders which were stacked neatly there in a pile.

'There's no way we're leaving with fingers or toes frozen,' Al told me, 'they have to be perfectly warm when we set off or we'll end up losing them.'

I took my feet out of their inner boots and massaged them back to life. The smaller toes felt curiously waxy to the touch, as if the skin was thicker than it should be.

By 2:30 a.m., fortified by a last cup of Bournvita and a few lumps of chocolate, we were outside the tent with crampons and neoprene gaiters fitted. Over the 'Michelin man' down suits we wore the red Berghaus wind suits with harness fastened over the whole ensemble. Movement was severely restricted by the thickness of this specialist clothing and I had to get Al to tighten my harness buckle up so it fitted snugly around my waist.

We arranged the rucksacks to carry the oxygen cylinders. With this, as with every other tiny part of the high-altitude survival jigsaw, attention to detail is critical. The oxygen bottle must be carried upright. If it falls in the sack the oxygen feed pipe could crimp and cut off the supply. Having tested my system at base camp, I now rolled up my Karrimat and inserted it in the pack. Slid into the roll, the oxygen cylinder was held in place firmly by the foam with the valve clear of obstruction.

There was the added advantage that if we had to bivouac for whatever reason, the Karrimat would be a very valuable asset.

I ran through a mental check-list as we put the final touches to the equipment. Ski goggles ready in the pocket of the wind suit. Spare glacier goggles in another pocket. Headtorch ready with two spare bulbs and spare battery. Two one-litre water bottles filled with 'isotonic' high-energy glucose drink. Walkie-talkie checked. Food—chocolate and Christmas pudding—ready. Stills cameras loaded with fresh film. Crampon repair kit. Spare carabiner. Figure-of-eight descendeur. Jumar clamps.

'Where's your drink?' Al asked.

'In the rucksack.'

'You're better off putting them inside the down suit next to your skin.'

I did as Al said, zipping up one of the plastic nalgene bottles into the suit just above the harness. The Sherpas were clearly ready to go. My mind raced through the mental check-list searching for the one missed component, the one small forgotten item which would bring the summit bid to a grinding halt.

There wasn't one. We were ready.

Without a word, we turned away from the tents and started our climb up into the night. Lhakpa led, with Mingma and Gyaltsen behind, then Al and myself at the tail.

After the suspense and tension of the preparation it was a sheer relief to be moving. Those first few steps had, for me, a truly epic quality. I knew we were in an incredibly privileged position—a position thousands of mountaineers would give their eye-teeth (and perhaps a lot more) to share.

We were leaving camp six bang on schedule on as near as the North Face ever gets to a perfect night. We had liquid, food, an adequate supply of oxygen and the assistance of three very strong Sherpas. Our equipment was tried and tested, we were as fit as one can be above 8,000 metres with no major sickness or injury to cope with.

It doesn't get much better than that. The 'window' was open. For the first time, I allowed myself the luxury of thinking that we might just make it. If our luck held.

In the precise minutes of our departure from camp six, as we later learned from the Hungarian climber who was with him in the tent, Reinhard died.

The Sherpas set a fast pace up the first of the snowfields lying above the camp. Al kept up easily but I found myself lagging behind. The thin beam of light from the headtorch, seemingly so bright when tested in the tent, now felt inadequate for the task, illuminating a pathetically small patch of snow.

Catching up, I concentrated on watching Al's cramponed feet as they bit into the snow. The conditions were variable with an unpredictable crust. Frequently it gave way, plunging us thigh deep into a hidden hole.

I quickly learned not to trust the headtorch with its tuned vision effect. It confused the eye by casting shadows of unknown depth. Rocks could be bigger than they seemed. Holes in the snow lacked all perspective. Distances became hard to judge. Was Lhakpa's light ten metres in front of me . . . or fifty? I couldn't tell.

We crossed several old tent platforms, abandoned by previous expeditions. Each one was littered with the usual shredded fabric, splintered tent-poles and empty oxygen cylinders. A foil food sachet got spiked by one of my crampon teeth and dragged annoyingly until I could be bothered to remove it.

At each of these wrecked sites, Al, the mountain detective, would pause for a moment to cast his headtorch around the remains. Even now, on our summit bid, his fascination for them was as keen as ever.

The climb continued, step after step, up the snowfield towards the much more demanding terrain of the yellow band. Very conscious of our limited oxygen supply, I tried to concentrate on regulating my breathing; I knew from scuba-diving training how easy it is to waste air.

But the terrain of the North Face is mixed; both in steepness and in composition. Steep ice fields give way to shallower rock slabs. Demanding rock sections end in long traverses. Establishing a breathing pattern is virtually impossible. Mostly I found I was puffing and panting at a very fast rate and there was nothing I could do about it.

After an hour I found I was feeling better. The headache and nausea had faded away with the concentrated physical work of the climb. My feet and hands felt warm, and the weight of the rucksack was not as bad as I had feared.

Reaching the end of the larger of the two snowfields, we encountered the first bare rock. I watched in horror as the three pinprick lights of the Sherpas began to rise up what seemed to be a vertical wall. Surely it was an optical illusion? I had never heard anyone talk about any actual climbing before the Ridge. But, standing at the foot of the rock section, my heart sank. It was steep. Very steep. I was completely inexperienced in night climbing, and fear formed an icy pool in the pit of my stomach.

We were about to tackle the yellow band.

Worse, we would have to climb on rock with our crampons on. This is like trying to climb stairs on stilts. The spiked fangs act like an unwanted platform sole, elevating the foot away from any real contact with the rock. Using crampons on rock greatly increases the risk of a misplaced foothold or a twisted ankle. In a tight spot, where the feet have to move in close proximity, they are even more deadly. A spike can snag in the neoprene gaiter of the other foot, a mistake which invariably leads to a heavy fall.

On other mountains we might have stopped to remove the crampons, but here that was not an option. On the North Face of Everest, removing crampons every time you made a transition from snow to rock would waste hours of precious time and risk almost certain frostbite to the hands.

I paused for a brief rest as the others made their way up into the rock band. Turning off my headtorch, I let my eyes adjust to the dark. The sky was mostly still clear of cloud but I could see no sign of the moon. The only illumination came from the stars, which were as dazzling as I have ever seen them. The towering mass of Changtse was now far below us, I could just see the sinuous curves of its fluted ridge.

Further down, thousands of metres further down, the great glaciers were just visible, reflecting the dull metallic grey of the starlight against the darker shadows of their deep valley walls. The whole of Tibet lay beneath us and there was not a single electric light to be seen.

Taking off my Gore-tex overmitts, I reached up to the oxygen mask. Ice was beginning to constrict the intake valve at the front. I carefully broke the chunk away.

Then, my crampons clanking and scraping with a jarring metallic ring against the rock, I began the climb up. The route took a line up a series of ledges, linked by narrow cracks. It was a nasty scramble, involving strenuous leg and arm work to lunge up steps which were often uncomfortably high. More than once I found myself jamming a knee into a crack for support, or squirming up on to a balcony on my stomach.

'This must be the first step,' I yelled up at Al. He didn't reply and hours later, when we reached the real first step, I realised how far out I had been.

We came to a platform and took a few minutes' rest before beginning the next section.

The climb was littered with tatty ropes. Some were frayed, some were kinked from unknown causes, others were bleached white from exposure to the intense ultraviolet radiation here above 8,000 metres. Al sorted through them with a professional's eye, muttering under his breath.

Selecting the best of a bad lot, Al attached his jumar clamp and started up, sliding the handgrip of the camming device with each move. I waited for him to gain some height and then followed on. The crampons made every move a nightmare, as they had to be jammed into crevices or rested on protrusions to gain a purchase. Often I found my feet scrabbling frantically for a hold, the metal spikes grinding the flaking rock into granules of grit.

A steady barrage of small stones, and the occasional fist-sized rock, came down from above where the Sherpas were climbing. Normally this is avoidable by all but the clumsiest climber, but here every foothold had the potential to dislodge debris. Our ears rapidly became adept at guessing the size of an approaching missile as it clattered down the rock-face.

'Below!' A flat, briefcase-sized rock slithered down the face and spun off into the dark depths.

After sixty or seventy metres of ascent I made my first mistake. As I pushed down to lift my body weight up on a boulder foothold, my crampon slipped away with no warning, unbalancing me and crashing my knee into a sharp ledge. The down suit cushioned much of the blow but it still took me several minutes to regain my composure as a series of sparkling stars did cartoon laps of honour across my field of vision.

On that fall, as at many other times, my entire body weight was suspended on the rope.

Another twenty metres of ascent brought me to the anchor point of the rope I was climbing on. Shining the headtorch on to the fixing point, I could scarcely believe what I was seeing. My lifeline was attached to the face by a single, rusting metal piton which had been ineptly placed in a crack.

Out of curiosity I tested the solidity of the anchor point with my hand. It moved. With one gentle pull, the piton slid right out. I stared at it dumbly for a few seconds, incredulous that my recent fall had been held by this pathetic piece of protection.

Throughout the expedition the knowledge that fixed ropes existed on the more technical rock had been a reassuring notion. 'Get to camp six and then you're on the fixed ropes' was a much repeated mantra, implying that they were somehow safe. In that one heart-stopping moment as the piton slid out of its crack, my faith in the fixed ropes was destroyed. I resolved to rely on them as little as I could.

The incline eased off and I found Al and the three Sherpas waiting for me. As I arrived they continued onwards up a series of steps cut into wind-hardened snow. At the next steep section Lhakpa again led the way up the rocks, climbing strongly and steadily. The light from his headtorch rapidly went out of view.

I had a favour to ask. 'Al, can you let me go in front? I'm not happy at the back.'

'No problem.' Al unclipped his sling from the rope and let me pass. It was a generous gesture which I greatly appreciated.

I started up the next rock section feeling a lot more confident with Al behind me at the tail-end of the rope. This was partly psychological, and partly from the practical help he could give by shining his headtorch on to holds. I found myself moving easier and with more certainty.

As everywhere on Everest, the rock was fragmented and unreliable. Apparently solid handholds came away easily in flakes, boulders trembled under the weight of a leg, and a flow of gravel-sized stones seemed to be perpetually on the move.

Just inches from my hand a stone the size of a telephone directory fell out of the night. Impacting hard, it shattered into hundreds of pieces, showering me with splinters of stone. Mingma's warning cry from above came simultaneously. I saw his headtorch flash down the face.

'You OK?'

'OK.' We carried on up.

By now I had no idea of our precise position on the Face. From the

Rongbuk glacier the distance from camp six to the North-East Ridge does not look great. In fact, as I was discovering, it is a significant climb. It was now many hours since we had left the camp and my body was already feeling as if it had done a substantial day's work.

There was still not the slightest glimmer of dawn. I began to long for the first rays of light.

Now we started what I guessed was the final section of the yellow band; more steep slogging up an eroded fault in the rock strata. It began with a stretching high step of a metre or more up on to a ledge; another occasion when there was no choice but to rely on a fixed rope. Then, with the infernal crampons scraping horribly on the rock, we scrambled up for about thirty minutes, pausing every five minutes or so for breath.

Turning back for a moment, I saw that Al was free-climbing the section. He, like me, had no confidence in the fixed ropes, but, unlike me, had the experience to know he could climb the route without a fall.

As the ground evened off, we began another traverse to the right, across a field of dirty snow. A bright red rope had been laid across it— the newest protection we had seen so far. Clipping on, I wondered who had fixed it: the Indians, or perhaps the Japanese?

The line continued up through a crack and then on to a sloping rock plateau the size of a tennis court. Crossing it, I realised we had finished the first stage of the climb.

The horrors of the night climb ended as we took the final steps on to the North-East Ridge. The crumbling cliffs of the yellow band had been steeper, more complex and much more committing than I had imagined. Climbing them in the dark, with just the glowworm light of the headtorch, had been a nightmare.

Now, with the first rays of dawn to light our route along the Ridge, I reached up and turned the headtorch off. If all went well now, we could be on the summit within the next six hours.

The three Sherpas stood hunched over their ice-axes, alien figures in their goggles and oxygen masks. They had set a blistering pace through the dark hours and now rested as we waited for Al to join us on the Ridge.

One of the Sherpas—Lhakpa—had climbed to the summit before, but I knew the others had never been this high. Each had stalactites of ice clinging to the bottom of his oxygen mask where exhaled vapour had frozen into spikes several inches long. Mingma was having trouble with his mask. I watched him take it off to unblock the frozen pipe and remembered the expedition doctor's warning that we might be unconscious within thirty minutes if our oxygen supply failed.

My oxygen hadn't stopped yet, but the hard frozen shell of the mask was eroding a nagging sore where it rubbed at the bridge of my nose. I eased it away from my face for a moment to relieve the irritation. Then, sucking deep on the oxygen, I prayed it wouldn't let me down.

With the dawn came the wind, our greatest enemy. As Al picked his way carefully up to join us, the first few gusts of the day began to play along the North Face, sending up flurries of ice crystals. While we waited for Al to recover his breath, I moved carefully on to the crest and looked over the knife edge drop down the Kanshung—the Eastern—Face.

There can be few more terrifying sights anywhere on earth. Seen from my vantage point, the Kanshung Face was a sheer 10,000-foot wall of ice falling away beneath me, so steep it seemed almost vertical. Vast fields of ice—hanging glaciers—perch precariously on its walls. It is deeply etched with fragile fissures and crevasses. It wasn't hard to imagine the whole Face—all those billions of tons of ice—giving up its fight with gravity and peeling off in one monumental avalanche down into the valleys below.

When Mallory first saw the Kanshung Face during the British reconnaissance expedition of 1924, he pronounced it unclimbable. He would leave it, he decided, 'to others less wise'. Now, looking down the Face, I understood precisely what he meant. The fact that it has subsequently been climbed—and by several different routes—seems to me an incredible achievement.

The Kanshung Face is home to, and creator of, some curious winds. With day breaking, one of those winds was beginning. As I looked down the Face, a billowing cloud of ice crystals was moving vertically up towards me. It was like looking down directly into the gaping mouth of a power station cooling tower. This is the tail of the massive 'rotor' that Everest spins out of the constant north-westerly Tibetan gales. As the ice crystals come up to the Ridge, they are blown to the south-east in a deadly plume which can be thirty miles long.

Few people summit when Everest's plume is running.

Lhakpa shouted something to me which broke the spell and I turned back towards the group.

Now our climb along the Ridge itself was about to begin. From where we were standing, it looked incredibly complicated: a dragon's tail of switchbacks, dips and rocky steps. Two of these, the 'first step' and the second, are regarded as the most formidable of the obstacles on the North Face route, but it was the sheer length of the Ridge that most worried me.

Back in London, I had met Crag Jones, one of the four British climbers to have summitted via the North Face. We sat in a Soho coffee bar drinking cappuccino while Crag cracked his knuckles and rolled up his sleeves to reveal Popeye muscles and veins the thickness of climbing ropes.

'The first and second steps *are* problems,' he told me, 'but it's the size of the Ridge you want to think about. When you get on to the Ridge you have to realise there could be another twelve hours of climbing to get back to camp six via the summit. Twelve hours. It's a hell of a long day.'

From where I was standing, Crag was right. It was already looking like a hell of a long day and we'd only cracked a tiny proportion of the route. Lhakpa moved towards me and shouted, his voice muffled by the mask:

'We move fast. Move very fast. OK?'

He tapped his wrist to indicate that the clock was ticking away. At 8,600 metres we were the highest human beings on the planet; and we were dying a little more with every hour. In the Death Zone, you have to move fast to keep alive.

Now in full daylight, we set out along the lifeline of tattered ropes which snake along the Ridge, the legacy of previous ascents. With the night hours behind us, I felt a glimmer of optimism creep in. I was feeling strong.

Thirty minutes later we rounded a small cliff and found the first dead Indian climber. We knew that the three Indian bodies would still be there on the Ridge where they had died a few days earlier, but, ridiculously, I had completely forgotten about them.

Now, here was the first body, lying partly in the shelter of an overhanging rock and ringed by an almost perfect circle of windblown snow.

Al shouted through his mask, 'Must be one of the Indians.'

We would have to step over his outstretched legs to continue along the ridge.

The Sherpas stood side by side, seemingly rooted to the spot by the sight of the dead man. Their heads were bowed, as if in prayer; perhaps, it occurred to me later, they were praying.

I felt an almost irresistible urge to look at the dead climber's face. What expression would be fixed on it in those final moments of life? Terror? A smile? (They say that those who die of acute mountain sickness have a delusion of well-being in the final stages.)

But his head was thrust far into the overhang, the neck bent so his face rested against the rock. All I could see was the edge of his oxygen mask. From the mask ran that precious, life-giving tube to the oxygen cylinder which was standing upright against a rock. It was an orange cylinder, a Russian one like our own.

I bent down, using my ice-axe for support, to have a closer look at the gauge on the top of the cylinder. It read, of course, zero. Even if he had died before the cylinder ran out, it would have continued to spill its feeble trickle of oxygen into the atmosphere until it emptied.

He was wearing very few clothes, just a lightweight red fleece top, some blue Gore-tex climbing trousers and a pair of yellow plastic Koflach boots similar to our own. His rucksack lay nearby, flat and empty. I wondered about this mystery for a moment. What had happened to his high-altitude gear? His down suit? His Gore-tex mitts? We knew the Indian team had been well-equipped. That left only two possibilities: either he'd ripped them off in the final stages of delirium, or someone had stolen them from the corpse.

In a way I found the first scenario an easier one to imagine.

The tragedy of the Indian team was central to the film I was making. Seduced by Everest's siren call, they had pushed themselves well beyond their own limits of endurance and had failed to reserve enough strength to get down in the worsening conditions which preceded the big storm. Summit fever had killed them.

Yet, even though we had the video cameras with us to record the actuality of our climb, I could not bring myself to film the dead man lying so pathetically at our feet.

I knew that ITN and Channel 4 would want this most graphic illustration of Everest as killer but I couldn't bring myself to do it. Even the victims of war eventually find a grave—even if they are shoved into it by a bulldozer. This Indian climber would remain exactly where he lay now, frozen for eternity. His grave was the bleakest imaginable and to think that his family, his friends, would see the reality of that was too much to contemplate.

As we stepped over the legs of the corpse to continue along the Ridge, we crossed an invisible line in the snow . . . and an invisible line of commitment in our own minds. Altitude is an unseen killer. Human life, any life, does not belong in the Death Zone, and by stepping over the dead body we made the conscious decision to push further into it. The dead body had been the starkest reminder we could have that we were now reliant for our lives on our equipment, our own strength and our luck.

There was the irresistible feeling that it was the Indian who was perfectly in tune with this place, and that we, being alive, were the invaders. All places above 8,000 metres belong to the dead because up there human life cannot be sustained. Wrapped up like spacemen in our huge high-altitude suits, breathing through the mechanical hiss of the oxygen system, I felt for the first time in my life like an alien on my own planet.

Our assault on the Ridge continued.

By 7 a.m. we reached the first step. It was both higher, at about twenty metres, and more of a climb, than I had imagined. Overshadowed by the bigger cliff of the second step, it tends to get treated as an insignificant obstacle but, looking up at it with my ski goggles beginning to acquire a frozen internal layer, it looked daunting enough.

It was not possible to remove the crampons to cope with these changing conditions as unfixing and then refixing them would risk fingers to frostbite (it was about –35°F at that point), and also waste too much time.

The three Sherpas went up first and I followed. For three metres or so, the route led up an ice-filled crack on the left side of the cliff. Next came a traverse across to a rocky ledge and then a precarious scramble up between two rounded boulders. I jammed the front metal points of my crampons into a tiny rock crack and pushed up . . . all my weight relying on the insignificant hold.

I paused for some moments to gather breath after the strenuous move, and then tackled the crux.

The move required a delicate balancing act which I could have achieved easily at sea level. Up here in clothes which reduced all sense of being in touch with the rock, and with the added exposure of an 8,000-foot fall directly down the North Face as a penalty for a mistake, it felt epic enough.

I snapped my jumar clamp as high as I could on the best looking of the many ropes which were hanging beguilingly around the crux. It gave a sense of security to protect a fall but that was a psychological advantage rather than a real one. In fact, a fall would leave the unlucky climber swinging helplessly in open space underneath the overhanging section of the cliff. Assuming the rope held.

Moving out into the exposed position, I stuck a leg around the smooth edge of the ridge and planted it on to the foothold which, fortunately, waited on the other side. I had to sense its security rather than see it . . . the leg was out of my field of vision.

My left hand instinctively snaked up to try and find a handhold above. A tentative pull on a possible hold merely made it give way, and

I threw the cigarette-packet-sized piece of rock down the North Face beneath me.

Not many people can imagine that Everest is a crumbling wreck of a mountain. It looks as if it should be made of granite, but in fact it is friable limestone . . . the worst of rocks to climb at any altitude.

Locking my fist on to a ledge above my head, I took a deep breath and shifted my entire weight on to the out-of-vision foot. Then I swung over and around the rock, to the safety of the other side.

Lhakpa was waiting there. He put his thumbs up and I replied with the same. Another obstacle over. Another step closer to the summit.

Now the wind was definitely picking up and we were still only halfway along the Ridge. We began to push harder. The plume of ice crystals from the Kanshung Face was now billowing up more strongly on our left, a sign we could not afford to ignore. Whenever we stopped to regain our breath, I looked away to the north, the direction a storm would come from. Plenty of clouds were moving rapidly towards us but nothing so far looked too threatening.

I had been so wrapped up in the climb, I had completely forgotten my stills camera. The tiny Olympus had a brand-new lithium battery and a full roll of transparency film. Squinting through the eyepiece, I took two pictures of the terrain ahead and one shot of Al. Then we pressed on.

At several points, the route took us right on to the very knife-edge crest of the Ridge itself. Then, we would time the dash along the ice to miss the blasts of wind. I had never been able to imagine how climbers could be blown off a ridge. Now, I was acutely aware of that possibility. One of the theoretical ends for Mallory and Irvine had them plummetting off the Ridge and down the Kanshung Face . . . perhaps their bodies, or their ghosts, were close by?

One particularly hair-raising section of the Ridge, only a few metres long, involved stepping down on to what seemed to be a corniced section of crumbling ice cross-sectioned by a crevasse. The Sherpas, lighter and more agile than we were, ran across easily. I took each step with my heart in my mouth, expecting at any moment that the cornice would give way and leave me dangling over the Kanshung Face.

The ice held.

By 8.30 a.m. we reached the second step. This step is another cliff, steeper and more than twice the height of the first. There is no way around it, it has to be tackled head-on.

Back in the 1980s, a Chinese expedition had fixed a lightweight climbing ladder to the most severe part of the cliff. It had been destroyed in a recent storm and the Indian climbers and their Sherpas had fixed another in its place. I had been greatly reassured by the notion of the ladder. Anyone could climb a ladder . . . couldn't they? In my mind it had lessened the severity of the second step.

In fact the ladder, which I had always thought of as a friendly aid, was about to prove a significant problem in its own right.

At the foot of the second step two unexpected things happened: the first was my discovery that both my litre bottles of juice, boiled down from snow so painfully slowly at camp six the previous night, were frozen solid. Even the bottle I had kept next to my skin inside the front of my down suit was a solid mass of ice. At the time it seemed like an inconvenience. Later on during the day I was to realise in the starkest way possible the seriousness of that event.

Al checked his bottles too. They were also frozen solid. Now neither of us would have a single drop of moisture through the whole day. Many experienced high-altitude mountaineers would have turned back at that point.

The other unexpected thing was that Al leaned towards me to speak. 'Open up my pack,' he said. 'Put the oxygen up to four litres a minute.'

He turned his back to me. Taking off my overmitts, and going down to the finger gloves, I undid the clips closing his pack and found the oxygen regulator valve inside. It was a difficult, fiddly job in the close confines of the rucksack. I clicked the regulator round to read four and closed the pack.

Now Al was pumping twice as much oxygen into his system as my rate of two litres a minute. I could understand his desire for more gas to tackle the second step, but even so his request surprised me. We both knew the risks of pumping up the oxygen too high. It runs out twice as fast and, with your body tuned in to operate at a higher level, you come down with a bigger crash when it ends.

'OK. It's on four,' I shouted to him. For a fleeting moment I thought I sensed something more than just tiredness in the way Al was moving. Was he having a harder time than he was revealing?

It was a measure of our increasing disorientation that neither of us thought at that stage of dumping the two litres of frozen liquid. Now we were climbing with two kilogrammes of superfluous weight on our backs up the hardest rock-climbing section of the North Face route.

The first six metres or so were simple enough. A tight squeeze through a chimney filled with ice led on to an easier graded ledge with a snow bank against the cliff. I used the jumar clamp to help my ascent, sliding the device up as high as my arms would stretch, then pulling up where it gripped against the rope. Someone had rigged a virtually new, 9mm rope on this lower part and that helped considerably.

The crampons scratched and bit into the rock steps like the claws of a cat trying, and failing to climb a tree. Then came a big step up. I tensioned my foot against a ripple of protruding rock to my right, and, cursing the crampons to hell, just managed to ease my body up on to the ledge which led to the ladder.

I paused for a long moment to catch my breath. The beat of my heart was sending a pounding rush of blood through my head. I was aware of my pulse-rate being higher than I have ever sensed it before. My breathing was wild and virtually out of control. For one panic-stricken moment I thought my oxygen had failed. Then I realised I could still hear the reassuring hiss of the gas and told myself to calm down.

I was standing more or less exactly in the place where Mallory and Irvine were last seen alive, spotted by telescope from the North Col camp. Their 1924 climb had been the hardest, and perhaps, the greatest, of the pre-war efforts on Everest.

There had been no ladder for them on the second step. If they'd tried it, one of them may well have fallen, taking his partner with him to certain death. The horror of imagining that final moment had always eluded me until now. Now I had no trouble in imagining a fatal fall from this spot. It was the most exposed and dangerous part of the climb.

My friend the ladder was the next obstacle. I put a hand on it and felt it sway and flap against the sheer face it was attached to. I had always imagined it to be solid. I began to climb.

The first problem was caused by the crampons. The metal spikes snagged against the rungs, or grated against the rock and prevented me from getting a proper footing on the ladder. Unable to look down, blinkered by the goggles into a front only view, I had to sense as best I could when my feet were in the right place.

My breathing rate went up again . . . the greater volume of escaping moisture running up through gaps in the mask and freezing inside my goggles. Halfway up the ladder I was almost blinded by this, and I ripped the goggles up on to my head to be able to see. We were all aware of the dangers of snow blindness but I felt I could take the risk for the next few crucial minutes.

The ladder had a distinct, drunken lean to the left. This, coupled with the fact that it was swaying alarmingly on the ragbag selection of pitons and ropes which held it, made it extremely difficult to cling to.

My Gore-tex overmitts were hopelessly clumsy in this situation. I could barely cup them tight enough to cling to the rungs. But, having started with them on, I could hardly remove them now; and any lesser protection would almost certainly result in frostbite from contact with the frozen metal of the ladder.

The 'friendly' ladder was anything but. I resolved to move quickly to get off it, and off the second step, as soon as I could.

Reaching the top rung, I assessed the next move. It was a hard one: a tension traverse using only the strength of the arms. The objective was to swing up on to the ledge which marked the end of the second step. To do it, I would have to cling on to a collection of rotting ropes tied to a sling of dubious origin. Then, with no foothold, I would have to tension as many spikes of my crampons as I could push on to the Face, and then in one fluid motion swing chimpanzee-like up to the right.

Down at base camp I had talked about filming this stage of the climb when Brian got there. Six weeks later this now seemed a supreme joke. Firstly, there was never any chance of Brian getting here; secondly, the thought of filming in this most deadly of places was the last thing on my mind. This was a survival exercise pure and simple.

Trying the move, I realised that there was a critical moment of commitment when the body would be neither supported by the ladder, nor safely on the ledge. To complete the climb of the second step, I would be, albeit for a split second, hanging over the North Face by the strength of my arms alone.

I tried it . . . and failed. Clinging to the ladder, I retreated several rungs to get some rest while my breathing rate subsided. Without sufficient oxygen powering the muscle tissue in my arms, they were tiring extremely quickly. Instinctively I felt I would have one or perhaps two more tries in me before I weakened to the point where I would have to retreat.

It was several minutes before my runaway breathing came down to a controllable rate. I tried the move again, and this time succeeded. With both arms fading fast, I pulled up on to the ledge and then stumbled the few metres of rocky slope to the top.

From this new vantage point on the Ridge, the summit pyramid was for the first time fully in view. The four of us waited for Al to come up the second step and then continued.

For the next hour we continued to make good time, climbing up gradually on the mixed ground of snow and rock. I paused several times to take photographs but by the fifth or sixth shot the camera began to behave strangely, winding on erratically and failing to close the automatic lens cover. On the seventh shot the Olympus ground to a halt and gave up completely in the sub-zero temperatures. That left me with no SLR camera as my Nikon F3 had similarly succumbed to the cold down at camp four.

Cursing this piece of bad luck, I unzipped my down suit and put the camera against my thermal layer beneath the fleece in the hope the body warmth might revive it (it never did). Then I took out that eight-dollar plastic 'fun' camera I had bought in Kathmandu, and realised that this recreational toy was now my only means of taking stills. On the cardboard cover was a picture of a bronzed woman in her bikini playing with a beach-ball. Feeling utterly ridiculous, I stared through the 'eyefinder' (basically just a hole in the plastic) and clicked the first of the twelve shots available.

The camera breakdown brought back the old nightmare; would the video cameras work in the −40 degree winds? The thought of them giving up now was too much to contemplate.

Once or twice I looked back down the ridge we had come up. The figure of Al, bright red in his Berghaus wind suit, was dropping further behind. Somewhere in my oxygen-starved brain a few connections were still working. Al had not asked me to click his regulator back down to two litres.

He was still climbing on four litres a minute . . . and he was dropping further and further behind. On two occasions we waited for Al to catch us up, and then we reached the third step, where we stopped ourselves for a rest.

The third step is nothing like as demanding as the previous two, but it comes higher into the climb. Beyond it is the steep avalanche-prone ice-field of the final summit pyramid, the rock traverse, and then the summit ridge.

Grateful for the rest, I took off my pack and sat down, my heels digging into the ice to prevent a slide. Sensing the pressing need to drink, I pulled out the water bottle from where I had left it inside my down suit, half expecting it to have magically defrosted. Of course it was still frozen; what else could I expect in these temperatures?

Realising finally, and much too late, how stupid I had been, I took both bottles of ice and put them at the foot of the third step next to some abandoned oxygen cylinders. Two kilogrammes less weight to carry.

Al was resting further down the Ridge where it had flattened out into a broad expanse. I pulled out my camera and took a shot of him lying down on his back. Not far away was the second of the Indian bodies, lying with his face towards us and with no sign of pain or distress on his frozen features. Unlike the first of the bodies, which had shocked me when we came across it, I now felt no sense of surprise at the presence of the corpse—a sure indicator that my mind was occupied with other thoughts.

After a while Al joined us, and we were now contemplating the final stages of the climb. Lhakpa was increasingly agitated about the weather. The wind was now stronger than before, and the spindrift from the summit ridge was filling virtually the whole of our view to the south. The plume was starting to run in earnest, and the sinister howl of a strong wind at high altitude was beginning to fill the air.

I followed the Sherpas up the third step and we gained the steep ice of the summit pyramid. If all went well now we could be on the summit within the next two hours.

After one rope's length on the ice, Lhakpa tugged my arm and yelled above the wind:

'Where's Alan? No Alan.'

Looking back down the ice-field, I could see he was right. Al had not appeared at the top of the third step.

Every minute we waited now was putting our summit attempt in jeopardy. The weather was increasingly threatening. The Sherpas were looking to me for a decision. Should we leave Al where he was and hope his oxygen held out? Should we go back down and see if he had fallen and was lying injured at the bottom of the third step?

Of all the scenarios, the trial runs that had run like fast-forward movie previews through my mind, the possibility that Al would have a problem had never occurred to me. I was confused and shocked.

For what seemed like an age, but probably was no more than three or four minutes we looked back down at the windblown lump which marked the top of the third step. The wind played strongly across the snowslope . . . causing the four of us to turn our faces away from the blast.

My brain was struggling to come to terms with the situation and, luckily, a few synapses were still connecting. I ran through the options and realised that it was very unlikely Al had fallen: he was far too good for that. Also, he had the extra oxygen bottle, so there was no danger he would run out of air. Probably he was just resting or sorting out his gear.

That was the logical response. I convinced myself that he would follow us up in his own time. The pause gave my feet a chance to go numb; wriggling them inside the plastic boot, I could sense them freezing up. My hands were also, for the first time, beginning to freeze.

Something inside me made the decision.

'Let's go,' I told Lhakpa. The words were whipped away by a sudden gust. He stepped down the slope next to me to hear better. I didn't bother shouting again but just pointed up towards the summit. He nodded and tapped his wrist to indicate we were running out of time.

I tightened the wrist strap of my ice-axe, and followed the three Sherpas up the steepening ice.

Inside me a tiny voice was making a faint protest, posing a few umcomfortable questions: Shouldn't you go back to check? Shouldn't you consider the possibility that here nothing is certain—anything can happen? Some accident might have befallen Al, his oxygen valve might have frozen, he might have broken a crampon, he might have pulled out a rope anchor on the third step.

Pausing for breath, I looked back again at bottom of the snowface. Still no sign of Al. I carried on climbing.

Back came the soothing logic, extinguishing those glowing embers of doubt. Relax. He'll be fine. He's always run his own agenda. He's climbed K2. He's probably stopped for a call of nature. Perhaps he just doesn't want to summit with us . . . preferring to reach the top alone?

Three rope lengths up the ice-field. I looked back again. Nothing. I carried on climbing towards the rock which marked the end of the triangle. And this time I didn't look back.

I had crossed another of those invisible lines in the snow. That same force—the one which had been unlocked from its cage inside me back at the Col—had now taken complete control. I wanted the summit so much that I was turning my back on Al whatever had happened to him.

In that final hour there was really only one single focus in my entire being; the desire to reach the top of the world had become all consuming. It had extinguished my concern for my fellow climber, blocked my capacity for questioning my own actions, and turned me into little more than a robot . . . placing one foot in front of the other like a pre-programmed machine.

Summit fever had me body and soul, and now a new wave of strength seemed to flood power into me. I suddenly felt myself driving upwards almost effortlessly, and only having to stop because the Sherpas in front of me were moving more slowly. Even in my disorientated state it occurred to my mind to wonder where this new surge had come from. I was sure that by now my body should have been running close to the point of exhaustion.

What exactly was it that was propelling me up to the highest point in the world?

Now the Sherpas were tired. Lhakpa's lightning pace had run down like a discharged battery. At the start of the snow pyramid they were resting every five or six steps. At the top of the four-rope-length pitch, they were managing only one or two steps between rests.

8,750 metres. Just under 100 metres of vertical ascent to go.

The snowfield arched up, ever steeper, in a soaring curve towards what I imagined was the summit. But instead of continuing up the ice as I had hoped, Lhakpa led the way back into another of the rock cliffs which flank this final buttress.

My heart sank. More rock . . . again with the crampons.

In fact, as I saw when I examined the ice route in more detail, the top section was obviously prone to avalanche. Fresh avalanche debris, blocks the size of cars, lay scattered not far away. The way up the rock cliff was the safer of the two, if safe is the right word.

First came a traverse along another tiny ledge, eroded into a fault in the rock. Clipping on to a rope which looked like it had been there for decades, I carefully made my way along, swinging my right foot far out to avoid snagging the left. Midway—about fifty metres—along the ledge, an outcrop forced a fine balancing manoeuvre to ease the body around a bulge and back on to the ledge on the other side. At that point, the rope was forced to rest against the rock. The wind had beaten it down to just one single frayed strand, about the width and strength of a piece of knitting wool. And about as much use in stopping a fall.

I found myself laughing as I shifted my cramponed feet into position to make the move.

The drop falling away beneath us here was the most sheer yet. We had made our way across the Face and were now positioned almost exactly below the summit, far to the right of the great couloir. The small stones and flakes of rock which we all unavoidably kicked loose, didn't bounce their way down as they had before . . . they just fell out of sight into the abyss.

My face sliding against the rock to press as much of my weight as possible away from the fall, I inched nervously around the obstacle and then rested, gasping for breath. Only then did I realise that I had held my breath during the move . . . a wave of blackness, a desire to faint, swept over me as I struggled to get oxygen into my body. Regaining my composure, I carried on along the decaying ledge. I had thought I was moving faster than the Sherpas, but they had already rounded the corner and were out of sight.

At the end of the traverse, the route stepped up abruptly in a series of ledges similar to those we had encountered on some of the night stages. I used my arms to pull myself up wherever possible, still stubbornly reluctant to trust my weight to the crampon points.

On one of the steps my safety sling got snagged into an old piece of rope and caught me in mid-move. I had to fall back on to the ledge and regain my balance before clearing the snag and continuing on.

After perhaps twenty minutes of climbing, we emerged on to the upper slopes of the summit pyramid snowfield, having effectively bypassed the more avalanche-prone section and gained about fifty metres of height.

During the detour, the wind had increased again. Now the snow ridge, and the skyline above us were cloaked in snarling clouds of air-borne ice. The wind was fickle, blowing with unpredictable violent blasts. The upward view was the most intimidating, with a huge circulating mass of ice particles twisting like a miniature tornado above what I presumed to be the summit, just twenty metres of steep ice above us.

We found some shelter in the lee of a rock outcrop and waited there to gain our breath for the final push. So close to the summit, I found myself barely able to wait. An irrational wave of paranoia swept over me; we were just minutes away . . . what if it was snatched away from us at the final moment?

Lhakpa looked at his watch again and then spoke to Gyaltsen. I couldn't hear their words but, in my paranoid state, I imagined them discussing how dangerous the wind would be on the top . . . agreeing that we should turn back. . . .

Then my senses snapped into gear, and I recognised my paranoia for what it was: the insidious beginnings of high altitude sickness where irrational thoughts are often the first stage. Since leaving the tent eight hours before, I had not drunk a single drop of fluid. My body was dehydrating dangerously.

Lhakpa led the way up painfully slowly into the cloud of spindrift, with Gyaltsen and Mingma behind him and myself at the back. There were no ropes here and I took care to dig as many crampon spikes as I could into the ice. Halfway up, I took out the plastic camera and framed it vertically for a shot of the three Sherpas as they rested.

I hadn't thought that it might be a false summit. But it was. Reaching the crest of the snowfield, I was taken completely by surprise by what lay before us. Instead of the short final stage I had imagined, we were now standing at the beginning of the final ridge; with the great bulging cornice of the true summit waiting at the far end. Between our position and the top lay a series of switchback ice waves, blown into shape by the wind, and overhanging the Kanshung Face.

By some trick of perspective, or perhaps another irrational side effect of oxygen starvation, the ridge looked huge, and the summit seemed kilometres away. For another of those bizarre moments of doubt, I thought Lhakpa and the others would pull the plug and decide not to continue. The wind was blowing hard now, and more consistently. The plume was running and we were about to walk right into it.

Then I noticed the clue which revealed the true perspective of the ridge; a string or prayer flags which had been fixed to the summit was now hanging sadly down the side. I could clearly make out the individual pennants of coloured silk. That visual reference pulled the ridge back down to scale and I realised it was much smaller than I had at first thought.

The summit was just a few hundred metres away.

from K2: Dreams and Reality
by Jim Haberl

Canadians Jim Haberl (born in 1958) and Dan Culver attempted K2 via the Abruzzi Ridge as part of a 1993 expedition led by American Stacy Allison. Haberl, Culver and American climber Phil Powers set out for the summit from Camp 4 at 8050 meters (about 26,000 feet). Conditions were perfect.

A t 2:30 a.m. I moved out of the tent and stepped into my crampons. With clumsy overboots and the first movement of the day at this height, even that simple process was a struggle. My fingers stiffened quickly. It took me fifteen minutes to get organized. Then I left for the top.

The full moon radiated brightly in the cold night sky, casting my shadow to the right, making my headlamp unnecessary. I carried only a water bottle in my pocket and a small camera. Dan followed next, carrying a pack with his big camera and zoom lens, a video camera, water bottle and extra gear inside. The total weight on his back was ten kilograms, a significant amount at 8000 metres. Phil left camp last with a two litre water bag strapped inside his jacket, a small camera, our tiny drug kit of injectable Decadron in case one of us developed high altitude edema and the radio in his pocket.

We were at our physical limits as we climbed above 8000 metres toward the summit of K2. We were not roped together for the summit bid, a decision we all felt was the safest, and the moderate thirty to forty degree snow slopes provided an excellent path to the top. At that altitude it was doubtful any of us could check the fall of a partner without an anchor, and to build anchors in deep snow is a time- and energy-consuming chore. The conditions we found on K2 were better than we could have hoped for; the snow was soft and secure and the weather perfect. If one of us climbed faster and the others were caught by darkness on the descent, that person could shine a headlamp like a lighthouse to direct the others to Camp 4. For these reasons we decided it would be safest to climb without roping together. Each of us knew he was on his own.

There was a bitter wind blowing down from the summit and my feet and hands were painfully cold. I knew that I should begin to worry about frostbite the minute I lost that sense of pain. We carried no thermometer but the temperature was well below freezing. There was no chance to warm up cold toes and fingers, so I plodded ahead. The altitude kept our pace so slow it was impossible to generate any heat. At that great height, bodies adapt by increasing the red blood cell count. In turn, more oxygen gets to the cellular level, but the blood gets thicker and the risk of cold injury to the toes and fingers increases dramatically. Climbing without the aid of bottled oxygen had been a conscious decision based on style. That decision also increased the risk of our adventure. I was not thinking of biological processes or climbing styles. I was simply cold.

Despite the bitter temperatures it was stunningly beautiful. The icy air had snapped me fully awake and cleared my fuzzy head. A new feeling began to grow inside me: maybe we—I—really would reach the top. Our summit bid was starting out in cold but otherwise perfect weather.

Predictably, just before 6:00 a.m., the sun began to make its way over the horizon—hundreds of kilometres away and thousands of metres below us over China. I stared in wonder at the scene below my feet and prayed that the radiant warmth from the sun would quickly thaw my cold extremities and ease my fears of frostbite. I continued to kick steps in the soft snow, which was getting steeper as we neared the rocks and slopes above. The effect of the sun's heat slowed the wind descending from the summit and this, more than anything, helped warm our frigid bodies.

I led the way to a small rock ledge and stopped for the first break of the day after more than three hours of climbing. Each of us sipped water from our bottles, put on another layer of sunscreen, lifted our feet off the snow to let the sun warm our boots, and enjoyed the heat. The Bottleneck loomed directly above and appeared to be in good condition.

The Bottleneck is a narrow gully, only a few metres across, of steep, forty-five degree snow and rock, the technical crux of K2's summit day on the Abruzzi Ridge. Some years it is a demanding rock climb; other years it is covered in a thin layer of ice—strenuous and difficult at 8200 metres. Regardless of the conditions, the Bottleneck is always threatened by an intimidating wall of seracs—impending ice towers—which loom menacingly above. During our ascent, the gully was choked with snow from the previous winter, and we made progress in a controlled way, kicking regular steps and trying to conserve energy in the deep snow.

Phil led off from our break with Dan following. The sun continued to rise and our concerns about the cold were replaced an hour later with those of overheating. When I looked ahead at Phil, I could see the butt flap on his puffy down suit was dangling open for ventilation. As for me, I would never have dreamed I would climb towards the summit of the world's second-highest peak without a hat on.

As we neared the Bottleneck I was shocked to see Dan slip and fall, sliding by me in the soft snow. But before he had gained any momentum, he was able to stop himself with his ice axe and climb back into our line of steps behind me. It was just a little stumble which amounted to nothing more than lost effort. The three of us quietly returned to kicking steps in the snow.

Phil climbed through the Bottleneck and waited. I could see him sitting on a rock at the top, watching. I followed his steps across a rocky section to where he was sitting, cautiously placing each crampon on the small holds of rock. I decided that later in the day, on the way down, my route would be a few metres further to the north in the deeper snow of the gully to avoid delicate rock climbing at this great height. Climbing down is always harder than climbing up.

I yelled at Dan to stay in the gully and bypass the rock Phil and I had climbed. Dan was still forty metres behind.

From the top of the Bottleneck we traversed left above rock cliffs and continued our ascent on snow slopes toward the top, still 350 metres above. Our way to the summit was now only a matter of perseverance and time. We each withdrew into our private mental shells, focused on the task. Our pace was steady but slow; I counted breaths between each step—my mantra—and soon I was up to fifteen deep breaths for every step. I had a new definition of slow, but gradually the terrain fell away below me.

Phil was in front, methodically kicking shin-deep steps in the soft snow, and though I was following his track I could not catch up to him. After we passed the seracs, Phil went up and right in a broad snow corner created by the meeting of the hanging glacier and a snow slope to the left. The snow in the corner was hideous—loose and unconsolidated for over 100 metres. It seemed that every step broke away as it was weighted. Although it was safe, it was a very frustrating and energy-consuming section.

While Phil wrestled with the corner, I traversed out to the left and dug a quick test profile in the snow. I was looking for avalanche hazard, knowing the quickest and easiest way down would not be in the corner Phil was presently climbing, but down the slope if it was safe. Deep snow made climbing up that slope impossible, but on descent it would feel very secure. My profile observations confirmed that the snow was stable and I made another decision for the descent.

I rested every once in a while but knew how important it was for us to keep going. Far below, the other members of our team arrived at Camp 4. Stacy, John Haigh and John Petroske looked like ants on a sidewalk from our vantage point just below the summit.

The views were spectacular. Mountains in all directions. These were the peaks I grew up reading about: Broad Peak and the four Gasherbrum summits to the east, the Latok peaks, the Ogre and Mustagh Tower to the southwest and Masherbrum and Chogolisa to the southeast. They all became part of me; no longer pictures in a book or words on a page, they would be real peaks in my memory. And K2. Now I could say I knew K2. I had climbed on its rock, slept on its flanks and huddled from the wind behind its ridges. And incredibly, we were near its summit.

On July 7, 1993 at 2:57 p.m., twelve hours after leaving Camp 4, Phil became the ninth American to reach the top of K2 at 8611 metres. He looked out at Gasherbrum II, an 8000-metre peak he had climbed in 1987, and later said, "It looked tiny." I could see him near the top, less than 200 metres from me but still a formidable distance away at my present pace. Phil radioed Base Camp from the peak to find that the entire Strip was tuned in. Barry Blanchard, who was at K2 with fellow Canadians Peter Arbic and Troy Kirwan attempting a bold, alpine-style ascent of the South Pillar, jested with Phil, "I can't believe there's a hick from Wyoming on the summit of K2." In a tone mixed with pride and excitement Yousaf said, "Phil, I am taking your picture while you are on top of K2. You will not be able to see you in this picture but you will know you are there because I am taking it now, while you are on top of K2." Stacy came on the radio from Camp 4 and asked, "Phil, where are you?" Phil responded, "I'm on the tippy top!" He snapped a picture of himself and then turned around and began the descent.

Phil and I met on his way down. We hugged and spoke briefly together. Always concerned about safety, Phil asked if I would consider turning around due to the late hour of the day. His worry was that I was still some distance from the top and the descent would be challenging or impossible in the dark. I told him that I was feeling in control and would continue with my climb. I thought the descent would go quickly.

We talked about Dan and his progress. We were both troubled that Dan, who had kept up a good pace the entire climb to Camp 4, was now falling behind. Phil said he would speak with Dan and suggest he turn around and descend with him. He then asked if I wanted the radio and the high-altitude drugs he carried in his pocket. I declined that offer. I stood and watched Phil cautiously pick his way down the route toward Dan, several hundred metres away. I noticed that Dan had left his pack far below, finally dropping the weight which was slowing him down; even a few kilograms at that height can make a difference. They embraced. The Swedish team in Base Camp watched that show of emotion through their powerful telescope. Phil asked Dan to descend with him but Dan said, "I gotta go." Phil continued on his way down to Camp 4, descending out of sight, leaving the radio and the drug kit in Dan's pack. Dan and I exchanged a wave of acknowledgement, then we both returned to the task at hand—the final metres to the top.

Fifty minutes after Phil, I reached a point only five metres below K2's grand summit and stopped to wait for Dan. We had decided long ago to try to make the first Canadian ascent of the mountain together. So I carved a platform and sat down in the afternoon sun. A more magical experience would be hard to imagine.

I stared out at the countless mountains below me and simply absorbed the wonder of it all. In every direction lay peaks and glaciers: some world famous, many unnamed, all part of a remarkable creation. It was a wondrous time for me, alone in that place, only faintly aware that I was sitting at 8600 metres on one of the world's most challenging and treacherous mountains. It was 3:50 p.m., and time seemed to stand still.

Forty-five minutes later, Dan climbed into view. Together we took the final steps to the top. It was one of my life's extraordinary moments.

I snapped two photographs of Dan to capture the instant. We had shared a dream and realized it in almost storybook fashion. I thought of my family and friends, people who had supported me through the years, allowing me to reach such a place. Years of climbing and mountain experience had led to that moment. Dan and I hugged on K2's peak. My breathing got even more difficult as an emotional lump formed in my throat.

With the ascent of K2, Dan, a man who had taken to mountaineering only seven years before, joined a rare band of adventurous climbers who had reached the summit of both K2 and Mount Everest—a feat accomplished by fewer people on Earth than have flown in space.

On the top Dan took off his mitts and with cold fingers fumbled with the two cameras he had carried up inside his suit. First he shot some video then some stills. He took photographs with us holding the Canadian flag, then environmental banners designed to raise the profile of two wilderness land-use issues we were concerned about back home in British Columbia: clear-cut logging in Clayoquot Sound and a huge strip mine near the Tatshenshini River. Neither of us could have known that the Tatshenshini River had been preserved in its entirety only two weeks before, yet both of us knew how exploring British Columbia's wilderness helped shape our lives.

Time drifted past. My hands got cold. By 4:55 p.m. it was time to leave the top. The wind had shifted and the weather was changing. Our luck had run out. Very suddenly the afternoon air began to lose its heat and the pleasant pinnacle of K2 became a place of potential danger. I had stuck around on the summit for over an hour and knew it was time to go. We turned our backs to K2's peak and carefully began the process of descending to Camp 4.

Each step down the mountain required concentration. I was very aware of the risk of stumbling or catching a crampon, careful of every foot placement and consciously assessing the quality of the snow to make sure there were no surprises. The upper mountain consisted of hard-packed snow, compressed by the wind which pours across K2's ridges and faces. After half an hour of carefully choosing our way, we gratefully stepped into the deep snow of the sheltered slope where I had earlier dug my observation pit. Here we relaxed somewhat and plunged down in the soft snow for twenty minutes. Everything was going well; we were tired but descending steadily.

It was 6:15 p.m. by the time I traversed to the Bottleneck, only 300 metres above Camp 4. Dan was several minutes behind and I decided this was convenient as we could downclimb the Bottleneck separately. I continued facing out and very carefully began the descent of the gully. Occasionally, as the soft snow gave way and my crampons scraped on the rocks below, I instinctively fought to keep my balance. Fatigue and terrain combined and I had a few awkward stumbles in the Bottleneck, but slowly the worst of it was behind me.

Camp 4 was just below and, as in the morning, my crampons dug confidently into the hard surface. I began the traverse towards Camp 4 and glanced up to see that Dan was entering the Bottleneck. Summit day was almost over. Finally. I wanted to relax and enjoy our success.

Seconds later my brain was brutally invaded by a loud, crashing noise, a noise which in an instant shattered the silence and the harmony of the day. I spun around to see Dan cartwheeling violently through the snow, rolling by me at high speed. I stared in horror. All I could see was Dan tumbling faster and faster, his blonde hair in the tangle of the fall. As he hit the hard snow below me his limp body began gaining momentum. Only a miracle would stop him.

There was no miracle.

I watched Dan hit some small rocks 100 metres below then continue to fall down a broad chute gaining speed with every passing second. He disappeared from my sight. I wanted not to believe.

My throat seized up in a swell of emotion. Weakly I croaked for help. Camp 4 was only 200 metres away. I yelled for help again, hoping that someone would hear. Then I cried out for Dan and listened. Nothing. I followed the line of his fall and carefully picked my way down through the rocks. The marks in the hard snow became farther and farther apart, spans of more than thirty metres, as his body had bounded down the face.

Gravity.

I found his hat.

My legs were tired and the steepening terrain of the South Face was the last place I wanted to be. I stopped on a ledge and stared down the huge expanse of the mountain at my feet. There was no sign of Dan. Nothing. I yelled his name for what seemed the hundredth time. There was no response. I sat down on the ledge in disbelief.

Dan was dead.

The salty taste of the tears rolling off my cheeks into my cracked lips brought me slowly back to the world of reality. I knew in my head that Dan was gone, yet my heart was yearning to refuse that logic. I was alone, sitting on a ledge just below 8000 metres and looking down the immense South Face of K2, wondering where Dan's body would come to rest. I took no solace then, in the thin cold air, knowing that Dan's spirit would remain with many of us forever. Thoughts like that were for another time. For me it was time to brave the descent of K2 without him.

Through the haze of emotion and altitude I assessed my situation. First, I had to climb back up to Camp 4, and painstakingly regain the several hundred metres of terrain which I had lost trying to find Dan. Time was still moving relentlessly ahead and glancing at my watch I realized we—rather, I—had been climbing for over fifteen hours above 8000 metres. I was physically exhausted and had just ridden an emotional roller coaster to the bottom of the big hill. It had been three days since my last morsel of food. Darkness would eclipse the Karakoram mountains in less than an hour. I had to shift into a pattern of decisions which would allow me to survive. I remembered vaguely that the wind had shifted too—a storm was coming.

It was time to be careful, not a time for mistakes. I felt weak and sad but determined to make it safely back to Camp 4. It took half an hour for me to manage the terrain back to the ridge. As I climbed slowly over the crest of the ridge I met Stacy, John and John. They were all geared up with ropes, first aid equipment and the energy to help with a rescue. There was nothing they could do. I told them through tears that Dan had died; then I fell backwards in the snow. John and John helped me to my feet and we all shared an embrace. The first of many. I remember walking carelessly across the flat ridge to the tent.

Phil was making hot drinks as I crawled into our tent. I tried to reflect on what had just happened. In the background, I could hear Stacy talking to Yousaf in Base Camp, relating the news of Dan's fall. Yousaf would take it hard; he and Dan had become good friends.

Dan. I wondered if he was out there somewhere? I fought to get my boots off in the cold. Insulated overboots always make it tougher to reach the laces. Maybe he was badly hurt. I pulled my down sleeping bag around my shoulders and slumped to the back of the tent. Was he bleeding? Barely clinging to a rock? Phil passed me a cup of warm water and I sipped it appreciatively. If anyone could survive such a huge fall it would be Dan. God knows there had been other close calls. I felt very tired. Could he still be alive? My imagination tried to dominate my logical brain.

I knew Dan was dead.

Very quickly it turned to night and the wind was building from the south. I knew he was dead.

The hot water tasted good. My cool fingers wrapped around the warm mug and gratefully absorbed the heat. I still could not imagine the thought of anything but water. No food. The night air was getting colder by the minute but my sleeping bag was warm. After one more drink I was finished for the day. I needed some sleep.

The storm came to full force around 3:00 a.m. I guess we knew it would; the wind shift and the plummeting barometer had warned us. I coughed through the night keeping both myself and Phil awake. Phil was anxiously listening to the cough, hoping I did not develop any fluid. It remained a dry, irritating hack which was good; no high altitude edema in my lungs. Phil leaned against the tent wall to reduce the stress from the powerful wind on the poles and waited for daylight. There were five of us camped at just over 8000 metres: Phil, Stacy, John Haigh, John Petroske and myself. At first light, Stacy looked outside her tent and announced that the visibility was only ten metres. Gusts of wind lashed at our small tents, threatening to tear them from the mountain. My thoughts went out to Dan, wishing him well, knowing I would never see him again.

By 8:00 a.m. we had packed up our tents and equipment and left Camp 4. We stumbled from wand to wand towards Camp 3 in fierce winds and near-zero visibility. The fifteen metre spacing of our glacier wands now seemed barely enough. Phil led the way, assessing our route for any new avalanche hazard from wind-loaded snow. Ice crystals driven by the wind stung my face. The noise was constant and intense. There was no relief from this unrelenting attack on my senses. Just surviving helped me to forget.

We dragged ourselves into the snowcave at Camp 3, grateful for a quiet break from the ruthless, hurricane-force winds outside. The silence and comfort of the cave was a remarkable contrast to the pounding of the mountain's storm only two metres away. I ripped the goggles off my face and peeled two centimetres of wind-driven ice from around the edges.

Soon there was warm water on the stove and the comfort of a small hole in the snow with five friends crammed inside. The respite from the storm allowed thoughts of Dan to once again surface in my brain. It was going to be a difficult time. I leaned back, closed my eyes and saw Dan. I could not get him off my mind. Again I wondered if he had survived the fall and was hurt but still alive on the South Face somewhere. These thoughts were illogical. I had seen his fall. I had watched him die. Still my mind invented several images. I hated this picture of Dan: bloody, alone and waiting to die, the storm raging around him. With great effort, I drove those visions from my head.

Dan was gone.

After a brief two-hour break at Camp 3 we slid out the cave's entrance to face the elements once more. Instantly, we were back into survival mode. The wind slapped my face without mercy. Exhausted, I turned my back and prepared to descend. Phil had left his pack outside the snowcave's entrance and it was gone; blown off the mountain. His camera, clothing, sleepingbag—everything. Gone. We had to get off K2 to escape the storm and the deadly effects of high altitude.

From the snowcave entrance we had fixed ropes as a guide, but the weather continued to batter us as we rappelled through the Black Pyramid, dangling on the lines. The wind manhandled me again and again, throwing me into the rocks. John Haigh was lifted by gusts and slammed into the mountain. What had taken only an hour in calm weather turned into three hours of stress and survival in the intensity of the storm. Without the preparation and effort of the past month, our descent would have been impossible. At least the way was familiar and manageable; we just needed to be careful.

I reached Camp 2 at 2:30 p.m. and had already decided to stay the night. I was too weak to continue and was worried that I could make a mistake if I pushed on. Phil, Stacy and John Haigh left for Base Camp, arriving there just after dark. Peter Arbic and Ghulam hiked out to meet them and while Peter coiled the rope Ghulam hugged his friends and said only, "Sorry." Late that night, Phil sat in Ghulam's tent drinking tea. Ghulam said, "Now, you promise, never return to K2." Phil promised. John Petroske had volunteered to stay in Camp 2 with me. Together we waited out the night at 6700 metres.

The storm continued into the night's darkness. John and I curled deeper into our sleeping bags and hoped it would go away. Both of us were happy that our team had made the effort and that our tent was sheltered behind the small rock ridge at Camp 2. The other tents—the Swedish and Dutch—were being pummelled harshly by the weather and were on the verge of being destroyed. John and I were alone on K2.

We woke at first light on July 9 to find the storm raging unabated. After a brief radio contact with Base Camp, relieved to hear that Stacy, John Haigh and Phil had reached there safely the night before, we crawled out of our tent and faced the powerful winds and driving snow. We had rested for sixteen hours which helped us to concentrate despite the noise and fury of the wind. We set up each rappel with care. Neither of us wanted a mistake.

Two hours later, just after 10:00 a.m., we rappelled into Camp I and dove into the small tent, still wearing all of our equipment. Neither of us worried about the impact of a careless crampon on the delicate nylon walls. Escape was all we craved. We would come back later to clean our gear from the mountain.

After thirty minutes inside our shelter at Camp I, we stepped back into the storm and continued down the ropes leading to Advanced Base Camp. It took two hours to reach the bottom of the Abruzzi and I felt very weak. It had been more than four days since I had eaten anything and my energy had been sapped by the days above 7500 metres combined with the emotional drain of Dan's death. The weight of my pack was too much and I abandoned it right there. I would come back and get it another time.

From Advanced Base Camp I gratefully followed John's lead across the Godwin-Austen Glacier towards Base Camp. Finally, we were off the mountain.

The walk was frustrating. We were tired and impatient to be in Base Camp as soon as possible, but the warming snowpack on the glacier would barely support our weight. Every few steps one of our legs would poke through the surface crust. I felt like screaming. The struggle to recover from knee-deep holes was sucking the last reserves of my strength. I was letting go. Sensing that we were off the mountain and past any real hazard, I let my guard drop and nearly abandoned my physical will to continue. We had crossed this familiar terrain more than fifteen times during June and early July while preparing for our final ascent of the mountain, but this trip across the Godwin-Austen Glacier was the slowest and most difficult.

Then we heard a loud crack high up in the clouds on K2.

I saw John look up. Wearily I followed his gaze and saw nothing, only the thick, low ceiling of clouds shrouding the surrounding mountain walls, completely blocking our view of the upper slopes of K2 and. Broad Peak. We shrugged our shoulders and turned our energy back to the disheartening snow.

Two steps later the loud rumble turned into a huge avalanche pouring out of the clouds. The South Face of K2 had released its storm snow.

Run!

Where? There was nowhere to go. After an instant of panic, John and I turned our backs to the onrushing snow and dropped to our knees. At least there was a kilometre of flat glacier between us and the base of K2's South Face to take some of the energy out of the avalanche.

It hit with such force John was immediately blown from my side. I felt the air being sucked out of me. I could not breathe. I was being pushed along the flat glacier on my hands and knees by the force of the blast. The wind was overwhelming. It was as though I was caught in a turbulent riptide, completely helpless in the power of the avalanche's wave. I prayed that the sweep of snow contained only powder, no chunks of serac ice or large rocks. Their impact would surely be crippling. Or deadly.

The powerful initial blast must have lasted only a few seconds but it seemed like several long minutes. Then the speed of the avalanche gradually slowed and snow began building up around me. Fortunately, when its energy was spent the deposit was only twenty centimetres of loose snow. I marvelled at the might and the mercy of nature's forces.

I looked around and saw John, five metres away, wrapped in the rope like a Christmas present. He stood up and dusted himself off. We smiled weakly at each other and I said, "John, let's just go home."

We stumbled across the flat glacier toward the moraine where our Base Camp was located. In the distance, I saw four people coming to greet us. As we neared I could see it was Phil and my three Canadian friends: Troy, Peter and Barry. They had come to accompany John and me on our last steps into Base Camp.

The meeting was filled with emotion. I felt secure in their arms but the affection and friendship of their long embraces again brought my feelings of sorrow and loss to the surface from my purposely hidden reservoirs deep inside. I let go, too tired to care about anything else. Tears poured out.

The final few hundred metres among the scattered rocks to our Base Camp were unusually quiet. Thankfully. Snow was falling lightly and the Dutch, Catalonian and British teams were resting inside their tents as we crept silently through their camps. My spirit was at rock bottom. I had no energy to tell our story. Had I been less tired and thinking more clearly I would have known that it did not matter—each climber, no matter the country, knew the makings of our tale. Though it was personal for me, for K2 it was generic. K2 kills climbers.

Everyone kept tent doors closed and left our account for another time. They knew that in a few days or weeks—during the next clear weather from the north in China—they might be feeling as I was, living their own tragic saga after a summit bid on the mountain.

Walking into Base Camp stirred yet more emotion. Reunited with my friends, Dan's friends, made me feel like I was the luckiest person alive. All of us wept.

Death is trying for those who are left behind. To attempt to express our deep feelings and pain is something few people have much practice at. Probably a good thing. All of us stopped trying to talk about what had happened and instead escaped the foul weather inside our dining tent. I sat in a back corner and listened to the others while I sipped at a bowl of hot broth from Ghulam's kitchen. It had been five days since my last scrap of food. My stomach was still queasy but the soup was delicious.

Eventually, after a second warm drink and some moments of uneasy conversation, I excused myself and went to the tent Dan and I had shared in Base Camp. I wanted to get out of my harness, boots and suit; I reeked of days-old urine. Now that I was off the mountain I could not stand my own stench. The inner layers of my clothing were stuck to my body. I wanted to get out of everything associated with K2.

The tent was just as we had left it, although the platform of rock and ice it rested on had melted slightly after six days. As a passing thought, I realized I would have to move our tent again soon. Inside, everything of Dan's was still there. All his books, his journal, letters from home to be opened after the summit, good luck charms sent by friends hanging from the roof, pictures taped to the tent wall—everything. My emotional purging was going to take a long time.

I peeled off my suit and long underwear. I stripped down to nothing and threw all the disgusting inner layers out the door into the snow. I smelled terrible.

My skin tingled in the cool air.

I stared in disbelief at my naked body. I had withered away to nothing. My muscles had shrivelled and gone; my legs felt soft and flabby. I saw only skin and bones. K2 had taken its physical toll of me. Changing into clean cotton, I crawled inside my sleeping bag and slept deeply for the rest of the afternoon.

from Everest the Hard Way
by Chris Bonington

Six expeditions failed on Everest's massive and technically difficult Southwest Face before British climber Chris Bonington, born in 1934, returned to the Face for his second attempt in 1975. Dougal Haston and Doug Scott made the summit push, and Bonington let them tell the story in his 1976 book about the trip.

Doug Scott

I caught Dougal up at the bottom of the Rock Band and carried on up into the foot of the gully. I cleared the rope of ice as I jumared up, conscious of the struggle that Tut must have had, firstly traversing into the gully and then clambering over the snow-covered boulder jammed against it halfway up. I noted the new perspective with interest, for the ropes led through a huge gash—a veritable Devil's Kitchen of a chasm 300 feet deep into the rocks, whereas the rest of Everest had been wide slopes and broad open valleys. At the top of the gully I followed Nick's rope out and up steeply right. I clipped onto the rope, using it as a safety rail, rather than pulling on it directly with my jumars, for he had warned me that the rope was anchored to pegs of dubious quality. It was awkward climbing with a framed rucksack, especially as the straps kept slipping on crucial hard sections. Nick had done a first-class job leading it without oxygen. I was glad to get to his high point and hammer in extra pegs.

Ang Phurba came up the rope next, for Dougal had stopped lower down to adjust his crampons which kept falling off his sponge over-boots and also to disentangle the remains of Nick's rope. Ang Phurba belayed me with all the confidence of a regular Alpine climber. I think he is the most natural climber I have ever met amongst the Sherpas. After only thirty feet of difficult climbing I tied off the rope and Ang Phurba came up to me. I stood there exhausted from having climbed a vertical ten-foot block with too much clothing and too heavy a sack. From there I led out 250 feet of rope to a site for Camp 6. Ang Phurba came up and we both kicked out a small notch in a ridge of snow which could be enlarged to take our summit box tent. Dougal came up with his crampons swinging from his waist.

Dougal Haston

I hauled onto the proposed site of Camp 6. Straight away my energy and upward urges came rushing back—there ahead in reality was the way we'd been hypothetically tracing for so long with fingers on pho-tographs and making us forget everything else was the fact it looked feasible. There was a steepish-looking rock pitch just ahead, but after it seemed like unbroken snow slopes to the couloir. It looked as if progress was inevitable as long as the others were successful in their carry. Ang Phurba kept muttering about a campsite further up under some rocks, but this looked like wasted effort to us, as the traverse line started logically from where we were at the moment. Diplomatically we told him that we were staying there, it being mainly Doug's and my concern, as we were going to have to occupy the camp, and he started off down, leaving his valuable load. We began digging in spells, with-out oxygen, but using some to regain strength during the rests.

Mike, Chris and Mick arrived one after the other, looking tired, as well they should be. Carrying heavy loads at over 27,000 feet is no easy occupation.

Doug Scott

Theirs had been a magnificent carry, especially Chris, who had now been at Camp 5 and above for eight days, and also Mick, who was carrying a dead weight of cine equipment. He had been at Camp 5 for five days, and Pertemba had worked hard practically every day of the expedition carrying heavy loads and encouraging his Sherpas, while Mike Thompson, who had never been above 23,000 feet before, had arrived carrying a heavy sack with apparent ease at 27,300 feet. We sat there talking confidently in the late afternoon. There was a strong bond of companionship as there had been all the way up the Face. One by one they departed for Camp 5 and they left us with the bare essentials to make this last step to the top of our route and perhaps the summit itself. I yelled our thanks down to Mike as they were sliding back down the rope. He must have known his chances of making a summit bid were slim, yet he replied, "Just you get up, that's all the reward I need." And that's how it had been from start to finish with all members of the team. It had taken the combined effort of forty Sherpas, and sixteen climbers, together with Chris's planning, to get the two of us into this position. We knew how lucky we were being the representatives of such a team and to be given the chance to put the finishing touches to all our efforts. Finally Mick left, having run all the film he had through the cameras. Dougal and I were left alone to dig out a more substantial platform and to erect the two-man summit tent. We were working without oxygen and took frequent rests to recover, but also to look across the Upper Snow Field leading up to the South Summit couloir. After the tent was up, Dougal got inside to prepare the evening meal, whilst I pottered about outside stowing away equipment in a little ice cave and tying empty oxygen bottles around the tent to weight it down. They hung in festoons on either side of the snow arête. Finally I bundled rope and oxygen bottles into our sacks for the following morning and dived into the tent to join Dougal.

Dougal Haston

Inside, we worked on plans for the next day. We had 500 metres of rope for fixing along the traverse and hoped to do that, then come back to 6 and make our big push the day after.

I was higher on Everest than I'd ever been before, yet thoughts of the summit were still far away in the thinking and hoping process. It had all seemed so near before in 1971 and 1972: euphoric nights at Camps 5 and 6 when progress had seemed good and one tended to skip the difficult parts with visions of oneself standing at the top of the South West Face, then reality shattering the dreams in progressive phases as realisation of certain failure burst the bubble. There had been an inevitability about both previous failures, but still carrying a lot of disappointment. Failure you must accept, but that does not make it any easier, especially on a project like the South West Face, where so much thinking, willpower and straight physical effort are necessary to get to the higher points. This time it seemed better. We were above the Rock Band and the ground ahead looked climbable, but I kept a rigid limit on my thoughts, contemplating possible progress along the traverse to the exit couloir, nothing more. If that proved possible then I would allow for further up-type thinking.

Our physical situation felt comfortable. Maybe that is a reflection of the degree of progress that we have made in our adaptation to altitude. Many the story we had read or been told about assault camps on the world's highest peak. No one ever seemed to spend a comfortable night at Camp 6 on the South Col route. Their nights seemed to be compounded of sleeplessness, discomfort and thirst. Here there was none of that. The situation was very bearable. We weren't stretched personally, didn't even feel tired or uncomfortable, despite a long day. The stove brewed the hours away—tea, lemon drinks and even a full-scale meal with meat and mashed potatoes. Each was deep into his own thoughts with only one slightly urgent communal reaction as a change of oxygen cylinder went wrong and the gas stove roared into white heat. Order was restored before an explosion, with Doug fixing the leak at the same time as I turned off the stove. Emergency over, we laughed, conjuring visions of the reaction at Camp 2 as Camp 6 exploded like a successfully attacked missile target. It would have been a new reason for failure!

Thereafter sleep claimed its way, and I moved gently into another world of tangled dreams, eased by a gentle flow of oxygen. The night was only disturbed by a light wind rocking our box and a changing of sleeping cylinders. One would need to be a good or very exhausted sleeper to sleep through a cylinder running out. From a gentle warm comfort one suddenly feels cold, uneasy and very awake. Just after midnight and the changeover, we gave up sleeping and started the long task of preparing for the morning's work.

Shortly after first light I moved out into blue and white dawn to continue the upward way, leaving Doug wrapped in all the down in the tent mouth, cameras and belays set up for action. There was a rock step lurking ahead that had seemed reasonably close in the setting afternoon sun of the previous day. Now in the clear first light, a truer perspective was established as I kept on thrusting into the deep-powdered fifty-degree slope, sliding sideways like a crab out of its element reaching for an object that didn't seem to come any closer. One hundred metres of this progress it was, before I could finally fix a piton and eye the rock step. It wasn't long, seven or eight metres, but looked difficult enough. Downward-sloping, steep slabs with a layer of powder. Interesting work. Grade 5* at this height. Much concentration and three more pitons saw a delicate rightwards exit and back, temporarily thankful, into deep snow to finish the rope length and finally give Doug the signal to move.

Doug Scott

I traversed across on his rope and up the difficult rocks to his stance. I led out another 400 feet over much easier ground, parallel with the top of the Rock Band. We gradually armed to the task and began to enjoy our position. After all the months of dreaming, here we were cutting across that Upper Snow Field. Dougal led out the next reel of rope.

Dougal Haston

The conditions and climbing difficulty began to change again. Kicking through with crampons I found there was no ice beneath. Rock

*There are six standards of climbing, Grade 6 being the most difficult. Grade 5 is quite steep and difficult and had certainly never before been tackled at this altitude.

slabs only, which have never been renowned for their adherence to front points. A few tentative movements up, down, sideways proved it existed all around. It seemed the time for a tension traverse. But on what? The rock was shattered loose and worse—no cracks. After I had scraped away a large area a small moveable flake appeared. It would have to do. Tapping in the beginnings of an angle, which seemed to be okay to pull on but not for a fall, I started tensioning across to an inviting-looking snow lump. Thoughts flashed through my mind of a similar traverse nine years before, near the top of the Eiger Direct. There it would have been all over with a slip, and suddenly, as I worked it out, things didn't look too good here, if you cared to think in those directions. Not only didn't I care to, I also didn't dare to think of full consequences, and chasing the dangerous thoughts away, I concentrated on tiptoeing progress. Slowly the limit of tension was reached and my feet were on some vaguely adhering snow. This will have to do for the present, were my thoughts as I let go the rope and looked around. A couple of probes with the axe brought nothing but a sense of commitment.

"No man is an island," it is said. I felt very close to a realisation of the contrary of this, standing on that semi-secure snow step in the midst of a sea of insecurity. But there was no racing adrenalin, only the cold clinical thought of years of experience. About five metres away the snow appeared to deepen. It would have to be another tension traverse. Long periods of excavation found no cracks. Tugs on the rope and impatient shouting from Doug. Communication at altitude is bad in awkward situations. One has to take off the oxygen mask to shout. Then when one tries to do this, one's throat is so dry and painful that nothing comes out. Hoping that Doug would keep his cool, I carried on, looking for a piton placement. A reasonable-looking crack came to light and two pitons linked up meant the game could go on. This time I felt I could put more bearing weight on the anchor. Just as well. Twice the tension limit failed, and there was the skidding movement backwards on the scraping slabs. But a third try and a long reach saw me in deep good snow, sucking oxygen violently. The way ahead relented, looking reasonable. My voice gained enough momentum to shout to Doug, and soon he was on his way. Following is usually monotone—sliding along on jumars. This one was not so. I could almost see the gleam in Doug's eyes shining through his layers of glasses as he pulled out the first tension piton with his fingers.

"Nasty stuff, youth."

I had to agree as he passed on through.

Doug Scott

I continued across further, using up one of our two climbing ropes, before dropping down slightly to belay. We had probably come too high, for there was easier snow below the rocks that led right up towards the South Summit couloir. However, avalanches were still cascading down the mountain, so we climbed up to the rocks in an effort to find good peg anchors for the fixed ropes. We didn't want to return the next day to find them hanging over the Rock Band. Dougal led a short section on easy snow, then all the rope was run out and we turned back for camp.

I sat in the snow to take photographs and watched the sun go down over Gaurishankar. What a place to be! I could look straight down and see Camp 2 6,000 feet down. There were people moving about between tents, obviously preparing to camp for the night. Mounds of equipment were being covered with tarpaulins, one or two wandered out to the crevasse toilet, others stood about in small groups before diving into their tents for the night. A line of shadow crept up the face to Camp 4 by the time I was back to our tent. I again sorted out loads and pushed in oxygen bottles for the night, whilst Dougal melted down snow for the evening meal.

We discovered over the radio that only Lhakpa Dorje had made the carry to Camp 6 that day. He had managed to bring up vital supplies of oxygen, but unfortunately the food, cine camera and still film we needed had not arrived. Anyway they were not essential, so we could still make our bid for the summit next day. There was also no more rope in camp, but I think we were both secretly relieved about this. Chris had always insisted that whoever made the first summit bid should lay down as much fixed rope as possible so that if that first attempt failed the effort would not be wasted. This made good sense, but it did take a lot of effort up there and we all longed for the time when we could cut loose from the fixed ropes. It was a perfect evening with no wind at all as we sat looking out of the tent doorway sipping mugs of tea. Finally the sun was gone from our tent and lit up only the upper snows, golden turning red, before all the mountain was in shadow. We zipped up the tent door and built up quite a fug of warm air heating up water for corned beef hash.

Dougal Haston

Five hundred metres of committing ground was a good day's work on any point of the mountain. The fact that it was all above 27,000 feet made our performance level high and, more to the point, we hadn't exhausted ourselves in doing it. This was crucial because deterioration is rapid at such altitudes. Over tea we discussed what to take next day. I still reckoned deep down on the possibility of a bivouac. Doug seemed reluctant to admit to the straight fact, but didn't disagree when I mentioned packing a tent sac and stove. The packs weren't going to be light. Two oxygen cylinders each would be needed for the undoubtedly long day, plus three 50-metre ropes, also various pitons and karabiners. Even if a bivouac was contemplated we couldn't pack a sleeping bag. This would have been pushing weight too much. The bivouac idea was only for an emergency and we would have hastened that emergency by slowing ourselves down through too much weight—so we tried to avoid the possibility by going as lightly as possible. The only extra I allowed myself was a pair of down socks, reckoning they could be invaluable for warming very cold or even frostbitten feet and hands. There was no sense of drama that evening. Not even any unusual conversation. We radioed down and told those at Camp 2 what we were doing, ate the rest of our food and fell asleep.

Doug Scott

About one in the morning we awoke to a rising wind. It was buffeting the tent, shaking it about and pelting it with spindrift, snow and ice chips. I lay there wondering what the morning would bring, for if the wind increased in violence we should surely not be able to move. At about 2:30 we began slowly to wind ourselves up for the climb. We put a brew on and heated up the remains of the corned beef hash for breakfast. The wind speed was decreasing slightly as we put on our frozen boots and zipped up our suits. Dougal chose his down-filled suit, whilst I took only my windproofs, hoping to move faster and easier without the restriction of tightly packed feathers around my legs. I had never got round to sorting out a down-filled suit that fitted me properly.

Because of the intense cold it was essential to put on crampons, harnesses, even the rucksack and oxygen system in the warmth of the tent. Just after 3:30 we emerged to get straight on to the ropes and away to the end. It was a blustery morning, difficult in the dark and miserable in the cold. It was one of those mornings when you keep going because he does and he, no doubt, because you do. By the time we had passed the end of the fixed ropes the sun popped up from behind the South Summit and we awoke to the new day. It was exhilarating to part company with our safety line, for that is after all what fixed ropes are. They facilitate troop movements, but at the same time they do detract from the adventure of the climb. Now at last we were committed and it felt good to be out on our own.

Dougal Haston

There's something surrealistic about being alone high on Everest at this hour. No end to the strange beauty of the experience. Alone, enclosed in a mask with the harsh rattle of your breathing echoing in your ears. Already far in the west behind Cho Oyu a few pale strands of the day and ahead and all around a deep midnight blue with the South Summit sharply, whitely, defined in my line of vision and the always predawn wind picking up stray runners of spindrift and swirling them gently, but not malignantly, around me. Movement was relaxed and easy. As I passed by yesterday's tension points only a brief flash of them came into memory. They were stored for future remembrances, but the today mind was geared for more to come. Not geared with any sense of nervousness or foreboding, just happily relaxed, waiting— anticipating. Signs of life on the rope behind indicated that Doug was following apace and I waited at yesterday's abandoned oxygen cylinders as he came up with the sun, almost haloed in silhouette, uncountable peaks as his background. But no saint this.

"All right, youth?" in a flat Nottingham accent.

"Yeah, yourself?"

A nod and the appearance of a camera for sunrise pictures answered this question, so I tied on the rope and started breaking new ground. The entrance to the couloir wasn't particularly good, but there again it was not outstandingly bad by Himalayan standards, merely knee-deep powder snow with the occasional make-you-think hard patch where there was no snow base on the rock. On the last part before entering the couloir proper there was a longish section of this where we just climbed together relying on each other's ability, rope trailing in between, there being no belays to speak of.

The rope length before the rock step changed into beautiful, hard front-pointing snow ice but the pleasure suddenly seemed to diminish. Leading, my progress started to get slower. By now the signs were well known. I knew it wasn't me. One just doesn't degenerate so quickly. Oxygen again. It seemed early for a cylinder to run out. Forcing it, I reached a stance beneath the rock step. Rucksack off. Check cylinder gauge first. Still plenty left. That's got to be bad. It must be the system. Doug comes up. We both start investigating. Over an hour we played with it. No avail. Strangely enough I felt quite calm and resigned about everything. I say strangely because if the system had proved irrepairable then our summit chance would have been ruined. There was only a quiet cloud of disappointment creeping over our heads. Doug decided to try extreme unction. "Let's take it apart piece by piece, kid. There's nothing to lose." I merely nodded as he started prising apart the jubilee clip which held the tube onto the mouthpiece. At last something positive—a lump of ice was securely blocked in the junction. Carving it out with a knife, we tentatively stuck the two points together again, then shut off the flow so we could register oxygen being used. A couple of hard sucks on the mask—that was it. I could breathe freely again.

Doug started out on the rock step, leaving me contemplating the escape we'd just had. I was still thinking very calmly about it, but could just about start to imagine what my feelings of disgust would have been like down below if we'd been turned back by mechanical failure. Self-failure you have to accept, bitter though it can be. Defeat by bad weather also, but to be turned back by failure of a humanly con-structed system would have left a mental scar. But now it was upward thinking again. Idly, but carefully, I watched Doug. He was climbing well. Slowly, relaxed, putting in the odd piton for protection. Only his strange masked and hump-backed appearance gave any indication that he was climbing hard rock at 28,000 feet.

Doug Scott

At first I worked my way across from Dougal's stance easily in deep soft snow, but then it steepened and thinned out until it was all a veneer covering the yellow amorphous rock underneath. I went up quite steeply for thirty feet, hoping the front points of my crampons were dug well into the sandy rock underneath the snow. I managed to get in three pegs in a cluster, hoping that one of them might hold, should I fall off. However, the next thirty feet were less steep and the snow lay thicker, which was fortunate seeing as I had run out of oxy-gen. I reached a stance about a hundred feet above Dougal, and with heaving lungs, I started to anchor off the rope. I pounded in the last of our rock pegs and yelled down to Dougal to come up. Whilst he was jumaring up the rope I took photographs and changed over to my remaining full bottle of oxygen. I left the empty bottle tied on the pegs.

We were now into the South Summit couloir and a way seemed clear to the top of the South West Face. We led another rope length each and stopped for a chat about the route. Dougal's sporting instincts came to the fore—he fancied a direct gully straight up to the Hillary Step. I wasn't keen on account of the soft snow, so he shrugged his shoulders and continued off towards the South Summit. I don't know whether the direct way would have been any less strenuous, but from now on the route to the South Summit became increasingly difficult.

Dougal Haston

The South West Face wasn't going to relax its opposition one little bit. That became very evident as I ploughed into the first rope length above the rock step. I had met many bad types of snow conditions in eighteen years of climbing. Chris and I had once been shoulder-deep retreating from a winter attempt on a new line on the North Face of the Grandes Jorasses. The snow in the couloir wasn't that deep, but it seemed much worse to handle. In the Alps we had been retreating, but now we were trying to make progress. Progress? The word seemed almost laughable as I moved more and more slowly. A first step and in up to the waist. Attempts to move upward only resulted in a deeper sinking motion. Time for new techniques: steps up, sink in, then start clearing away the slope in front like some breast-stroking snow plough and eventually you pack enough together to be able to move a little further and sink in only to your knees. Two work-loaded rope lengths like this brought us to the choice of going leftwards on the more direct line I had suggested to Doug in an earlier moment of somewhat undisciplined thinking. By now my head was in control again and I scarcely gave it a glance, thinking that at the current rate of progress we'd be lucky to make even the South Summit.

It seemed that conditions would have to improve but they didn't. The slope steepened to sixty degrees and I swung rightwards, heading for a rock step in an attempt to get out of this treadmill of nature. No relief for us. The snow stayed the same, but not only was it steeper, we were now on open wind-blown slopes and there was a hard breakable crust. Classic wind slab avalanche conditions. In some kind of maniacal cold anger I ploughed on. There was no point in stopping for belays. There weren't any possibilities. I had a rhythm, so kept the evil stroking upwards with Doug tight on my heels. Two feet in a hole, I'd bang the slope to shatter the crust, push away the debris, move up, sink in. Thigh. Sweep away. Knees. Gain a metre. Then repeat the process. It was useful having Doug right behind, as sometimes, when it was particularly difficult to make progress, he was able to stick two hands in my back to stop me sliding backwards. Hours were flashing like minutes, but it was still upward gain.

Doug Scott

I took over the awful work just as it was beginning to ease off. I clambered over some rocks poking out of the snow and noticed that there was a cave between the rocks and the névé ice—a good bivvy for later perhaps. Just before the South Summit I rested whilst Dougal came up. I continued round the South Summit rock whilst Dougal got his breath. I was crawling on all fours with the wind blowing up spindrift snow all around. I collapsed into a belay position just below the frontier ridge and took in the rope as Dougal came up my tracks. After a few minutes' rest we both stood up and climbed onto the ridge, and there before us was Tibet.

After all those months spend in the Western Cwm over this and two other expeditions now at last we could look out of the Cwm to the world beyond—the rolling brown lands of Tibet in the north and north east, to Kangchenjunga and just below us Makalu and Chomo Lonzo. Neither of us said much, we just stood there absorbed in the scene.

Dougal Haston

The wind was going round the South Summit like a mad maypole. The Face was finished, successfully climbed but there was no calm to give much thought to rejoicing. It should have been a moment for elation but wasn't. Certainly we'd climbed the Face but neither of us wanted to stop there. The summit was beckoning.

Often in the Alps it seems fine to complete one's route and not go to the summit, but in the Himalayas it's somewhat different. An expedition is not regarded as being totally successful unless the top is reached. Everything was known to us about the way ahead. This was the South East ridge, the original Hillary/Tenzing route of 1953. It was reckoned to be mainly snow, without too much technical difficulty. But snow on the ridge similar to the snow in the couloir would provide a greater obstacle to progress than any technical difficulties. There were dilemmas hanging around and question marks on all plans.

My head was considering sitting in the tent sac until sunset or later, then climbing the ridge when it would be, theoretically, frozen hard. Doug saw the logic of this thinking but obviously wasn't too happy about it. No other suggestions were forthcoming from his direction, however, so I got into the tent sac, got the stove going to give our thinking power a boost with some hot water. Doug began scooping a shallow snow cave in the side of the cornice, showing that he hadn't totally rejected the idea. The hot water passing over our raw, damaged throat linings brought our slide into lethargic pessimism to a sharp halt.

Swinging his pack onto his back Doug croaked, "Look after the rope. I'm going to at least try a rope length to sample conditions. If it's too bad we'll bivouac. If not we carry on as far as possible."

I couldn't find any fault with this reasoning, so grabbed the rope as he disappeared back into Nepal. The way it was going quickly through my hands augured well. Reaching the end Doug gave a "come on" signal. Following quickly, I realised that there were now summit possibilities in the wind. Conditions were by no means excellent, but relative to those in the couloir they merited the title reasonable. There was no need to say anything as I reached Doug. He just stepped aside, changed the rope around and I continued. Savage, wonderful country. On the left the South West Face dropped away steeply, to the right wild curving cornices pointed the way to Tibet. Much care was needed, but there was a certain elation in our movements. The Hillary Step* appeared, unlike any photograph we had seen. No rock step this year, just a break in the continuity of the snow ridge. Seventy degrees of steepness and eighty feet of length. It was my turn to explore again. Conditions reverted to bad, but by now I'd become so inured to the

---

*A vertical step of about 80 feet which is the final serious obstacle to the summit of Everest.

technique that even the extra ten degrees didn't present too much problem.

Doug Scott

As I belayed Dougal up the Hillary Step it gradually dawned upon me that we were going to reach the summit of Big E. I took another photograph of Dougal and wound on the film to find that it was finished. I didn't think I had any more film in my rucksack, for I had left film and spare gloves with the bivvy sheet and stove at the South Summit. I took off my oxygen mask and rucksack and put them on the ridge in front of me. I was seated astride it, one leg in Nepal, the other in Tibet. I hoped Dougal's steps would hold, for I could think of no other place to put his rope than between my teeth as I rummaged around in my sack. I found a cassette of colour film, that had somehow got left behind several days before. The cold was intense and the brittle film kept breaking off. The wind was strong and blew the snow Dougal was sending down the Nepalese side right back into the air and over into Tibet. I fitted the film into the camera and followed him up. This was the place where Ed Hillary had chimneyed his way up the crevasse between the rock and the ice. Now with all the monsoon snow on the mountain it was well banked up, but with snow the consistency of sugar it looked decidedly difficult.

A wide whaleback ridge ran up the last 300 yards. It was just a matter of trail-breaking. Sometimes the crust would hold for a few steps and then suddenly we would be stumbling around as it broke through to our knees. All the way along we were fully aware of the enormous monsoon cornices, overhanging the 10,000-foot East Face of Everest. We therefore kept well to the left.

It was whilst trail-breaking on this last section that I noticed my mind seemed to be operating in two parts, one external to my head. It warned me somewhere over my left shoulder about not going too far right in the area of the cornice, and it would urge me to keep well to the left. Whenever I stumbled through the crust it suggested that I slow down and pick my way through more carefully. In general it seemed to give me confidence and seemed such a natural phenomenon that I hardly gave it a second thought at the time. Dougal took over the trail-breaking and headed up the final slope to the top—and a red flag flying there. The snow improved and he slackened his pace to let me come alongside. We then walked up side by side the last few paces to the top, arriving there together.

All the world lay before us. That summit was everything and more that a summit should be. My usually reticent partner became expansive, his face broke out into a broad happy smile and we stood there hugging each other and thumping each other's backs. The implications of reaching the top of the highest mountain in the world surely had some bearings on our feelings, I'm sure they did on mine, but I can't say that it was that strong. I can't say either that I felt any relief that the struggle was over. In fact, in some ways it seemed a shame that it was, for we had been fully programmed and now we had to switch off and go back into reverse. But not yet, for the view was so staggering, the disappearing sun so full of colour that the setting held us in awe. I was absorbed by the brown hills of Tibet. They only looked like hills from our lofty summit. They were really high mountains, some of them 24,000 feet high, but with hardly any snow to indicate their importance. I could see silver threads of rivers meandering down between them, flowing north and west to bigger rivers which might have included the Tsangpo. Towards the east, Kangchenjunga caught the setting sun, although around to the south clouds boiled down in the Nepalese valleys and far down behind a vast front of black cloud was advancing towards us from the plains of India. It flickered lightning ominously. There was no rush, though, for it would be a long time coming over Everest—time to pick out the north side route—the Rongphu Glacier, the East Rongphu Glacier and Changtse in between. There was the North Col, and the place where, in 1924, Odell, who had climbed to 28,000 feet on the North Face, was standing when he last saw Mallory and Irvine climbing up toward the summit of Everest. Wonder if they made it? Their route was hidden by the convex slope—no sign of them, edge out a bit further—no nothing. Not with all the monsoon snow, my external mind pointed out.

The only sign of anyone was the flag; it was some time before I got round to looking at it. It was an unwelcome intrusion and there had been more to do than look at manmade objects. Still, you couldn't help but look at it, seeing as how it was a tripod and pole nearly five feet high with a rosary of red ribbons attached to the top. Take a photograph. Ah, yes! Dougal ought to get some of me. He hadn't taken a single photograph on the whole trip. "Here you are, youth. Take a snap for my mother." I passed him my camera. "Better take another one, your glove's in front of the lens. Now a black and white one." He's never been keen on photography, but he obliged.

Dougal Haston

We were sampling a unique moment in our lives. Down and over into the brown plains of Tibet a purple shadow of Everest was projected for what must have been something like 200 miles. On these north and east sides there was a sense of wildness and remoteness, almost untouchability. Miraculous events seemed to be taking place in the region of the sun. One moment it seemed to dip behind a cloud layer lying a little above the horizon. End Game—thought we. But then the cloud dropped faster than the sun and out it came again. Three times in all. I began to feel like Saul on the road to Tarsus. More materially, right in front of me was an aluminum survey pole with a strip of red canvas attached. The Japanese ladies in the spring hadn't mentioned leaving or seeing anything. Puzzlement for a moment. Then the only answer. There had been a Chinese ascent of the North East Ridge claimed, just after the Japanese ascent. Some doubt, however, had been cast on the validity of this, due to the summit pictures lacking the detail associated with previous summit shots. It was good to have the ultimate proof in front of us. Having to play the doubt game in climbing is never a pleasant experience.

Slowly creeping into the euphoria came one very insistent thought as the sun finally won its race with the clouds and slid over the edge. The thought? Well, we were after all on the top of the world, but it was still a long way back to Camp 6 and it was going to be dark very soon and then what would we do? We knew we could get back to the South Summit in the half light. On the previous nights there had been a very bright moon, and it seemed reasonable to assume we could retrace our steps down the Face if this came out. If it didn't, as a last resort we could bivouac. That, after all, was the reason for bringing the tent sac. I'd always reckoned a bivouac possible at such altitude, but that doesn't mean to say I looked upon the project with a great degree of enthusiasm. We finally turned our backs to the summit and set off down.

Our tracks were already freezing up, making the going reasonable. An abseil got rid of the Hillary Step with the rope left in place. Moving together we were soon back at our little cave. Much cloud activity didn't bode well for the appearance of a moon. The oxygen cylinders dribbled out their last drops of usefulness and became mere burdens. Standing vaguely waiting for some light to happen it was good to take off the tanks and mask. Lighter feeling but not lighter-headed. Slowly, as it clouded over, the choices were gradually cut down. We decided to have a look at the possibility of a descent in the dark, knowing the up-trail to be deep and maybe now frozen, but a tentative fifty-foot grope on the South West Face side of the ridge into the strong night wind with finger and toes going solid finally slammed all the alternative choices to a bivouac out of mind. Dropping back to the sheltered side I told Doug the news. There was nothing really to say. He started enlarging the hole.

Doug Scott

Dougal melted snow on the stove once again whilst I continued digging into the hillside. After we had had a few sips of warm water, Dougal joined me and we quickly enlarged the snow cave, digging away with our ice axes, pushing the loose snow out through the entrance. By nine o'clock it was big enough to lie down in; we pushed out more snow against the entrance and reduced it to a narrow slit. We were now out of the wind, which was fortunate, as already our oxygen bottles were empty, or our sets had refused to function. The little stove, too, was soon used up. So there we lay on top of our rucksacks and the bivvy sheet, wishing perhaps we had given more thought to the possibility of bivouacking, for we had no food and no sleeping bags. I was wearing only the clothes that I had climbed up in, a silk vest, a wool jumper, a nylon pile suit and my wind suit. I don't think we were ever worried about surviving, for we had read of other climbers who had spent the night out on Everest without much gear, although lower down. However, they had all subsequently had some fingers and toes cut off. What worried us was the quality of survival, and we brought all the strength of our dulled listless minds to bear upon that. I shivered uncontrollably and took off my gloves, boots and socks to rub life back into my extremities for hours at a time. We were so wrapped up in our own personal miseries that we hardly noticed each other, though at one point Dougal unzipped the front of his duvet suit and kindly allowed me to put my bare left foot under his right armpit and my other at his crotch, which seemed to help. Without oxygen there didn't seem to be any internal heat being created, so I mostly sat and rubbed and rubbed my fingers and toes. This was no time for sleep. It needed the utmost vigilance to concentrate on survival, keeping my boots upright out of the snow, keeping the snow off my bare hands and feet, warming my socks against my stomach, keeping my head from brushing snow off the roof of the cave. The temperature was probably—30° centigrade. It was so cold that at first when I left a sock on my rucksack the foot of the sock went as stiff as a board. Most of the night I dug away at the cave just to keep warm, hacking away at the back with the ice axe into the hard snow and pushing it out through the doorway. By the dawn it was to be big enough to sleep five people lying down!

Our minds started to wander with the stress and the lack of sleep and oxygen. Dougal quite clearly spoke out to Dave Clarke. He had quite a long and involved conversation with him. I found myself talking to my feet. I personalised them to such an extent that they were two separate beings needing help. The left one was very slow to warm up, and after conversations with the right one, we decided I had better concentrate on rubbing it hard. And all the time my external mind was putting its spoke in as well.

◆ ◆ ◆

Dougal Haston

I was locked in suffering silence except for the occasional quiet conversation with Dave Clarke. Hallucination or dream? It seemed comforting and occasionally directed my mind away from the cold. That stopped, and then it was a retreat so far into silence that I seemed to be going to sleep. Shaking awake, I decided to stay this way. We'd heard too many tales of people in survival situations falling asleep and not waking up. It seemed as if we'd both come to this conclusion and Doug's incoherent speech served to keep both awake. There was no escaping the cold. Every position was tried. Holding together, feet in each other's armpits, rubbing, moving around the hole constantly, exercising arms. Just no way to catch a vestige of warmth. But during all this the hours were passing. I don't think anything we did or said that night was very rational or planned. We were suffering from lack of oxygen, cold, and tiredness but we had a terrible will to get through the night; all our survival instincts came right up front. These and our wills saw the night to a successful end.

First light came, and we were able to start the process of preparing for downward movement. Checks showed an ability to stand up and move. Extremities had slight numbness, but no frostbite. Kidney pains were locking us in an almost bent-in-two position. Boots were difficult to get on. I gave up my frozen inner boots and used down-filled boots as a replacement. The sun came up, but with no hope of getting any warmth to our bodies. Movement was the only way, and soon we were across the cornice, saying adieu to Tibet and starting off back down the Face. The warmth of movement was almost orgasmic in its intensity as the blood started recirculating. Aware of the possibilities of lack-of-oxygen hallucinations and their potentially dire effects, we kept a wary eye on each other as we belayed down the first few pitches.

Doug Scott

We had not slept or eaten for nearly thirty hours, we had actually spent the night out in China, and we had done it at 28,700 feet without oxygen. Eventually we made the fixed rope and at nine a.m. fell into our sleeping bags at Camp 6. I put the stove on and looked around for something to eat and came across the radio. We had been so absorbed in surviving the night and the descent that at times it had all seemed so much like a dream, just the two of us and no one else in the world to share the cold swirling snow. The radio brought us back to reality; it crackled into life. Answering voices—Chris concerned, relieved— happy with the success. Put on a good voice, I thought, don't want to sound slurred, although I felt it. "No, I don't think we are frostbitten," I said, for by then our fingers and toes were tingling.

The quality of survival had been good.

from On the Heights

by Walter Bonatti

Ardito Desio, an early explorer of the Baltoro region, led the Italians' 1954 attempt on K2. After two months on the mountain, one climber was dead of altitude sickness, but six Italians and two Hunza porters were camped high on the Abruzzi Ridge. Among them: Walter Bonatti, at 24 the expedition's youngest climber, already on his way to becoming one of Europe's great alpinists.

July 28, morning, at Camp 7, 24,000 feet.

I felt like a stranger as I watched the departure of my companions who were preparing to make the final assault on K2. They were: Erich Abram, Achille Compagnoni, Pino Gallotti, Lino Lacedelli and Ubaldo Rey.

Three days earlier, when we first reached that height and fixed our seventh camp there, I too like them had had my share of hardships but was filled with eagerness and hope. Then for the nth time the weather had broken and we were kept prisoners in our tents for two long days and three nights. The first evening I had eaten something which had disagreed with me and from then on could only manage to sip a little lemonade. Now that the moment had come to watch my companions leave for the summit, the world seemed to collapse about me. I felt shaken and listless, no use to anyone, and I cursed the fate which stopped me from savouring that moment which I had so long awaited to settle accounts with K2. Twenty days had passed from the time when I had left base camp for the last time, in excellent health and with the advance party, and it seemed ironic that I was now in this state.

Slowly and laboriously, my five companions made their way upward, step by step; the stress to which they were subjected was obviously exhausting and made one think that only strength of will and hope was keeping them going. Their task for the day was to pitch the eighth camp and take with them everything necessary for the two who would remain up there. The two who occupied so advanced a position would almost certainly be predestined for the assault on the summit, although the final qualification for the last act would be their physical state and their own sense of duty. The others would be there to support them, but would go down again to Camp 7 to spend the night there and take up more supplies the next day.

As my five companions went farther and farther up the slope on which the sun was glistening I remained in the tent, a prey to depression. So intense and bitter were my thoughts that finally I was compelled to pull myself together. I decided to eat at all costs, even though I felt sick at the very thought; only thus could I recover a little energy and again take my place up there. I often had to close my eyes to swallow a little of the food available and force myself to think of something else; at times I felt I would choke from nausea but fortunately I managed to keep down all that I swallowed.

Little more than half an hour after I had been left alone in the camp Rey suddenly appeared in front of the tent. His face was twisted with fatigue and discouragement. In a few words he told me that, after little more than a hundred and fifty feet, illness had forced him to stop and leave his load in the snow. Never so much as at that moment did I feel that I could understand his state of mind without him having to describe it to me. Such blows are the hardest to endure for those who, like us, have lived for two long months on a mountain such as this.

The four men had by now become very small in the distance and were just about to be swallowed up by the mist which was growing thicker; the fate of K2 remained in their hands alone. A last silent look up there and we closed the tent behind us. It was like that all day.

No one had come up from below and at our radio appointment at half-past five with base camp we insisted that the Hunzas should bring up more loads. For this operation we asked base camp, with which it was possible to communicate by radio relay, to transmit our message to Camp 5, whence our supplies were to leave. The base camp gave us the weather reports which were at last favourable; the sky, they said, had cleared and a cold wind from the north promised a definite improvement (that was to be our last contact with base).

Towards evening two men were seen descending: Abram and Gallotti. So Compagnoni and Lacedelli were to be the lucky ones who would make the final assault. I felt an immense pleasure when Abram and Gallotti found me better; so the miracle had worked. They briefly described the layout of the new camp, said that first one ascended directly to the right, then up a sort of couloir and finally, now full on the east face, up another slope, not so steep as the former one, at the end of which the tent of Camp 8 had been pitched in the shelter of a huge serac. The altitude was 25,000 feet and it took four hours to get there.

Gallotti then told of his adventure which had ended almost fatally. "We left Achille and Lino to pitch the tent, while Erich and I went down. As usual we were not roped. The descent turned out to be slower than we had foreseen; we sank into our former tracks until suddenly during a traverse we went too fast and nearly had a disaster.

"Half-way down the last slope the snow must have balled up under my boots and before I knew what was happening I found myself slipping sideways. I made several attempts to stop myself with my axe but without result. I had already gained tremendous speed, when I unexpectedly found myself with my face to the slope. I gave a violent lick with my right boot against the face and the two front teeth of the crampon got a grip and a few feet farther down I found that I had stopped. I recovered my breath little by little and looked about me. I had covered between one hundred and fifty and two hundred feet in my slide and when it ended I had an indescribable feeling of wellbeing. But my guardian angel must have got a devil of a fright and lost several feathers in the fall. I once more began to move towards

Erich and the last few feet between me and the tents I covered on hands and knees . . ."*

July 29.

The dawn was splendid and I, considering the height we were at, felt very well again. My physical and moral well-being were such that I even felt like having a meal. Rey too seemed to have recovered; Gallotti and Abram, however, were worn out by the hardships of the previous day.

The day's plans were as follows: Lacedelli and Compagnoni were to go on up from Camp 8 to the mass of red rocks crowned by the summit and there, according to plan, at about 26,500 feet, it was hoped to pitch Camp 9, consisting of a tiny "Super K2" tent. Then they would make their way back to Camp 8 where our reinforcements were due to arrive. We in Camp 7 would bring everything necessary to pitch another two tents at Camp 8 which was to serve as our base and also two oxygen packs[†] for Compagnoni and Lacedelli on their final assault from Camp 9. Meanwhile the Hunzas we had asked for by radio the day before would set out from the lower camps by stages with supplies of oxygen, food and fuel.

Having prepared the loads with enforced slowness, we got ready to leave, but what we had always feared soon happened and this compromised the situation anew: Rey and Abram were forced to give up. No amount of encouragement could put fresh heart into them; they knew very well how important their mission was and what their refusal would mean, but they were now forced to stop just because earlier they had done more than was humanly possible. Almost without uttering a word, they laid their loads down on the snow and began to stumble down the slope.

These were terrible moments not only for those who turned back, but also for those who remained. Only those who have lived through

*From Gallotti's diary.
[†]Special packs equipped for carrying and using three oxygen cylinders.

such an experience can appreciate it. For the present Abram was to stay at Camp 7 with the hope of being able to recuperate a little and join us the following day. From Rey, however, there was nothing more to be hoped; he would have to go back. There were only two of us left.

Gallotti seemed so worn out that I wondered if he would be able to go on any farther. I did not have the heart to ask him to exchange his load for the oxygen pack left by Abram. This was the heaviest item of all but was absolutely essential. He certainly had not got the strength left otherwise he would have done so himself. The oxygen was precious for our companions up there, but one pack would have solved nothing. I therefore decided to put mine down too and to replace it with the food and equipment needed to pitch another tent at Camp 8. Up there we would discuss with Lacedelli and Compagnoni what we would have to do next.

I set out once more. The effort became greater and greater and I moved upward ever more slowly. No sooner had we mastered the diagonal traverse to the right than the mist enveloped us. The tracks on the snow left the day before by our companions had been blown away by the night wind and we were only able to find our way by the sticks providentially set up by them. Gallotti proved himself gifted with exceptional endurance; though he was almost at the end of his tether, he continued to follow me.

It was late in the afternoon when we sighted the tent; the mist had hidden it from us till we were only a hundred feet or so from it. Compagnoni and Lacedelli replied to our shouts. When we reached their tent, they appeared to be in a state of extreme fatigue. They told us that they had spent many hours trying to cross the ice wall above their tent. They had only gained three hundred feet or so before, having left their sacks behind, they had had to return totally worn out. All in all, the situation seemed very uncertain, so that we left our discussion until later and Gallotti and I, before darkness fell, set ourselves to dig out a small level space on the slope in order to put up the tent and get under shelter.

After a meagre supper (we had not eaten since morning) we all crowded into one tent to discuss what to do next. The sky outside was studded with stars and it was very cold in the open.

After a long argument we finally came to the conclusion that if there was still any hope of conquering K2 we should have, somehow or other, to bring the oxygen up to Camp 9 the following day. It was far too risky to try to make the last assault without it. It was not possible to divide the work to be done over two days for that would have meant exhausting our already very low supply of food and fuel, including that which should already be on its way with the Hunzas; it would also mean that our physical state would be still further weakened, since at such altitudes one's condition rapidly deteriorates even when doing nothing. Last but not least, the chances of a change in the weather with its inevitable consequences would be multiplied. There had already been many such changes during the climb. The use of open-circuit oxygen apparatus, which would ensure a regular supply of oxygen for from ten to twelve hours, and which would reduce the effective altitude by about 7,000 feet, would undoubtedly be a considerable advantage; it would mean that we should be able to climb to 27,000 feet in the conditions prevalent at 20,000 feet.

We thus decided that Gallotti and I should go down to Camp 7 the next morning to pick up the two oxygen kits and bring them up to Camp 9 in the course of the day. Meanwhile Lacedelli and Compagnoni, who would go on upwards to pitch Camp 9, would not pitch it in the place planned, that is to say under and to the left of the great barrier of red rocks, but as far below as possible, perhaps three hundred feet farther down the slope, to allow us two to complete our exhausting mission: more than six hundred feet of descent and then a climb of at least six hundred feet with a load of nearly 45 pounds on our backs and at an altitude of 26,000 feet. It was a very hard task and, if the success of the K2 expedition had not been at stake, it would most certainly have been rejected, but considering all things it was the most suitable. If the plan were to succeed we should have to spend the next night in the tiny tent of Camp 9, all four of us huddled together, much as we were then, and await with impatience the longed-for dawn of victory.

All that evening Compagnoni had looked obviously exhausted. Doubting if he would be able to endure the effort of the assault on the summit, I was more than once tempted to ask him to let me take his place; but in the end I didn't. I felt that such a suggestion, made by me rather than by him, would have been tactless. Furthermore I was worried by the fact that before the final assault we still had a very active day's work ahead of us, full of unforeseen events. I was in fact torn between the feeling that I would have to take Compagnoni's place, the scruples which in our present situation prevented me from doing so and finally, without a shadow of presumption, the fear that, in my place, Compagnoni would not succeed in bringing the oxygen up to Camp 9. It was almost a relief when Compagnoni, perhaps guessing my thoughts, said to me: "If you are still in good shape tomorrow up there at Camp 9, it might well be that you will have to change places with one of us." In reality, this was not a very likely possibility in view of the extremely energetic day I had ahead of me, which made me think that for that day at least it would not be reasonable to take matters further. "If tomorrow evening there is any further reference to Compagnoni's words," I thought on returning to my tent, "it will mean that we have all four reached Camp 9 and two of us with our burden of oxygen; for the moment, that is all that matters."

In the tent Gallotti complained of a sharp pain in his left foot due to the cold. I helped him massage it until feeling resumed and we then tried to settle down for the night.

The next morning, though we had been getting ready from six-thirty, it was eight o'clock before we were ready to start; at that altitude putting on reindeer-skin boots takes about half an hour. Our surroundings were the most inspiring that any mountaineer could imagine. We may also have got that impression from the fact that at last we could see the long-desired summit. The serac above the camp hid the middle section from us, but probably for that very reason the peak itself surmounted by its hanging ice field seemed to us so clear and so near that it looked as if we could climb it in a few steps. The sight above us was, however, much restricted by the outline of the slope where we were, but nonetheless was of awe-inspiring beauty. Below us was enthroned Skyang-Kangri or Stair-case Peak, a superb summit of nearly 25,000 feet, which the expedition led by the Duke of the Abruzzi had failed by sheer bad luck to conquer in 1909 after reaching an altitude of over 21,000 feet. Seen from above, with its three huge steps which outlined its mass, it made one think of an enormous staircase in the skies. The horizon seemed infinite, composed entirely of peaks and ice-fields, and, especially towards the Kuen-Lun, of a remarkable pale azure in which sky and mountain seemed to merge. We said "Good luck!" to our companions and left them.

Though unladen, we advanced slowly. As the snow blown by the wind had once more obliterated our tracks, we tried to make very short steps in order to make the track easier for the ascent. Gallotti had not forgotten his slide of two days before and when he came to the same spot he kept his eyes as wide open as possible.

We finally reached the oxygen packs. Meanwhile Abram and the two Hunzas, Mahdi and Isakhan, were climbing upward from Camp 7 where they had arrived the day before. Bravo, Erich, so you managed to master the crisis! Among their burdens were also light mattresses and sleeping-bags, which looked very attractive to Gallotti and me who had had to sleep the previous night on a single mattress and to share a sleeping-bag.

When, with the oxygen on our backs, we again reached the path we had just descended I had the privilege of seeing one of the finest examples of perseverance and will-power that a man could possibly imagine. I, the least experienced, was in the lead and then, between me and the other three who were following, Gallotti, whose pace was so laboured that his halts were longer than the time he spent in climbing. Sometimes he halted with his face buried in the snow, then, as if remembering how much depended on the arrival of the oxygen up there, he found, I do not know how, the strength to carry on. His face had become swollen and disfigured by the effort and by the time he reached Camp 8 he could not have taken another step. What Gallotti had done was something of a miracle and that in itself would have made the ascent of K2 worthwhile.

Though a good step forward had been made, we were still far from the two who were waiting for us at Camp 9 and this goal seemed farther away than ever since the situation had again worsened. It was no longer possible to count on Gallotti. Abram did not say a word but it was clear from his face that there was little to hope from him. Isakhan was moaning like a baby; he had a very high fever. Mahdi was the only one who was still in excellent condition. He was a remarkable man and had always been the best of the Hunzas. In my opinion he was the only one of them who could stand comparison with the best of the Nepalese Sherpas whom, though I had never known them personally, I had often heard praised. It would have to be Mahdi who would go with me to Camp 9 with the oxygen packs, but how was I to induce him to make such an effort without letting him believe that he too might have a chance of reaching the summit? That was the lever which would serve to enlist the services of the proud and stout-hearted Mahdi. But before broaching the subject we made a good soup for all of us with the few cubes available; it is easier to argue on a full stomach. Then, beginning with the promise of a reward in rupees when victory was ours, we put the proposal to Mahdi, giving him the impression that he might be able to go on up to the summit with me, Lacedelli and Compagnoni. It was a necessary deception which had, however, a grain of truth in it. Mahdi accepted. After he had been fitted out with clothes provided by Gallotti and Abram, except for shoes, which proved to be impossible, we hastened on our way. Abram in the meantime was feeling better and declared himself ready to accompany us as high as he could, taking turns with us in the transport of the oxygen. We put on our crampons and made a final inspection of the equipment. There was no lack of rope and we also had a pair of karabiners; we also took a little bag of tools, spare valves and minor spare parts for the breathing apparatus, and a torch; then we were ready to start.

Time had flown. It was half-past three in the afternoon and we had only four hours of daylight left. Our companions would begin to worry when they did not see us appear. A deep line of footprints rising towards the right showed us the route to follow in order to reach the wall above the tents. We were crossing an area in shadow and the temperature was noticeably lower. Our muscles were numbed and, contrary to an hour before, no longer responded to our efforts. It was the effect of the long halt, but even more it was the crippling weight of the breathing apparatus on our backs, made still worse by the inexorable effect of the rarification of the air. All this meant that the person carrying the oxygen packs could only take them for three or four steps, made very drowsy and with great effort, before handing them on to someone else.

At the foot of the wall, about a hundred feet high, there was a very wide and deep crevasse. The path crossed the only point where the two lips of the crevasse came close to one another. The upper lip was composed of a shelf of unsubstantial snow. The repeated passage of our companions had so damaged the edge of the shelf that it was very uncertain whether we should be able to cross with so great a weight on our backs.

By half-past four we emerged on the slope above the wall but we were so filled with anxiety that we could not look at our surroundings and shouted to our companions with all the breath that we had left. They heard us and replied. We were overjoyed. But where was the tent? A long white line, broken here and there, which rose before us on the long slope marked their tracks. This became straighter and straighter until it broke off under the seracs of the summit. But just before the last feathery ridge the tracks moved slightly leftward and then disappeared. It seemed that they must continue still higher up, towards a steep outcrop of rock. We were still able to follow them as far as the base of a mass of rock and then—nothing. Lacedelli and Compagnoni must certainly be there, in a tent hidden from our sight by the great spur. "Lino! Achille! Where are you? Where have you pitched the tent?" "Follow the tracks!" a voice replied from above us. We resumed our climb in the tracks of our companions. We felt easier now that we heard our friends' voices. We imagined that the tent would be there where the tracks stopped and that we should have no further difficulties. Though we were aware that we should have to make a great effort to get there before nightfall, we believed that there was no reason to be afraid.

Step by step, halt by halt, our climb went on. We crossed a zone of great crevasses, concealed by thin and fragile snow-bridges and I was very happy to think that when we once more retraced our steps K2 would be ours. A sense of euphoria due to this thought seemed for a moment to make our heavy labour easier.

However, this state of mind was not to last long. The higher we climbed the greater was our suspicion that the tent and our companions were not to be found behind the spur. Seen from where we were it did not seem to be big enough to conceal any tent, no matter how small; on the other hand there was no other place more suitable to pitch a camp. The slope was a continual succession of steep rock slabs and snow right up to the great red barrier. We became anxious and imagined the wildest hypotheses: perhaps the marks which we were following were not footprints but the trail of some rock which had broken away and rolled down the slope? But in that case where could Lacedelli and Compagnoni be? Perhaps right over on the far side of the right-hand slope? No, that was not logical. The danger of an ice-fall would have been too great; but they might have found shelter in some small cleft which we could not see from where we were. What if they had gone on till they had reached the altitude we had first agreed? But no, that was not what we had arranged. Then too, the way there, considering the heavy snowfall, would have risen straight up the slope to below the rock barrier and their tracks would have been easy to see. . . . But the wind might have wiped them out. . . . With the same anxiety as before we went on calling the names of our companions. Their brief response had come from the direction of the boulder. They must be there, we thought, no longer daring to think otherwise. The disappointment would have been too bitter.

Meanwhile the sun had disappeared behind the crest of K2 and the air was biting. Everything around us seemed changed as if we had found ourselves by magic on some other mountain. Up to a short time before every fold of the slope had been bright and sparkling in the sun, but now an opaque gloom cast a feeling of chill severity over everything. The whole atmosphere had become mysterious and made me feel incredibly small and fragile. Never as at that moment did I feel the power of K2 and of all the Himalayas around me. The spell of "twenty-six thousand feet" took complete possession of me: I think that I was afraid.

Suddenly, reality shook me out of that ecstasy which in a certain sense I could have wished would never end. With all those sensations coming one after the other, I felt as if I were transported far from this world by the most fantastic imaginings. Abram complained that one of his feet had lost all feeling. Dear, good Erich, how I wish there were sufficient words of admiration when I think of all you had done up till then. You had decided to turn back when we were still on the ridge. But two hours had passed since then and you were still dragging your way up, sharing the weight of the oxygen with us, since you knew that every foot of hard work you saved us increased the chances of success.

Without wasting a moment we took his foot out of the great boot and took it in turns to rub violently until a sharp pain let us know that the danger was past. One most moving farewell and then for a minute or two we watched the slow descent of our companion. It was half-past six in the evening.

We reached the great hogsback which divided the eastern from the southern slope and then suddenly found ourselves confronted, on the left and just below us, by an enormous ice couloir which fell in a single bound down to the Godwin-Austen glacier. It was this ridge which had been the obstacle which seen from below had interrupted the long thread of the footprints, here and there obliterated by the wind. The tracks went on along the whole ridge and then, as we had already seen from below, rose sharply along the steep slope. Seen from here, it showed a steep channel which began below the seracs of the summit and then widened out more and more until it finally merged into the perspective below us. Then the tracks crossed this channel decisively leftwards, rose once more straight up the precipitous face and finally reached the rock mass. But beyond was still a mystery.

After descending the snow ridge Mahdi began to moan from the cold and show signs of hysteria. I would have liked to be able to fly, if only to see where those two above had managed to conceal themselves. It would be dark in half an hour and we still did not know for certain which way to go. "Lino! Achille! Where are you? Answer!" Everything was silent. Perhaps they could not hear us from the tent, but why didn't they show a sign of life? We would all of us be more at ease.

We had now reached the point where the crossing of the channel began and rather than follow the tracks of our companions we decided to take a short cut towards the rock mass.

The slope became more and more perpendicular and dangerous and it sometimes seemed as if our hearts must burst with the effort. We could not even lie down for a moment on the snow or we would have ended up 10,000 feet below. Ah, those cylinders, those cursed oxygen cylinders! They seemed to crush us by their weight, our loins had lost all feeling and my poor back could no longer stand the strain. Up to a short time before I had been able to relieve the burden by walking crouched, but now the slope was very steep and I was forced to walk askew, with no sense of balance. Sometimes the pain was so acute that it seemed we must collapse; then we would hang on to an ice-axe planted in the snow and give vent to inhuman groans, which gave us some measure of relief.

What irony it was to think that what we were carrying would in time become our greatest relief. We were carrying pure oxygen, 45 pounds of precious freight which in a few moments could restore us to the same conditions as those 7,000 feet farther down. How simple it would be to turn one of those valves! What did it matter that we had no masks? The air around us would soon become impregnated with the precious gas. I could not help thinking upon what a slender thread the conquest of K2 depended.

The sky began to grow darker and our cries more and more anguished, more and more desperate, but still there was no reply. We could not believe that we would not find the tent up there above the rock. But why didn't Lacedelli and Compagnoni reply? We must now be very near, within about a hundred and fifty feet. "Achille! Lino! Why don't you answer?" Both of us stood still, with no breath left and with the snow half-way up our legs. In another few minutes the already faint twilight would become black night. Like a madman Mahdi began to shout incomprehensible words, words which naturally I could not understand; but it was clear to me that he was in a state of great excitement.

This could not be allowed to go on. With a jerk, I freed myself from the weight of the oxygen and, summoning all my forces, hoisted myself up to the top of the groove till I reached a point a little above the top of the rock. Lying flat on the snow, with my sight clouded by the effort, I could see that there was no tent on the far side of the rock which looked quite smooth; a short line of tracks, half-obliterated by the wind, continued to rise obliquely to the left along the steep face of rock and ice. I experienced a violent sense of shock. For a moment I felt as if I were fainting. My heart sank and I could no longer even think. When I got up again, a long time had passed since the shock. It was pitch dark. Mahdi was beside me and I could see his eyes gleaming in the darkness. I could find no words to tell him what had happened. I was aware that my throat was very dry and I instinctively put a handful of snow into my mouth. I was quite indifferent to the cold.

I recovered a little and then, taking off my gloves, fumbled in my various pockets till I found the flashlight. In vain I tried to make it work. Perhaps the extreme cold had affected the battery. I remembered that, in order always to have it available, I had put it into an outer pocket. I could not manage to make it work.

There was no longer any doubt about it. Our companions were at the foot of the great red barrier. But why had they done it? How were we to tackle that sheer face in the darkness and rejoin them? We would have to go back to Camp 8. But how were they to find the oxygen the next morning? "Lino! Achille! Answer. Can you hear us?" The most absolute silence reigned, broken every so often by terrible howls from Mahdi. Then I had another idea and with great trouble managed to make my companion understand. This was to reach the tent by climbing directly up the rest of the snow couloir to the height of the great red barrier and then crossing below it along a long snow ledge which from where we were did not seem very steep. In this way we would save about five hundred feet of diagonal climbing in the dark over snow slabs and very dangerous rocks. Mahdi received the proposal almost with indifference and resumed his howling. I made my way down again on hands and knees to recover the oxygen.

When I rejoined Mahdi, who in the meantime had climbed about seventy-five feet, he was furiously brandishing his ice-axe towards the heights, cursing everybody. I could not see his expression because of the darkness but I believe that his face would have made one afraid. When I became aware that his despair was passing the bounds of reason, a shiver of terror ran through my body, I felt a sense of dismay when I realised the terrible possibilities. I again took off my burden of oxygen and shouted to Lino and Achille. Still silence. Mahdi was still beside himself. His excitement and his hysteria made him do the most unreasonable things. Sometimes he went up, sometimes down, sometimes sideways. He was no longer conscious of the burden on his back and swayed violently. At every movement I expected to see him rolling down. I could only keep him still by force, but in those moments of madness he was stronger than I. Then he calmed down a little and I, concealing my fear, managed to induce him to keep still. If he had not sunk so deeply in the snow, who knows how many times we might have slithered right to the foot of K2?

By now the situation had reached a point where I could no longer even consider returning to Camp 8 as a possibility. I thought of what it could mean if Lacedelli and Compagnoni did not find the oxygen. Which would be the lesser evil? To descend now would mean certain death for us; Mahdi was out of his senses and would rush down at any moment with myself after him, but I felt that I could no longer control him. I considered the last desperate alternative, to spend the night here in the darkness. Instinctively, I began to thrash about with the ice-axe, with the idea of cutting a step on the slope wide enough for both of us to sit, one beside the other. Meanwhile, among all the thoughts rushing through my mind and the memories which kept chasing one another, one thought stood out more and more vividly; the anticipation of our miserable end. The more I rebelled against it the more it hammered at my eardrums. It seemed sometimes as if my head were about to split. Was I going mad? Suddenly I surprised myself by shouting: "No, I don't want to die! I must not die! Lino! Achille! Can't you hear us? Help us, curse you!" and breaking into violent threats.

When this fearful crisis was over I felt as if I had awakened from a nightmare. I realized that I had dug quite a large level space. Mahdi too seemed quieter now; at intervals he moaned from the cold and replied to every proposal of mine with a tearful "No, Sahib!"

The point of the ice-axe soon struck hard ice and forced me to stop digging. The space now seemed sufficiently wide to hold us and I sat down to test its size; I found that its lower edge reached my knee and the upper was the exact height of my head. Mahdi, who up till then had sat motionless a short way away while I was working, seemed to take heart and replied with an unexpected "Yes, Sahib!"

Though by now we were almost resigned to our fate, we called once more to our companions with all the breath we had left. But our throats were so dry and voiceless that we even found it hard to pronounce their names.

Then, incredibly, on the ridge just under the rock barrier a light was lit. "Lino! Achille! Here we are! Why didn't you answer?" In a very distinct voice Lacedelli excused himself, but pretty roughly. Knowing his good nature, I was unwilling to take his words too seriously. One of the effects of the rarification of the air is extreme nervous sensibility and irascibility. After all, I thought to myself, it was only a short while ago that I was inveighing against them, insulting them and cursing them. "Have you the oxygen?" he went on. "Yes," I replied. "Good! Then leave it there and come up at once!" "I can't! Mahdi can't make it." "What?" "I said Mahdi can't make it. I can look after myself but Mahdi is out of his senses and is crossing the face right now."

In fact while this dialogue was going on Mahdi, shouting deliriously, had risen like lightning and was walking hesitantly towards the steep ice slope and the light, quite unaware of the very great danger he was in. Not only could he not benefit from the light, but he was dazzled by it. "No, Mahdi! Turn back! No good!" I went on shouting. But he, blinded by the hope of life which the sight of the light had given him, went on his rope-dancer's way. Suddenly the light disappeared. Our friends, I thought, were getting ready to come to our aid. Mahdi, on the darkened slope, had again begun to yell like a madman: "No good, Lacodelli Sahib! No good, Compagnoni Sahib!" He was in the grip of a second crisis. But his god still protected him and he managed to return to me.

We waited in vain for our friends to reappear. We began to call again, to implore them, but no one gave a sign of life all night long. I felt as if a fiery brand were being seared into my soul.

Between promises and prayers, I managed to induce Mahdi to sit down alongside me. He wanted to return to Camp 8 at all costs and twice I had to hold him back on the edge of headlong flight. I took the crampons off my feet to make the circulation easier and did the same for Mahdi who, numbed by the cold, would have left them where they were rather than take off his gloves and put them on again. Our throats and lips were dry and burning. Fumbling in my pockets I found three caramels which provided our only sustenance. We each put one in our mouths but were at once forced to spit them out again, since we had no saliva. The night was calm but every so often the whistle of the wind could be heard, and the cold soon made itself felt. I would have liked to know the time but could not bring myself to look at my watch. I felt relief at being able at last to remain seated; from the morning until eight o'clock that night we had only rested for a couple of hours at Camp 8, and they had been mainly spent in getting reorganized. Now that we were at last able to remain still, we sometimes managed to forget reality, but only too briefly. Conditions were quite bearable for the moment since we had only just ceased working and our muscles had kept their warmth, but what would it be like later? I would have liked to think about nothing, but I found it impossible.

The sky was studded with a myriad of stars so bright as to cast strange reflections on the snow. In fact it seemed to me that it had been much darker an hour or so earlier. There was no moon, yet all the summits around us could be distinguished clearly. In the valleys an immense sea of cloud grew more and more dense, covering all the mountains up to a height of more than 25,000 feet. "What a wonderful sight," I was able to think in my few calm moments. All the high summits of the Karakoram seemed to be born magically as dark skerries rising out of the milky sea. There were the summits of the Falchen Kangri and behind them the Gasherbrum peaks, the highest of them the Hidden Peak. K2 dominated all these colossi and it seemed almost impossible that we were up there on it. Instinctively I looked above me and, as if to confirm what I had been thinking, K2 seemed to defy me, revealing the clear-cut shadow of its horrific ice cascade which seemed to cut into the arch of the sky. Only above did it look like a peak; below; it was like the sword of Damocles suspended over two tiny humans. If only the minutest part of that enormous hood were to break away, we would be swept away like fragile straws without hope of salvation.

As fear alternated with hope and memory with regret, the terrible cold numbed our limbs, which were shaken at intervals by long shivers. We clung to one another, limiting our contact with the ice around us as much as we could. Many times I noticed that some part of my body began to lose sensitivity and fought with every means at my disposal to overcome the numbness caused by the ice. Often movements of the joints or violent massage of the affected part were not enough, so I seized the ice-axe to beat repeatedly wherever the chill had attacked me. This method was not only efficacious in restoring the circulation but also removed any fear of becoming faint for lack of oxygen.

Suddenly the first gust of wind and snow beat in our faces like a blow; then another and yet another. In a short time the blizzard had completely enveloped us with whirls so savage and violent that it managed to fill our clothing, both inside and out, with an icy powder. Soon it was no longer possible even to shout to ease our torments and we were scarcely able to protect our noses and mouths with our hands to prevent being suffocated, while our eyes were almost blinded. Like shipwrecked men in a stormy sea we hung on to life with every fibre of our being so as not to be overwhelmed. The struggle became more and more desperate and unequal and we no longer knew if we were fighting for our lives or if we continued to live at all.

Three times the snow almost buried us; it filled up the space in which we sat and three times we cleared it away again by every means at our disposal. Each of us was now fighting for himself, drawing on his last resources. Then suddenly I heard a howl alongside me, a human howl and not the howling of the wind and I instinctively stretched out my hand towards a flying shadow. I was only just in time to stop Mahdi making for the precipice. I shall never know if this act was dictated solely by a desperate instinct to return to Camp 8. Then, scraping with my hands, I managed to dig a hole along the side of the wall to hide my head in, trying to find shelter. And still the storm raged.

The wind dropped at dawn. A sea of cloud still covered everything to within a few feet of us. The sky cleared little by little and a star began to shine. How many hours that inferno had lasted I do not know. I only know that my body felt as if it no longer belonged to me. I could no longer feel either my feet or my hands; my legs would not support me and all the rest of my body, particularly my arms, was shaking with continual tremors which I was unable to control. It was something that I was still able to think rationally.

I watched impotently the departure of Mahdi who, disfigured and paralysed by the cold, suddenly began to totter down the slope without waiting for the first rays of the sun which were by now very near us. I asked myself with anguish if he would manage without falling. I did not know what to say. Suddenly, about a hundred and fifty feet below me, he stopped on the slope and remained there for a long time motionless. At last he moved and with my heart in my mouth I sat watching his tottering descent, broken every few steps by a painful halt. What a relief when I at last saw him get to the end of the first seven hundred feet of exceedingly steep slope! Now he could stumble and roll as far as he liked; the danger of a precipitous fall was over. Poor devil, what a state he must be in! Who knows if he understood why we had to spend the night without any sort of shelter? That night, before the blizzard began, in order to curb his impatience to return, I had promised him among other things a large sum in rupees and he had stayed; would he curse me now for having done so? Yesterday evening I had been filled with fears for his life and now he was going back alone. Had I been mistaken in my decision? God alone could judge.

Like a sublime vision, the sun suddenly rose above the sea of cloud creating countless bands of light and shade. Soon the warmth of its rays restored me to life and calmed somewhat the violent tremors which continually racked my whole body. I took off my gloves. My poor hands were unrecognisable but they began to recover their sense of touch and to hurt me. At last I could look at my watch; it was a few minutes to six. What had happened to my two companions up there? Even now I was not able to see the tent. I went on massaging myself all over, extracting the snow from every cavity where it had been pressed by the blizzard. It had encrusted my heavy beard and formed a carapace of ice around my face which I was still unable to break through. I dug out the oxygen packs which had been buried by the blizzard, put on my crampons and began the descent. It was incredible how insecure I felt even though completely unladen; I had to plant the ice-axe at every step and hang tightly on to it in order not to fall down. I left behind me those seven hundred feet of steep and dangerous slope and then, though my steps were still uncertain, I felt my sense of balance increasing. Soon I was no longer cold.

With uncertain steps I made my way into the maze of crevasses. Then a cry from above reached me. I looked up there behind me but was still unable to see anything except the multicoloured cylinders which I had left there. I continued my way down.

Here was Camp 8. Keep it up, Walter! One more effort and you are among friends, in the tent, in the warm. Now it became easier to cross the crevasses. I had only to let myself slide and there I was. A swoop into space and I found myself twelve feet farther down, plunged in the snow up to my waist. With a surge of feeling I saw once more the two tents of the camp. They were just there in front of me but, as though playing with me, they never seemed to get any nearer. It was the result of the slackening of tension which one feels in every enterprise when the end is near.

A few steps from the tents I found myself face to face with Isakhan, who had come out to get some snow to melt. It was a relief when he told me that Mahdi had just arrived and he had put him in his tent. I took off my crampons and went into the tent with Abram and Gallotti. The latter said: "A little before seven we were awakened by the tent flaps being thrown open. Mahdi was facing us in a state of great agitation, showing us his martyred hands and feet. His toes especially were blackened and injured in a most distressing way. His explanations, in a voice overcome by weariness, were far from clear and left us in a state of grave apprehension. Erich and I looked at one another without the courage to make any guesses."* A little later I arrived.

Poor Mahdi!† My mind wandered in imagination, re-living dramatic scenes. I saw him once more, the Mahdi of a year ago, when he made the descent from the face of Nanga Parbat, bearing on his shoulders a man with a frozen foot—Hermann Buhl, the lone conqueror of that peak.

I recounted the drama of that night briefly to my friends and perhaps even then I was not fully aware of what I had been through. I was, however, entirely unscathed.

At five-twenty that afternoon Isakhan appeared in our tent with these words, spoken in English: "A Sahib is about to climb K2!" We rushed outside. There was a great lump in my throat and I could no longer control my emotion. Two tiny dots were slowly and steadily advancing along the slope of the ridge, which had assumed the bluish hues of the twilight.

At eleven o'clock five hearts were exulting at the same victory in the same tent. They were Erich Abram, Pino Gallotti, Achille Campagnoni, Lino Lacedelli and I. At that moment I forgot everything else in the world.

During the night it snowed.

---

*From Gallotti's diary.
†He had to undergo various amputations on his fingers and toes at the Skardu hospital.

from Everest: The Unclimbed Ridge
by Chris Bonington and
Charles Clarke

The 1980s saw climbers bring light-weight alpine tactics to Everest's harder routes. Chris Bonington in 1982 led a bold alpine-style attempt on Everest's Northeast Ridge. Peter Boardman and Joe Tasker, who had collaborated on some of the era's most daring ascents, set out for the summit on May 15. Bonington's task was to establish a camp on the North Col to safeguard the pair's retreat. Meanwhile, he used a telescope to follow his friends' progress on the ridge.

t was always difficult getting up before the sun warmed the tent, which happened at about nine. Even then, I lay for a long time in a stupor before thirst and hunger drove me out of the warmth of my sleeping bag. It was another perfect day, cloudless, almost windless, a pleasure to be out. I staggered over to the mess tent and for the first time that morning, peered through the telescope. I started at the snow shoulder, behind which hid the Third Snow Cave. No sign of them there, so I swung the telescope along the crest of the Ridge leading to the First Pinnacle. Still no sign. Could they have overslept? And then I saw them, two small, distinct figures, at the high point they had previously reached on the First Pinnacle. To get there they must either have travelled very fast, or perhaps had even set out before dawn. They certainly knew that they had to cover a lot of ground that day, for to have a good chance of reaching the summit they had to reach Point 8393 that evening.

The image through the telescope was so sharp I could actually see their limbs. For the rest of the day, either Adrian or I watched through the telescope as Pete and Joe slowly made their way along the Ridge. But now their progress had slowed down. They were on new, and presumably difficult ground. We assumed they were leaving a fixed rope behind them for they had with them about three hundred metres of rope. Their slowness was not surprising. They were now at around 8250 metres above sea level. They must have had around fifteen kilos each on their backs, with their sleeping bags, tent, stove, food, fuel and climbing gear. It was difficult to tell how hard the climbing was but I suspect it was harder than they had anticipated. I wondered if anyone had ever climbed to that standard at that height before. They were now higher than all but five peaks in the world.

We spent the day cooking, drinking and eating, but constantly going back to the telescope to gaze up at those tiny figures. I longed for three o'clock, so that we could turn on the sound, have some kind of contact with them, hear how they were, what the climbing was like—but most of all just to hear them. It was five to three. I opened up the radio and started calling.

'Hello climbing team, hello climbing team, this is Advance Base, do you read me? Over?'

The set crackled in my hand, but it was just some distant voices speaking Chinese. The Pinnacles, etched black against the sky, were stark and jagged. I tried again. It was now past three but there was still no reply. I was not unduly worried. Perhaps their set had failed, but more likely they were so engrossed in the climbing they either forgot to open up, or just did not have time. I could clearly see one figure on the Ridge, outlined against the sky, half way between the crest of the First Pinnacle, and the black tooth of the Second. The other figure was just below the skyline, moving very slowly.

We now called on the half hour through the rest of the afternoon but there was no reply. At nine that evening, the sun already hidden behind Everest, we looked up at them for the last time and called them yet again on the radio. One figure was silhouetted in the fading light on the small col immediately below the Second Pinnacle, whilst the other figure was still moving to join him.

They had been on the go for fourteen hours. It was only twenty minutes or so before dark, so they had to find somewhere to spend the night at the foot of the Second Pinnacle, either a snow cave, or more likely a small ledge cut out of the snow on which they could pitch the tent. But what was it like up there? The Ridge was obviously narrow and the slopes on either side seemed steep, but there was plenty of snow on the eastern side. The only problem, perhaps, could be that it was too soft and insubstantial.

We had our evening meal, looked up at the Ridge, whose black serrated edge could be seen clearly against the inky blue of the clear, star-studded sky. There was no twinkling of a light and presumably they were camped or holed up on the other side. I slept deeply that night but next morning immediately went over to the telescope.

There was no sign of them. Perhaps they were already on their way. It was another brilliant, clear day and the absence of a snow plume from the summit indicated that there was little wind to trouble them. We knew that they would be out of sight on the other side of the Ridge for a hundred metres or so, since on the north side the way was barred by the sheer rocky buttresses of the Second Pinnacle. I had a feeling that they would try to get back on to the north as quickly as possible, both because the snow on the east would probably be insecure and also to have some kind of contact with us, even if their radio was no longer working. There also seemed to be interconnecting ledges across rocky slopes on this side.

At this stage we were not unduly worried. We leisurely packed our-rucksacks, had one last brew, and then, leaving a note for Charlie to let him know what was happening, set off for the North Col. This time we retraced our descent route and made steady, uneventful progress. I had brought with me a pair of binoculars and every ten minutes or so I gazed up at the Ridge, hoping to see Joe and Pete. From the slopes leading up to the Col we had an excellent view. Beyond the Second Pinnacle there was a very small col. The crest of the Ridge then levelled out for what, I estimated, were about three rope lengths, before dropping away to the col beneath the Final Pinnacle. We knew from photographs that they then had to come on to this side of the Ridge, for there was a sheer rock buttress on the eastern side. To the north there was a line of ledges which we thought would give easy access on to the North Face.

I explored each point where I thought they might come into sight and then swung the lenses back down the Ridge. Our field of view was so good that they would have been clearly visible had they returned to the crest or northern side of the Ridge. But there was nothing. Just rock and snow and ice. I could not stop myself praying that they were all right. I found myself crying in the intensity of an anxiety that had crept up on me almost unawares. I chided myself. Nothing to worry about yet. They're just on the other side of the Ridge.

We were now on the ramp leading up the centre of the North Col. Our steps from two days ago were covered with wind-blown snow and again I was very happy to let Adrian do the trail-breaking. It was six in the evening before we reached our previous high point. I took a tentative look at a narrow arête of snow. It looked feasible, but steep and frightening, something to be attempted in the morning when we'd be feeling fresh.

'Come on, Adrian, we'll stop here for the night. It's safe enough with this crevasse between us and the slope.'

I started digging a platform beside the crevasse. Adrian was appalled at the exposure of our perch but I tried to reassure him that it was perfectly safe. 'Once in the tent you can forget the drop.'

It was a wonderful dusk, the sky cloudless, with hardly a breath of wind. To one side the North East Ridge was black and massive, while below us the East Rongbuk Glacier swept away in a vast white highway. On the other side of the glacier stretched the gentle snow peaks flanking the Lhakpa La and behind them towered the solid rocky triangle of Khartaphu. The very peace of the scene was soothing. I was glad to be high once again, glad to be climbing with Adrian and sharing with him our own modest adventure of reaching the North Col.

The following morning we struck the tent and I set out along the fragile crest of the arête which we hoped would by-pass the crevasse.

As so often happens, it was easier than it looked, and although it steepened into a nearly vertical drop into the huge crevasse below us, I had the security of the rope paid out by Adrian. Cutting big bucket steps, I worked my way down, then shouted to Adrian to anchor the rope so that he could follow. We now had the rope in position for our return. Soon we had both cautiously abseiled down it and were able to break out on to the easy ramp we had seen from below. Once more I was pleased for Adrian to take the lead on straightforward ground. As we went up, we were still searching the Ridge every few minutes but still there was no sign. Although we were getting anxious, we could not help enjoying the sensation of being on new ground, of finding our way up to the North Col. There were intriguing reminders of our predecessors. An old cable-laid nylon rope hung from a huge over-hanging boss of snow. Could it have been left by the Chinese in 1975? Further up, by a formidable, narrow ice chimney, projected a butane gas cylinder, French 1981 vintage, no doubt. This route seemed too hard for us and we continued up the ramp to the foot of an acutely-angled snow slope that seemed to lead to the crest of the Ridge. Once again I went into the lead, kicking my way up the steep, but secure snow, until suddenly my head poked over the crest. I had reached the North Col.

It was a sharp knife-edge, dropping away steeply on the other side with the fresh vista of Pumo Ri, shapely and elegant, in the near dis-tance and behind it the great bulk of Cho Oyu. I moved cautiously along the knife-edge to where it broadened into an easy slope, and buried a deadman snow anchor. While Adrian jumared up the rope I was able to look around. The ridge opened out into a wide dome just above the lowest point of the Col. It would provide both a good camp site and an excellent viewpoint of the North East Ridge. In the concen-tration and very real joy of climbing that final pitch to the Col, there had been no room for my growing worry about Pete and Joe, but now it came creeping back. I got out the binoculars and searched the line of Ridge again but to no avail.

But what of the Americans in the Great Gully of the North Face? I started searching for them and picked out a collection of tents, tiny coloured boxes, clinging beneath a sheer sérac wall. There was no sign of movement, but a line of tracks wound sinuously across the slope, taking a route round the huge icefall that barred the Great Gully at about half height. There was another camp, tucked below a rocky overhang just near the side of the couloir, and I could just discern some more tracks. Surely they also would be going for the summit in such perfect weather?

By this time Adrian had joined me. He shared with me a sense of elation very similar to that which I experience on reaching a summit. I suppose it was because this was our chosen objective. Just after he arrived we saw two tiny figures descending the fixed ropes on the American route. Could they be Pete and Joe, who had somehow got across on to the North Face without us seeing them? But this was clutching at straws. Our logic quickly told us that these were Americans, perhaps on their way down from a successful summit bid.

We dug out a platform for the tent and spent the rest of the day taking it in turns to examine the North East Ridge. It was now 19th May and I was very worried. Pete and Joe had been out of sight for two nights and almost two days. From this viewpoint we could see just how short a distance they would have had to cover before we could expect them to come into sight on our side of the Ridge after turning the Second Pinnacle.

That afternoon, Adrian picked out some movement at Advance Base. Could it be *them*? Could they somehow have retreated all the way down without us seeing them? But no. There were three figures. It could be the American skiers, or perhaps it was Charlie who had come up with some Tibetans. We opened up on the radio at six o'clock. There was no reply from Pete or Joe, but Charlie, reassuring and cheerful, came on the air. I immediately told him of my fears. Charlie recalls:

At six p.m. on 18th I had a crackly radio link with the Col.
I was about to berate Chris about the mess but his mes-

sage was anxious, high pitched, almost unintelligible. They had not seen them . . . 'I am concerned . . .'

'I share your concern,' I replied.

I share your concern . . . my world of elation was quick-frozen, replaced, not yet by sorrow or pain, but by a curious reality. I was in a high camp, with two Tibetans for the night. Three miles away on the North East Ridge something had happened or was happening. Two miles away on the North Col Chris and Adrian were safe. We were 6000 miles from home. I talked bleakly to my diary:

The Ridge is very much a spectator sport from down here up to the Second Pinnacle. Then there is obviously some dead ground. I'm not sure how the view compares from the North Col. I think we must prepare for a disaster. But there is still hope. If the situation is the same tomorrow I shall have almost given up.

However, we had all this on Kongur last year and everyone was OK.* On the positive side they could have shot off early on the 18th, gone out of sight, conquered the 'great problem'. On the 18th they could be out of sight still, in all probability camped between the two steps, summit tomorrow and back to the North Col.

The outcome will be quite simple. They'll either come bouncing in or drag themselves in in various degrees of injury or illness: or, we'll never see them again. I cannot really accept them as lost, but then it took a while for Mick's loss to sink in.† Oh God.

I did not sleep well that night and as soon as it was light enough I was gazing up anxiously through the binoculars. Another perfect day but still no sign. We opened up on the radio on the hour throughout

---

*The summit party were out of contact for ten days in 1981.
†Mick Burke's death on Everest in 1975.

the day, but with little hope of a reply since it was unlikely that we should hear them unless they were in direct line of sight. I now searched not only the crest but the glacier at its foot, just in case they had fallen.

That night Adrian went outside for one last look up at the Ridge.

'Chris, come and have a look at this, I think I can see something. It could be a tent.'

He handed me the binoculars.

'It's about a third of the way along the Ridge, above and beyond the Pinnacles, just below the crest. Look, there are three slight bumps. Go down from the left-hand one. There's a bit of a gully, and there it is, on a kind of ledge. It's just a little orange blob. It could be a tent, couldn't it?'

It was certainly on the line from the Final Pinnacle on to the North Face. Then why hadn't we seen them? They would have been in view, moving slowly, for a long time. But that little orange blob was a slender strand of hope. I pushed logical doubts aside. That could be Pete and Joe. Perhaps they had reached the top and were on their way down. They could be with us tomorrow. Neither Adrian nor I slept that night. I imagined what they would have to say, what they had done, how they would look, convincing myself that it was undoubtedly their tent and that they were on their way down. The night crept away so very slowly. We had arranged a call to Charlie at eight and I expressed my hope.

'There's a faint ray of hope. Last night Adrian saw a small red patch that could be a Sumitomo tent. It's on about the right line. But we haven't seen any figures and, of course, it's possible that it's a ruined tent from a previous expedition. It's on rock rather than snow, which means it doesn't stand out quite so well. It's not a hundred per cent but at least it's hopeful. Over.'

But as the light on the North Face improved and we gazed at the distant little blob, our hopes dwindled. There was no sign of movement. It was the wrong colour, being orange when the outer of the Sumitomo was a deep red and its inner a bright yellow. It was also the wrong shape, looking more square than domed. It was perhaps a box tent abandoned by the French the previous year. The weather had been so clear and our viewpoint so good, that surely we should have seen them if they had reached the end of the Pinnacles? Our hopes vanished and despair set in. They had now been out of sight for four days—to cover a distance of about three rope lengths at the least, eight or so at the very most. Four nights above 8250 metres. If their progress had been so slow, surely they would have decided to retreat. We had already seen the effects of spending four nights at 7850 metres.

The only explanation must be that a catastrophe had occurred. What if one of them had fallen and was injured? Surely the other would have retraced his steps to signal us for help, particularly since we assumed they had left a line of fixed rope behind them? It would have meant retreating only two or three rope lengths. Or could both of them have fallen sick or be so incapacitated by exhaustion that neither could move? This seemed unlikely. They were well acclimatised, and though perhaps tired from our long siege, they knew how to pace themselves and had been at these altitudes without oxygen before, on Kangchenjunga and K2. One of them could perhaps have collapsed, but not two. That left a grim interpretation. That they were both dead. Either one had fallen, pulling off the other, or perhaps one of those fragile ice flutings had collapsed, sweeping both of them down the huge Kangshung Face. I could remember its immense scale, just how steep the upper part of the Ridge had seemed, and how insubstantial and dangerous Dick had found that pitch on the First Pinnacle.

Below us Charlie had also spent a sleepless night.

> I was washed over by different waves of emotion. I fought with pain because I loved them. They were the personification of what I had once wanted to be, but I had not that combination of physique, skill and drive to push high on great peaks. They courted danger, yes, in the huge scale of the undertaking but not because they were reckless. Not Pete and Joe. There are, I think, some climbers who can—

in the fervour of their ambition, intoxicated by danger and excited by the prospect of success—push aside all fear and feelings, take great risks and, moving fast, often alone, survive enough times to gain a reputation. To me these climbers are as one of the faces of Buddha, who lived as a hermit practicing extreme asceticism, emaciated beyond measure before gaining enlightenment by this supreme sacrifice. I wondered if Pete and Joe, like Buddha returning after his enlightenment, would come back to the world of man and accept the dish of fresh curds from the village girl on the Full Moon Day of May. For Peter and Joe there was, I feel, that Middle Way: they believed that hard high-altitude climbing was a reasonable sport within mountaineering. Statistically dangerous, yes, but with care, stealth and speed, within reason. They had affirmed their faith in high altitude by repeated visits, they knew and respected the arena of avalanche, storm and stonefall. They had pushed hard and fast at the summit of Kangchenjunga, retreated in the face of avalanches from K2. They were wily and sometimes very frightened. They never showed self-indulgent elation when successful.

I talked it over with Adrian and then at mid-day with Charlie. There seemed nothing to gain by staying on the North Col. We left the tent in place, anchored to a snow shovel and its valance securely wedged down with snow. We also left the radio, the cooking gear, all the remaining food and a note welcoming them back and telling them what we had done.

We held ourselves tightly in control. Although I had very little hope of their survival I could not bring myself to admit it. Besides, we were still on the mountain and needed all our concentration to return safely to Advance Base. By the time we reached the sérac wall where I had left a fixed rope, the clouds had engulfed us and the wind was beginning to whip stinging snowflakes into our faces. Adrian, who wears glasses, was almost blinded as they misted up. He was also feeling the debilitating effects of spending three nights at around 7000 metres. We were both very, very tired as we stumbled down the slope, thankful for the marker wands we had placed to guide us down.

Back on the glacier we could begin to relax, and then, having reached the rocky moraine, we were able to take off the rope and walk down in our own time. I pulled ahead, forcing myself over the broken rocks covered in fresh snow, to get back to the camp. At last it was in sight and Charlie was coming towards me.

'They've had it. I'm sure they've had it,' I muttered.

'I know.'

We held each other and wept.

from Everest Canada:
The Ultimate Challenge
by Alan Burgess and Jim Palmer

The Khumbu icefall, an arena of massive ice towers and yawning crevasses, lies at the bottom of Everest's standard South Col route, posing risks to both climbers and porters. A 1982 Canadian expedition accepted those risks. Here British climber Alan Burgess (born in 1958), best-known for the hard climbs and high spirits he shares with his twin brother Adrian, describes the consequences.

I lay barely awake, just aware of a weak light and cold air in the narrow, frosted opening of my sleeping bag. The radio crackled somewhere in the background, in a neighbouring tent. The noise drew my thoughts together. I realized that I was in Camp I. I could see now that the tent was bent under a lot of new snow, its dark shadow a third of the way up the walls. The radio crackled again and I could hear Bill March's muffled voice, which meant it was two tents over. I tried to understand the significance of this. He had to be speaking to Base Camp. Or maybe people in the icefall. But no. There wouldn't be people in the icefall. Or could there be? There seemed to be a lot of snow. For some minutes, I listened, catching the odd word here and there, and slowly I realized that he *was* talking to a carry. So they had left Base! I sat up and, feeling the altitude, immediately took a few deep breaths. I unzipped the door and forced my head out, frost condensation falling around my shoulders. Snow fell inside the tent. There must have been 18 inches of new snow at Camp I. Now I began to take in the seriousness of the problem Bill could be trying to deal with on the radio. How long ago might people have left Base Camp? My watch said 5:15. They could be two hours into the icefall by now! Maybe too late to turn back! But maybe there was less snow below—maybe there was *none* in Base Camp. I heard Kiwi Gallagher's voice. I couldn't understand much, but I did hear something about "no snow at Base," and some discussion about personnel locations. More reports came in, filling in gaps in my mental picture of the situation, until I realized that Sherpas and climbers were spread right through the middle of the icefall, over two hours in, and still over two hours from the top. Pat Morrow was in the lead, above "the valley" and was into snow so deep that he was requesting trail-breaking assistance down from Camp I. They had been lured into a vulnerable situation, and were now pushing upwards to get out of it.

I pulled my head back into the tent. Tim Auger was lying in his sleeping bag next to me, and I could see that he was waking. I was about to tell him about our probable recruitment as trail-breakers, when, strangely, I lost the thread of my thought. I wanted to say something to him but couldn't find words, as a new, uneasy feeling took over completely. Something was wrong. Tim sat up, blinking, listening, looking at nothing. I heard an avalanche. It kept going, getting louder. The tent started to shake. Tim and I looked at each other, as the floor shuddered and air blast snapped and tore deafeningly at the walls. It was a big one. Very big. In the roar, Tim's lips moved inaudibly, his eyes large, but I didn't answer. I just stared back at him, my entire consciousness flooded with the roar. It seemed a long time until, with a hollow rattle like distant thunder, it stopped. A very heavy, eerie silence returned. Tim and I were still rigid, staring at each other.

We both shouted to Bill, but immediately heard the radio. Pat Morrow. He said that he had almost been caught in the avalanche. He said that they were above it, but it went lower down. He thought that there were some Sherpas behind but he didn't know how many.

The radio was now crackling wildly. It was impossible, as we hurriedly pulled on boots and gear, to tell who was speaking. Somebody was saying that Base Camp got air blast too. God! It *must* have been big! Pat was going down to count people. Other voices spoke hurriedly, shouting words that we couldn't understand, but then, quickly, Kiwi's voice and others were imposing order. I realized that they were mobilizing from Base Camp for a search.

Once equipped, I went across to the Sherpa tent to explain to them what was going on, or at least what little I knew. Bill was standing nearby, now fully equipped, the radio at his hood. As I passed, he glanced at me, and our eyes shared our fears. Dave McNab was in their tent door, dressed and buckling on crampons. Then Rusty Baillie came on the radio, his voice clear but halting, explaining that there had been Sherpas above him, but they must certainly now be dead. He couldn't see anymore. The avalanche had actually hit him and he had been covered up to the waist. Peter Spear had also been covered, but they had found him again.

The radio messages were now clear and precise. Kiwi was coordinating from Base Camp, and teams were moving up quickly. Bill told me to stay with Sungdare, who had a touch of snow blindness and was ill, and Gyaljen Phortse. Bill, Dave, Pat, Nawang Karma and Tenzing Tashi clipped onto the rope and disappeared over the snow crest, down into the icefall.

This left me alone at Camp I with the two Sherpas and no radio. Sungdare and Gyaljen Phortse were in the tent just behind mine, 20 yards up the hill. I made my way up, knee deep in snow, and called from outside their door. They unzipped and let me in. Sungdare, a tall, confident, experienced mountaineer, was lying on his side, his knees pulled up and his arms across his face. Snow blindness is painful and illness is discouraging, but I knew he was feeling more than that. Gyaljen Phortse sat staring at the wall. Normally he was an effusive and friendly person, but now his eyes were dead and expressionless. All he said was, "When it snows like this we should be in Base Camp." There was nothing to say in reply.

I changed their gas cartridge and made them some tea. I had Sungdare roll around and sit up to check his eyes and alertness. He appeared to be all right. I suspected that, even before the avalanche, it had been his instincts and experience that had made him feel too sick to go out on a dangerous morning. Such illness can be a polite Sherpa statement of opinion on objective hazards.

I worked outside for a while, digging out the tents and gear and restacking equipment, and then went back into my own tent to make some breakfast, drink some tea, and contemplate the situation. I wondered how the team would react if there had been deaths or serious injuries. I thought, too, of the Sherpas I knew well from other expeditions, and hoped they were all right. In particular, I hoped that Pema Dorje was in the clear, because I knew his anxious mother had pleaded with him not to join our expedition.

Some of my thoughts were practical. We were racing the seasonal jet stream, which was coming lower every day now. At some point it would reach the 29,028 foot level of Everest's summit, and we had to get there first. I made calculations: the speed of loads through the icefall and up to the camps. Only so many backs to carry them, only so many days to do it. One day it might snow too much. Maybe two days. Maybe a week.

Where could we draw the line? How long could we use up resources and time before we even got out of Base Camp? Maybe we had been pushing too hard. But maybe there was no other way to succeed.

A few hours later Tim Auger, David McNab, and two Sherpas returned. They were very subdued. The Sherpas went to Sungdare and Gyaljen Phortse's tent, and Tim and Dave came into mine. I began to prepare tea and food for them.

"All the Westerners are OK," Tim said. That was good to hear. But Tim continued, "Some Sherpas have been killed. We dug out one body. Pasang Sona. They spent an hour, Steve [Dr. Stephen Bezruchka] and Rusty, trying to revive him. But it wasn't any use. They thought there were two others missing, but they couldn't be sure till they did a real check at Base. They'll radio up when they know who."

The avalanche had covered acres with a compressed mixture of snow and ice blocks, so that as the recovery teams clambered through a landscape of teetering, crevassed devastation, in falling snow and grey cold, almost every probing pole hit something hard. After a time, their sense of desperate urgency became deadened; eventually they realized that they had been lucky to find Pasang Sona because of a visible piece of rope that led to him. It was hopeless looking for the others.

It had been a very close call for Peter Spear. As he wrote afterwards:

> We had heard many avalanches but this one got louder and louder and louder. . . . I looked up through the snow . . . and there was a massive avalanche 50 metres wide and hundreds of feet high coming directly at me. I shouted "avalanche!" at Rusty and tried to dive behind my pack to survive the blast. . . . I was still clipped onto the climbing rope, the wind blast . . . hit me . . . I was hurled and tumbled and bent and bashed by the snow which came cascading over me.

When it stopped, only part of his face and one forearm were clear. He was able to clear his nose and mouth, but was in tremendous pain. His body was pressed in a desperately contorted position, with tremendous tension on the rope at his harness. It was Rusty who found him, after digging himself out, and Rusty and a Sherpa dug him free. Peter felt tremendous relief when the Sherpa slipped a knife down and sliced the rope. His clothes were completely packed with snow, which they quickly beat out, and Rusty supplied a down jacket for the walk back to base. They met the rescue party moving up the ropes.

Peter's diary noted the joy he felt at the sight of them, and they noticed that, as chipper as he seemed to be, he still showed the effects of shock and pain.

Tim related afterwards his feelings as he went down to help with Bill and Dave. "I remember Bill stopping . . . and hollering back to us . . . 'All of the climbers are accounted for,' meaning all of the team members." From further down, though, they heard a shout, "No, we're missing some people." Tim said he knew that when he saw the devastation, the silent, packed field of white, he knew that anybody missing must be dead. He said the realization was ". . . just numbing. It makes your whole body dull."

The men worked quietly, the orders and reports curt and perfunctory, as the shock set in. Tim wrote in his diary:

> While digging from the bottom end of the buried fixed rope, a hand was uncovered and the grim reality became clear. It took an eternity to clear the white cement from Pasang's body. . . . James [Blench] asked Bezruchka, "What do we do?"
>
> Bezruchka replied, stifling tears, "We should try CPR (cardio pulmonary resuscitation). If it was me I would like someone to try. "
>
> We put the cold, lifeless body in a sleeping bag with Rusty to try to warm him while Dave McNab and Bezruchka did CPR for almost half an hour. The attempt at resuscitation proved useless and it was obvious that he was dead.

By 9:00 a.m. they realized there was no chance of finding anyone alive, or even of finding other bodies. They decided to bring Pasang Sona's body down. Speedy noted that, as they brought the body down, it was "dark, snowing, and misty" reminiscent of the mood in "a Wagnerian tragedy." Peter Spear wrote that the event was awakening in many the realization that "Everest is not a mountain to be toyed with."

It was a very quiet evening in Base Camp. The final count had been made, so there was no doubt who was where. The body on the stone altar outside was of Pasang Sona. He was 40 years old, from Kunde, and had been on three previous Everest expeditions and on Annapurna I.

Dawa Dorje, one of the two Sherpas whose bodies were not recovered, was also 40. He was from Thame and I knew him well from the winter Annapurna IV expedition. He was a real gentlemen, well dressed, clean cut, and young looking. He had climbed all over in Nepal, and was one of the most experienced Sherpas.

The youngest killed was Ang Tsultim, from Khumjung. He was 20 years old, and this was his first climbing expedition. He had previously worked only with trekking groups.

After sending messages to the families, writing the official report, and collecting the Sherpas' few belongings, Bill wrote:

> It was difficult to sleep that night and I awoke at 1:00 a.m., crawled out of the tent and made my way down to the body. Two Sherpas stood as silent sentinels; it was a beautiful starlit night, with the bright moonlight making the valley like day. A silent prayer was said and I grieved quietly and deeply at the loss we had suffered.

At the same time, in another tent, diary notes of a different tone were being written by Don Serl:

> I'm going home. The trip is dead for me and there seems no real reason or cause to revive it. I think we fucked up badly, and that three lives have been spent teaching us a lesson I doubt we can or will learn. We were far too casual about the other hazard of the icefall—the avalanches. The seracs and so on proved not to be the problem at all, and diverted our attention from the real danger, which none of us recognized in its full scope.
>
> This shortcoming on our part cost those lives, and to say now that "we'll be extremely cautious" is hollow, and probably incorrect, as I believe we *still* don't have the ability to predict this sort of avalanche danger from the shoulder. In fact, it may be really unpredictable, and I'll not willingly walk into that situation now that I realize it exists. . . . And now three Sherpas are dead. . . . I can't accept that . . . my portion of responsibility should include returning to the mountain.
>
> I climb for joy, and challenge and danger too, sure, but

there's no way I'll be able to enjoy any more of this trip, and there's too little to life to pass it doing things one doesn't enjoy, at least when one has a choice. So it's away for me. I'm going back to climbing between me and the mountain, where *I* bear the costs, such as they may be, of my errors. Honesty. Directness. Not some horrible situation where three men die and the process can carry on. That's a perversion of any value I care to hold. That's *destination*, not *path*, if ever I saw it. . . .

If, as Rusty suggests, expeditions are emasculating this area, through the deaths of the best and most vital Sherpas, there's a moral question for you. Maybe that in itself justifies self-contained expeditions.

Probably does. Will think about that later, more. Now, to try to get some sleep. May be a bit tough.

from Fragile Edge
by Maria Coffey

Many Himalayan climbers have written about death. But Maria Coffey (born in 1952) is not a high-altitude mountaineer. She shared her life with one—Joe Tasker, whose 1982 disappearance on Everest's Northeast Ridge is described by Chris Bonington and Charles Clarke in Everest: The Unclimbed Ridge *(page 105). The following year, Coffey traveled with Hilary Boardman—the widow of Tasker's partner on the Ridge, Peter Boardman—to the mountain that had claimed both men.*

L hasa was two hours away by minibus along a dusty road, through brilliant light and a landscape of intense and sharply defined colours. Rolling brown hills were the backdrop to a lake of bluest water, and the hues of a newly renovated Buddha shone where the image had been hewn into a rock face. But Lhasa itself, on first impressions, lacked colour. Grey, squat buildings, their corrugated-iron rooves glinting in the sunlight, were laid out along concrete streets down which young Chinese soldiers sauntered or cycled. There seemed little evidence of the fabled ancient city which existed until the Chinese invasion in the 1950s. Then the Potala came into view, the exiled Dalai Lama's palace, a vast architectural wonder shimmering on a hill, the most awe-inspiring building I have ever seen. I craned my neck to keep sight of it as the bus left the city limits, took us along arbutus-lined roads past a gravel works where lorries backed from a gate and belched exhaust fumes, and finally drew up inside the large compound of the 'Guest House', the barracks where all foreign visitors stayed. Someone had been gardening: colourful flowers broke through the dusty soil and brightened the entrance to the reception desk and the communal dining hall. Joe and Pete had stayed here, too: their expedition stickers were on the glass doors.

Hilary and I shared a room which opened out onto a courtyard of sun-yellowed grass and a view to the steep and rocky hillside behind. There was a rudimentary bathroom four doors away with sporadic running water, two toilets and a trough-like basin. Our beds were narrow, high and hard, and piled with eiderdowns for the cold nights. We left our luggage on the polished wooden floor and returned to the dining hall for lunch. Sunshine streamed through the windows of the high-ceilinged room, which reminded me of a school hall. At the tables sat other tourists, mostly elderly Americans or Germans.

'I don't want to talk to anyone here,' said Hilary firmly, and I understood her reticence. It was not easy for us to explain to strangers the reason for our presence in Tibet. But, as food was being served, a face familiar to me from photographs was suddenly at our table. Pertemba, a Sherpa guide, had stood with Pete Boardman on the summit of Everest in 1975 after an ascent by the South-West Ridge. Hilary had met him in Nepal and, later, during his visit to England. He greeted her now with tears shining in his eyes. The news of Pete's death had only recently reached him. We had heard he would be in the Rongbuk Valley around the same time as us, leading a small trekking group, but this meeting in Lhasa was unexpected and Hilary was visibly shaken. They withdrew to another table to talk, and after lunch I joined them. Pertemba gave us the feeling that he totally understood the motives behind our journey, and, like Hilary, he did not accept the theory that Joe and Pete had fallen to their deaths down the Kangshung Face.

'I would have known if Pete had died violently,' said Hilary. 'I would have sensed it.'

Pertemba nodded; perhaps they fell asleep, totally exhausted, and simply did not wake up.

I listened, but my mind that afternoon could not dwell on death. I was concerned with re-creation, with trying to picture Joe sitting in this dining room, relaxing and laughing after a meal. There was comfort in this but also a growing tension. Each day now was bringing me physically closer to the place, and therefore also to the fact, of his death. Reaching Everest was our goal, but we could not stay there for long; soon I would have to turn away from the mountain and accept that I was leaving him behind me.

Hilary and I rested in our room after lunch, silently wrapped in separate thoughts and tired by the sudden increase in altitude. But we roused ourselves: our time in Lhasa was limited and we decided to visit the old part of the city. Dong and Zhiang drove us back along the grey roads to the edge of the Parkhor, a market street encircling the sacred Jokhang Temple.

'We will wait here for you,' said Dong. 'Please return in two hours.'

'Why don't you come with us?' I asked, unthinking.

'No, no, we wait here. Two hours, please.'

Later, when I saw the remains of monasteries that the Red Guards had ripped apart, the machine-gun bullet-holes strafed across what was left of the walls, I began to see why Dong and Zhiang hung back. Whatever the rights and wrongs of their recent history, the Tibetans understandably resented the presence of Chinese, particularly those in uniform, in the parts of their world that they had managed to salvage from the horrors of the Cultural Revolution.

The Parkhor had obviously escaped the worst of the ravages, for it gave me a strong and immediate sense of old Tibet. Once again, as in Hong Kong, we slipped quickly from one world into another, and my first impression of Lhasa, its military-camp atmosphere, dissolved away. Makeshift stalls of wood and canvas stood on sunlit cobbles. The houses that lined the street were constructed of timber and roughly hewn white-washed boulders held together with clay. Their upper storeys seemed to overhang precariously, tipping forward with bright red and blue window shutters, colourful flower boxes and fluttering prayer flags. Some houses had shops on the street level, their doorways opening into dark, cool interiors. Market vendors called to us and poked out their tongues in the traditional greeting as we wandered along looking at the jewellery, the blocks of tea, the rancid yak butter and the sacks of barley flour. One stall was simply a large rug spread on the ground, round which members of the Khampa tribe, from eastern Tibet, bargained intensely over turquoise bracelets and brass cymbals. They were beautiful, impressive men with sharp, fierce features and long, black, ribbon-braided hair, and they paid us no heed as we stopped in our tracks to gaze at them. As the only tourists in the market place that afternoon, however, we did attract a lot of attention. An old man with a long white beard stopped and regarded me in amazement. He encircled one of my thin wrists with his fingers and poked gently at my upper arm, obviously intrigued by the lack of muscle. Turning his attention to Hilary, he compared her strong arms with mine and then went on his way, wreathed in smiles of sheer amusement. Two Buddhist nuns in brown robes came by, their shorn heads covered by white headdresses with starched, wing like pieces protruding at ear level. They seemed delighted by the sight of us and laughed merrily, especially when a little girl ran by and smacked me playfully on the bottom.

Bicycles were the only vehicles in the street, and the tinkling of their bells was a continuous background noise. The cyclists wove between the shoppers and browsers, there was no pushing or shoving and a feeling of gentleness and ease pervaded. After the uniformity of dress in China, these people were full of visual contrasts. The myriad colours of waistcoats, aprons, headscarves, belts and hats were layered with dust and dirt but still bright against the black or brown cloth of their dresses, loose trousers and shirts. Turquoise encased in silver adorned ears and wrists. And wide, generous smiles opened up across stolid features to express amusement and delight: smiles which cheered me throughout the journey despite the people's poverty and their tortuous history.

Hilary began to feel dehydrated from heat and altitude, so we looked for somewhere to buy a drink. The first shop doorway round which we put our heads opened onto a room full of leather hides hanging from low ceiling beams. Men working at wooden benches laughed and beckoned to us to enter. Our next try was more successful and we walked into a cool, dim room and across a stone floor polished by years of footsteps. The walls of the shop were of darkly-stained wood, and the place was empty except for a counter at one end. On this far wall shelves reached to the ceiling and held row after row of bottles filled with mysterious, brightly-coloured liquids. We spoke not one word of Tibetan between us and the shopkeeper laughed as we hummed, hawed and finally pointed to a bottle containing a thick, yellow liquid which looked like concerntrated fruit cordial. The light outside made us squint so we found a wooden bench in the shade of a tree and settled down to investigate our purchase. A shaven-headed monk sat nearby and his saffron robes reflected the liquid that we sniffed at and sipped cautiously. He watched our investigations with open curiosity. Whatever was in the bottle may have been a fruit drink, but it definitely had a strong alcoholic content.

'Do Tibetan monks drink alcohol, Hilary?'

'I wouldn't have thought so. Shall we . . . ?'

'Let's offer it to him. He can only refuse.'

He enfolded the recapped bottle within his robes in a swift, smooth motion, chuckling with glee. While Hilary went off in search of a tap I took out my camera, but the monk shook his head and turned his face away. Within minutes a group of children had formed round the bench, gesticulating excitedly for me to take their photographs. I did so and they held out their hands, not, as I first presumed, for money, but for the Polaroid pictures they were expecting to see emerge from the camera. I was sorry to disappoint them and felt suddenly ashamed to be a tourist.

The Jokhang Temple, a shrine of great holiness, stands at the centre of the Parkhor. Pilgrims were circling the temple clockwise, spinning brass and wooden prayer-wheels and sending out incantations on the wind with each revolution. The more devout measured the distance by prostrating themselves full-length on the ground. A hollow-faced young man, clad in loose sacking, prayed loudly as he repeatedly threw himself down and drew himself up again to his full height. The wooden slats tied to his hands and knees for protection made loud slaps as he hit the cobbles. The small boy with him was going through the same ritual of devotion, and from their weariness and dirt-smeared skin it seemed that they were nearing the end of a long journey. An old man sat on the cobbles near the temple, his eyes shut and his head moving to the rhythm of his chanting and clapping. Other pilgrims stood against the wall turning prayer-beads through their fingers. And there were beggars; one woman bared sagging, wrinkled breasts and held aloft a baby's bottle, while at her side a child held a newborn baby. Close to the temple the sense of devotion heightened and the crowd increased, streaming through the two large entrance pillars, across flagstones hollowed out in places by hundreds of years of prostrations. There was a huge prayer wheel and I waited in turn to spin it, sending its hundreds of carved incantations out onto the breeze. Prayers for Joe and Pete, I thought. We could not go in—it was time for us to return to the minibus. Drawing reluctantly away from the milling devotees we retraced our steps through the market place, past the grisly meat stalls where the red of the flesh and the dripping blood were intensely bright in the afternoon sun, and back into modern-day Lhasa.

It had been a wondrous afternoon, and my senses felt assaulted by the array of sights, sounds, smells and colours. But the new experiences had been poignant. At every turn I had imagined Joe, visualized him filming in the market place and laughing as children crowded around him. The stages of grief are well understood, and I knew that I was going through the 'searching' process, seeking out a lost mate in a place I knew he had been, re-creating him, not yet fully accepting that he was dead. But knowing it did nothing to alleviate the hurt.

Back at the Guest House we washed our hair at the tap in the courtyard. Sitting on the step with our heads wrapped in towels, we enjoyed the last of the day's warmth in that sheltered spot and wrote postcards. Beyond Lhasa there would be no communication with home.

'What are you going to tell people?' asked Hilary.

'Weather great, food Chinese, wish you were here.'

She threw a damp towel at me. In truth, it was hard composing the postcards. Briefly I described my impressions of Lhasa and my feelings about the next stage of the journey. There were many people who would want to hear from us, who had helped us in various ways over the past months and who would appreciate a card from Lhasa; it was worth the effort.

Sitting up in bed after dinner, Hilary read aloud from Pete's diary the account of his visit to the Parkhor: it was a strange echo of our afternoon. My head ached and my fingers were tingling, both the effects of suddenly arriving at 12,000 feet from sea level. I reached for the sedatives, anxious to sleep, and stepped outside into the courtyard to gaze at the stars appearing in the sky above Lhasa, until the cold and the effects of the drug sent me to bed.

Pete's diary recorded that he and Joe had walked from the Guest House to the lake behind the Potala before dawn one day, to photograph the sunrise. Hilary had asked Dong over dinner if we could do the same, but he and Zhiang had organized a day of tightly-scheduled sightseeing which they did not want us to miss.

After breakfast the next morning, we all set off for the Sera Monastery aboard a minibus. As the Potala came into sight Zhiang said something to the driver, and we swung off the highway and onto a side road. Dong turned round.

'This is a quick way to the lake.'

It was just as Pete had described it in his diary, totally still and perfectly reflecting the splendour of the palace. A mist hung about the Potala, increasing its aura of mystery. I felt that it could vanish into thin air at any moment. Groups of Chinese soldiers, off-duty but still in uniform, horsed about on the lakeshore and took photographs of each other against the awesome backdrop.

At Sera, Dong and Zhiang once again hung back and we entered the courtyard of the monastery without them. Stone steps led up and into a great dark hall supported by carved wooden pillars and festooned with *thankas,* long strips of intricately-painted silk that were suspended from the ceiling and reached almost to floor level. Shafts of sunlight, alive with dust motes, pierced the gloom, and the air was thick with the smell of rancid yak-butter candles and burning juniper twigs. The religious paintings on the walls had recently been renovated and their reds, blues, greens and golds stood out brightly in the dim light, unlike the grease- and smoke-darkened colours of the *thankas* and the entrance pillars. Along the walls stood large, peaceful, golden Buddhas, representations of past incarnations of the Dalai Lama. At the back of the spacious hall were a series of small, windowless rooms, illuminated by candle-wicks that floated in vats of the strongly pungent yak butter. Statues of spirits, some welcoming and benign, others darkly fearsome, were crowded together in the gloomy interiors and threw long and flickering shadows on the walls. A rope slung between posts guided the progress of pil- grims past these deities and I joined the shuffling press of people, mov- ing slowly along amidst a murmuring of prayers. Now and then there would be a halt, bumping us all together, as someone reached forward with a gift to add to the white scarves, money, jewellery and photographs of the Dalai Lama with which the altars were festooned. I was conscious of being a curious tourist, and of the wealth displayed by my clothes, my watch and the camera hanging from my neck, but the people around me did not seem to notice. With bowed head and clasped hands, I reached back to a Catholic childhood to find expression of my respect for their devotion.

Later that day, in the Drepung Monastery, the absence of pilgrims gave me the feeling that we were in a museum, and a scattering of monks was the only indication that the building housed a religious community. I broke off from our group and went alone up flights of nar- row stairs, along a dark and low-ceilinged corridor and onto the flat roof. Sunshine burst through the opened door and made me fumble for my glacier glasses. On the edge of the parapet was a row of golden figures, guarding the building against intrusion. I approached them slowly, try- ing to recall why they seemed so familiar. And then the memory washed over me: Derbyshire; logs crackling in the fireplace; our heads bent together over photographs. A February night, six months before. Joe and

I had looked at this rooftop together then: there had been a picture of it in one of his books on Tibet. Leaning against a wall, looking past the statues to the tin rooftops of Lhasa reflecting the sunlight, I wondered if he had climbed up to this roof, too, and if perhaps he had remembered that same night. A low chanting began and broke into my reverie. At a nearby altar an elderly monk was prostrating himself before the Buddha. My presence seemed not to disturb him, yet minutes later he was angrily gesticulating at the two young Chinese soldiers who walked past, obviously upset by this physical representation of the force which had attempted to desecrate his faith.

Hours slid by, and the effort of trying to absorb so much was exhausting. It was early evening before we returned to the Guest House. I was sleepily finishing dinner when two men came to the table and introduced themselves.

'We are journalists, from Holland,' said one. 'I believe you are the wives of the two British men who disappeared on Everest.'

My head snapped up. I was suddenly awake. Some of the reporting in British newspapers about Joe and Pete had left me wary of the press.

'We are covering the Dutch ascent of the North Col. We have just returned from Rongbuk. You are leaving for there tomorrow?'

Hilary had told me about the team of Dutch climbers with whom we would be sharing the Base Camp. She and Pete had been friendly with two of them in Europe, and she was looking forward to a reunion.

'No. We're going to Kharta first.' Hilary looked tense. 'Why are you in Lhasa?'

'There has been an accident,' said the man. 'An avalanche. A climber is badly hurt and we are here to send a report back to our newspaper in Holland.'

Her face was already pale.

'Who?'

The journalist paused.

'Eelco Dyke—you know him?'

Listening to the account of what had befallen Hilary's friend, a cold, eerie feeling crept over me. I had the sensation of picking up some residual echo from the walls of the spacious dining hall, some remnant of conversations that the survivors of Joe and Pete's team must have had there, in that same room, on their way home after the disappearance. Leaving her deep in conversation with the two men, I wandered back to our room and fell into a disturbed sleep. In my dream Joe was alive, he was with me in my Manchester house and we were eating a meal together. It was so realistic and normal that I awoke in confusion and had a few seconds of mental struggle before I remembered where I was and why. It was not a good start to the day, and I could barely hold back my tears over breakfast.

The truck that would take us to Everest was parked outside the dining hall. Tele, our driver, was busy warming up the engine, checking the numerous tyres and loading gear onto the back. It was a big, lumbering workhorse of a vehicle; wooden slats along the sides rattled, and chains hanging down from the hinged rear flap clanged as we bumped along unpaved roads. It belched out exhaust fumes, stirred up clouds of dust and shook every bone of its passengers' bodies, but it proved to be totally reliable. Tele was a tiny, birdlike man whose skinny legs would scramble in and out of the truck at great speed. He barely reached above the steering wheel, and it was a wonder to me that he drove the heavy beast with such surety. He had a wide, gap-toothed smile and usually wore a woolly hat but no socks, a fact which bothered me throughout the trip. Dong suggested that Hilary and I sit in the driver's cab but we declined, wanting the panoramic views from the open back of the truck, and prepared to accept the choking dust and chill winds that went with them. Zhiang joined Tele, and the rest of us settled down amidst the piles of gear, following Dong's instructions to pad ourselves against the bouncing of the truck. We were sweating inside salopettes and down jackets, but soon we would need the protection of these as the altitude increased and the temperature dropped.

We rumbled through the streets of Lhasa and onto the Friendship Highway, past the Buddha cut into the rock and across the long bridge spanning the Brahmaputra River. It was a gradual climb through a barren landscape of brown and purple hills and a vast expanse of space, sky and intense light. The road led over a series of passes and between these we crossed plateaux, each higher than the last. At Khamba La Pass dozens of squares of white cloth, each with a holy inscription, were tied to sticks held in place by a small cairn. The little flags flapped wildly in the wind at 15,700 feet, sending prayers onto the air currents. I cut a piece from my long silk scarf and tied it to one of the sticks, then stood back to watch how the wind whipped my little flag about, and how its colours were bright against the blue of the sky. Joe used to wind that scarf around his neck when he was rock-climbing in England; sometimes a corner would work loose and the wind would blow it against his face as he stood at the bottom of the crag squinting up at the route. At every prayer-flag cairn that we passed I left a piece of that scarf, feeling impelled to do so without really knowing why. Perhaps it was a ritual of mourning, or a gesture of my attempt to accept Joe as part of Tibet.

The road skirted Yamrock Lake for thirty miles, and every few hundred yards birds rose from the rushes on the shore in a frenzy of flapping wings and startled cries. When the lake was out of sight behind us on the dusty plateau, we stopped at a petrol station. It was a rudimentary affair, a low clay building with the tank on the roof and pipes that ran inside, through measuring cylinders by the counter and out of the wall to the yard. There were no pumps: the drivers filled up their own cans with petrol and decanted these into the tanks of their vehicles. A young Tibetan girl sat behind the counter, calculating the cost of each transaction and taking money from the customers. Despite the overpowering fumes she smiled cheerfully. While I held a funnel for Tele, Zhiang helped him to pour the petrol until the truck's large tank overflowed, and we found room for the reserve cans in the back. The smell of petrol mingled with the dust as we drew away, making us cough and cover our mouths with scarves.

I hunched in the back of the truck, withdrawing from my companions and the surrounding landscape, and letting jumbled thoughts of the past fall around my mind. The bumpy road, the rattling vehicle and the lashing of wind and dust all faded into fantasies of being in Joe's car, driving to the pub on Saturday nights, watching his profile in the light of the dashboard as we talked and laughed. Easy, uncomplicated music playing on the tape deck, music that matched the sweeping lines of the Derbyshire Dales and the winding, unlit roads. Parking next to a stone wall and walking arm in arm down the steep hill. Up the steps and into the warmth and light of the crowded bar, where friends with flushed faces greeted us and offered drinks. A long, long way from this rutted and potholed road in Tibet. Resentment welled up. I was too young to be going through this, everything had been cut short just as it was beginning. Joe's talents had been flourishing, there had been so much more for him to do. And all those lost opportunities, the conversations and the times together that I had looked forward to and which now were never to be. Regret: it was such a hopeless feeling.

Behind my closed eyes was a screen across which memories flitted, going in and out of focus. One took shape: leaving the airport after Joe flew to Hong Kong, and driving his car back up to Derbyshire, to the factory which had bought out part of his business and which now housed his shop. One of the secretaries took the keys from me.

'I'll pick the car up just before he gets back,' I said numbly.

'Now don't go running off on any holidays after this expedition,' she told me, with mock sternness. 'We all felt so sorry for him the last time.' Joe was popular with the girls there, sent them cards from his trips and joined in with their Christmas parties.

'No,' I replied, 'I won't. I won't do that again.'

It was not until I was reversing my little Beetle out of the factory yard that the anger hit me. Why should I have felt so guilty when she said that? Why had I needed to reassure her that I would be there for him when he returned? What the hell did she or any of the other girls know about life with such a man, anyway? He breezed into the office, flirted with them all, impressed them with his ease and friendliness and brought a touch of glamour and excitement into their lives. But what did they know of the stress and the fear that I lived with, or of the jealousies and insecurities that plagued me? Could they handle such a relationship? Had they thought of that when they tut-tutted about my going to Corsica so soon after his return from Kongur? I almost turned the car around and marched back into the office to confront her. But the innocence of her remark dawned on me as I drove away. There was no reason why she or anyone else should understand the complexities of loving a man like Joe; I certainly had had precious little idea at the beginning.

A tingling in my cheeks and the soles of my feet brought me out of the daydream and back to the truck. I wiggled my toes inside my boots and looked up. The road was dog-legging steeply, giving wide-angled views back across the valleys and plains. Two boys waved from a sulphur pool set against a rock face. On the Kharo La Pass, at 17,000 feet, the road ran close to the jumbled crevasses of a glacier and we could see up to the place where it originated, on the mountain which rose up another 4,000 feet. The altitude was making my palms tingle, too. I rubbed my hands together and scolded myself for the slip into maudlin thoughts, for it was a privilege to be in that high, wild place and have all senses intact to appreciate it.

Midway down the other side of the Kharo La Pass we stopped for a lunch of tinned meat, biscuits and lychees beside a mountain stream. I wandered along it to find a private spot. When I returned, with my face washed clean of dust, Tele handed me a posy of wild flowers. Hilary had one, too.

'He rushed around looking specially for the flowers he wanted,' she said.

Far away, on a hillock that rose sharply from the plateau, the outline of Gyantse's ancient fortress was etched against the sky in the clear afternoon light. The sight was entrancing and grew gradually closer and larger until finally we skirted the city, the third largest in Tibet. The walls of the fortress were like giant bared teeth, high above us. The truck trundled on, Gyantse began to recede and the light of the afternoon softened towards evening. A farmer in a dusty hamlet paused in his work to wave. I plugged into my Walkman, to a tape called 'China', and for a while my sadness and concerns ebbed away and were lost in the beauty of the Tibetan plateau.

Twelve hours after leaving Lhasa we drew into the military camp at Xigaze and fell out of the truck, dusty and aching. It was already dark and we were ushered straight into a dimly-lit dining room where one table was laid with a meal of rice, meat and dried fish. Relieved that the constant motion of the day had finally stopped, we ate everything and slaked our thirsts with cup after cup of green tea. The stars were out by the time we left the dining room, and the air was sharply cold. Our room had an Everest sticker on the door.

'Maybe Pete and Joe slept here,' Hilary wondered aloud.

The large, speckled mirror reflected two dusty, dishevelled figures; we cleaned up using the washstand and jugs of cold water before crawling beneath the eiderdowns. It was good to be stretched out in bed, to relax tired muscles and rest aching bones. My mind would not calm down, though: it continued to spin. I was beginning to think of Joe on the mountain, to visualize where he lay and what he looked like. Not knowing what had happened to him was hard to bear and made acceptance of his death more difficult. Some little part of me still harboured the hope that they would miraculously appear. For weeks after first hearing of his disappearance I would step towards the ringing telephone, unable to suppress a thought of 'maybe'. One afternoon I stood in a greengrocer's in Manchester, waiting to buy fruit and listening absently to the news on the radio behind the counter. The last item came on, an 'interest story' before the weather.

'The mountaineer who was pronounced missing presumed dead after falling from a Himalayan mountain has turned up in a Nepalese village, alive and well.'

As his name was announced and the accident he had survived described, I left the shop, empty-handed and in tears. It could not have been Joe or Pete, it was far too late, and yet those first few seconds had brought me a flash of impossible but undeniable hope, and I felt crushed and cruelly tricked. Chris Bonington had told me that the chances of anyone surviving a fall down the Kangshung Face were almost negligible. He had also explained that if something had happened to hinder their progress near the summit of Everest—an injury perhaps—they wouldn't have survived for long as at that altitude, especially without an oxygen supply, the body rapidly deteriorates. So there was no hope. And yet, deep in my psyche, I was clinging to one final, disintegrating straw. Which was why approaching the mountain was difficult: I sensed that being there, seeing with my own eyes the enormity of the challenge which Joe had taken on, would force me to begin to accept and to let go.

By 6 a.m. I was wide awake again and tense. Hilary stirred in the bed across from me. Our friendship was growing, accelerated by the experiences we were sharing. There was already a remarkable ease between us and we were tuning into each other's thoughts.

'We're going to see them today, Maria,' she mumbled sleepily, and I knew what she meant.

Xigaze, the second great city of Tibet, houses the Tashilumpo. This beautiful monastery, with its gleaming golden roof, is the seat of the reincarnate Panchen Lama and the home of an increasing number of monks, including some novitiates. Inside its large wooden gates is a small walled town with irregular flagstoned streets winding through buildings and courtyards. The place had a peaceful, self-contained atmosphere, but this was not enough to banish the sense of emptiness and the echoes from the past which seemed to resound through all the monasteries I visited in Tibet. At least in the Tashilumpo the monks seemed to be purposefully engaged in worship and work, and not just in showing tourists round. I felt calm within those walls and moved about slowly, taking in as best I could the images before me. Within a cavernous hall, shafted with light from the high, narrow windows and hung with huge *thankas*, yellow-swathed monks on rows of cushions chanted and bowed their shaved heads towards an altar. Hundreds of candles flickered around the huge Buddha, and the smell of burning yak butter, juniper and incense was strong. Two young men in brown robes walked among the rows carrying large brass jugs and pouring tea from these into bowls at the feet of their elders. The chanting echoed around the hall, insistent and intoned, until somewhere out of sight a gong was loudly struck and caused a sudden hush to fall. The monks sat still and silent as the low note of the gong reverberated around the raftered ceiling high above. Other tourists continued to walk around, pointing up to the silk *thankas* with audible comments. I wanted to put a finger to my lips, to signal them to be quiet. Perhaps it was the Catholicism I had been born into which made me stand back in the shadows, thrilled by the solemnity of the ceremony and reluctant to break the mystery of the moment. Our guide, a tiny, elderly monk, shooed me down the central aisle of the hall and into a room which held the tomb of the fourth Dalai Lama. It was a massive dome of mother of pearl, embedded with precious and semi-precious stones. Blatant wealth, when compared with the poverty of the Tibetans.

'I felt like this in the Vatican,' I whispered to Hilary. 'It's beautiful, but so confusing.'

'Let's go outside,' she said. 'I need some air.'

We slipped away and wandered into a small, sunken courtyard, bright with flowers and full of sunlight. A tethered goat chewed on a mound of vegetable peelings, and windows opened into spartan rooms.

'Perhaps those are living quarters,' I surmised. 'They remind me of the nuns' cells at my convent.'

'No wonder you and Joe get on,' she said. It was a long time before she could talk consistently of Pete and Joe in the past tense. 'You're both religious refugees.'

A young monk came out onto a balcony. He looked cross and waved us away. We hurried off to look for the guide, ashamed of our trespass.

Old and very precious texts were opened up for us in the library, the lives of Buddhist saints inscribed on thick pages bound in beautiful silk brocade. In a nearby room six monks sat on mats on the stone floor carving words on wooden blocks to be used for printing sutras, or prayers, in texts and on prayer-flags. One monk spied the book on

Tibetan monasteries which Hilary had under her arm and indicated that he would like to see it. They all left their work and crowded excitedly around, pointing to photographs.

Two young novitiates chopped vegetables for a broth in the kitchen, and giggled when we put our heads around the door. Huge cast-iron pots and a sooty kettle steamed on stoves fired with brushwood and yak dung, large brass ladles and funnels hung on the wall.

I visited the clean, white-washed outhouse in the main courtyard. There were only a few flies to be swatted away from the hole in the floor. A monk walking by averted his eyes as I emerged and a tiny goat scampered along behind him.

In a small, incense-filled room above the courtyard, twenty elderly monks sat on colourful rugs and floor cushions, facing each other in two rows. Robed in red and wearing an angular hat, each had arranged before him a bell, a set of small cymbals and a conch shell.

They were chanting, their upper bodies rocked to and fro slightly and they made strange hand movements as part of their prayer. One dipped a long-haired brush into a bowl and flicked the liquid around him. Suddenly, and in unison, they picked up the instruments: bells tinkled, air passed through a conch, the cymbals clashed and a low drum-beat sounded. Hairs rose on the back of my neck as the music rolled around the room and subsided once more into a low chant. Again I stood back, in a corner, humbled to be a witness to this ancient ritual. My stance had unconsciously become similar to Joe's—feet apart, arms across the chest, leaning slightly back—as if willing him to materialize and share the experience with me. The prayer was over; the room fell silent. There was only a shifting and rustling as the monks removed their hats, folded them flat and put them away inside silk envelopes. We left quietly, passed through the sunlit walls of the Tashilumpo and returned to the truck for the next part of our journey.

It was a long and beautiful drive, with no other traffic except for an occasional army truck. On the high, wide plains, white- and grey-walled villages would appear like tiny specks that grew and gradually took shape as we approached. A yak was tethered outside one, chewing contentedly against a backdrop of plateau, snow mountains and sky. Along steep valleys the road clung to purple and brown rock faces that displayed wind-eroded, fluted formations. Far below, irrigated farm-land ran along the riverbanks in solid strips of green.

We stopped for lunch at a windswept pass where a few wild, long-haired yaks grazed hopefully among the rocks. One had a prayer-flag fluttering from its horns. Hilary wanted to photograph gear donated to us by a climbing equipment company and I herded up the animals to be in camera range. It was peaceful there: prayer-flags in the wind, the ponderous yaks and, beyond it all, snow mountains on the horizon.

On the other side of the pass the road dropped steeply and was flanked by precipitous terraces rising from a rushing, whitewater river. I stared intently: the feeling of déjà vu was overpowering. And then I remembered—Joe had filmed this stretch of road: it had been shown on BBC television. I imagined him leaning out from the Land-Rover, asking the driver to slow down, wondering how that piece of footage would turn out.

We rounded a bend and an impressive mountain range came into view, the peaks shrouded in cloud. Makalu, Lhotse, Nuptse—heard the others identify them. Hilary clutched my arm and pointed.

'There it is, Maria.'

Above the clouds, impossibly high, was the summit of Everest. Denny banged on the roof of the driver's cab and we ground to a halt. With the engine cut, there was silence, save for the wind and the whirr and click-ing of cameras. I gazed and gazed at the mountain, immense beyond my imaginings. I could pick out the ridge where Joe and Pete were last seen. The image blurred, tears were washing down my face and collect-ing in the jacket collar pulled tightly around my chin. A sense of deso-lation hit me hard. A man I loved, a man who shared my life for over two years, had perished on that mountain, almost at the highest point on earth. A cold, hard place, relentless and utterly remote. There was a 'flag' of snow blowing from the summit of Everest; I shivered, imagin-ing the force and chill of the wind up there. So many people had said it, and of course I already knew: Joe had not wanted to die so young, but, if it was to be, he would have wished to end his life as he did, high in the Himalayas. There was a simplicity and a beauty in the manner of his death, no debilitating illness or sordid car accident but a strong and certain overwhelming by the forces of the mountain. As the truck started up I knelt on rucksacks against the cab, looking up at the ridge, drawn towards the sudden physical reality of Everest, as bewildered as a hurt child and in as much need of comfort. The road swung round, Everest went out of view and we began the approach to Xegur.

from Five Miles High
by Charles S. Houston and
Robert H. Bates

American medical student Charlie Houston, born in 1913, led a small American expedition to K2 in 1938. The party of five climbers and six sherpas, which also included Bob Bates, Bill Houseman and Paul Petzoldt, spent considerable time exploring alternate routes before attacking the Abruzzi Spur. Houston and Bates co-wrote the expedition book, Five Miles High; *here Houston describes his own summit attempt with Petzoldt.*

On Saturday the 16th, Petzoldt and I ambitiously started the primus at 5 o'clock, hoping to get away early. But at 7 when we finally started, a cold wind and threatening snow drove us back to lie in our tents for an hour. Then the sun broke through the clouds and we started off again. From previous inspection we felt that the right side of the buttress above Camp V was more hopeful than the steep snow gully, the beginning of which was just visible to the left.

I led off and traversed a steep snow-covered ice slope where crampons were necessary, but we were soon forced to climb directly up the right side of the buttress. The rock was very exposed and flaky, and in addition covered with powder snow, which made for considerable anxiety on the part of the leader and the second man. We found ourselves barely 200 feet above camp after several hours of hard work. To our great disappointment such difficult climbing clearly made this no route for supporting higher camps, and we turned back.

After the usual luncheon, our spirits rose again, and shortly after noon we turned to the left side of the ridge where we worked up a steep snow gully. Here the snow was very deep and fell away out of sight in the depths below, giving the climbing party an eerie feeling of insecurity. Fortunately, the snow soon led to the top of the buttress, and we climbed easily for several hundred feet. Paul's almost uncanny ability to smell out the best route several yards in advance was a great help, but we soon reached very nasty broken rock which gave rise to considerable profanity from the second man as small stones were knocked down on him. We persevered and came to a tiny nook at the foot of another large gendarme which seemed to be as difficult as the one above Camp V.

It was then 4 o'clock and the weather was getting stormy, so we turned back to camp, where we found Bates and House with the three Sherpas cosily ensconced in the tents it had taken them all afternoon to pitch. We all crowded into one small tent to devour a supper cooked by Paul which almost surpassed his previous culinary efforts. After supper some renditions from the *Oxford Book of English Verse* sent us off to our sleeping bags in a very contented mood.

The wind rose steadily all evening and we fell asleep to the ominous flapping of the tents. The outlook for morning was gloomy, and we woke at 5 to find ourselves completely surrounded by mist. Breakfast was started to the inevitable drip, drip, drip of frost melting on the inside of the roof. One of the dekshis, knocked over by a blowing tent wall, drenched someone's sleeping bag. The waiter, carrying breakfast to the other tent, almost froze his hands in the wind. All in all it was a nasty morning.

At 8 the weather had improved slightly and we decided to push on to Camp VI carrying our sleeping bags. The support party planned to start several hours later and establish one tent with food at Camp VI, while Petzoldt and I made an attempt to go still higher. We started off bundled in windproof suits, mittens, and helmets. Once out of the shelter of the ridge we felt the full force of the wind, which, laden with cloud and snow, howled through the rocks. Immediately beards frosted over and hands and feet became numb. We realized the imminent danger of frostbite, and, fearing that we soon might not be able to find our way back through the storm, returned to camp. The others, who had evidently been worried about us, came from their tents with hot drinks, and Pasang greeted us with, "Just like Nanga Parbat, sahibs," and then proceeded to pull off boots and rub frozen feet into consciousness.

We spent the rest of the day encouraging our spirits with continuous feasting. Lunch began as usual and was continued with small tidbits until time for tea. Tea in turn was prolonged into high tea, and finally into supper. Then, after long conferences, comparisons of this and previous weather, and general optimistic imaginings, we found it necessary to take a small sustaining snack to see us through the night. Even with that, when we turned in about 8 o'clock, our spirits were very low. The wind was increasing in violence, blowing heavy clouds from the west. Driven snow froze on the tents and the temperature was steadily falling. Our snug sleeping bags were very welcome.

To our surprise, Monday the 18th was one of the most perfect days we had yet seen. Every peak about us stood out brilliantly clear, topped with purple and pink in the early morning light. The wind had disappeared, the new snow had been mostly blown from the rocks, and, best of all, the morning's sun warmed our tents rapidly. In this calm weather breakfast was pleasant to prepare, and Petzoldt and I got away before 8, carrying our sleepers and a light lunch. We reached the perch which was to serve for Camp VI well before noon and left our loads. Petzoldt then started off to the left of the buttress and almost immediately was stopped by steep snow-covered slabs. After an hour of futile attempts to find some route over which these could be crossed, we turned back and tackled the right side. This seemed on first inspection to be even more severe, but I found a chimney about 20 feet straight up which was climbed with some difficulty. At the top of this an airy traverse, still on the right side of the ridge, was secured by several pitons and brought us to a platform barely 200 feet above the campsite.

The support party arrived about this time with tents, food, and the usual imprecations about falling rock. They had been subjected to occasional bombardments of small fragments, although the larger stones had fallen clear of them on either side of the ridge. As Petzoldt and I worked still higher, Bates and House, at first incredulous about the possibilities for pitching two tents, or even one, on the narrow shelf, set to work to achieve the impossible. The Sherpas, with their natural zest for masonry, constructed three dubious platforms and set up one tent for the reconnoitering party. The group then returned to Camp V, planning to bring up the final loads next day.

Petzoldt and I meanwhile were finding some trouble with the route above. In several places fixed ropes were necessary, and the ice in the gullies at either side of the ridge very effectively kept us on its crest. About 500 feet above camp, Paul lost a mitten, which blew over the edge and vanished in a second. This was serious, for to lose irretrievably so vital a protection makes one fully realize the narrow margin between warm hands and frostbite. About us the downy cloud which seemed always to hang in this part of Abruzzi ridge was dank and clammy but we reached a point from which we could see easy going for several hundred yards before starting back toward camp. The blessed support party had blown up air mattresses, laid out sleeping bags, and even melted a few precious spoonfuls of water. Tea was soon ready and, during the usual pemmican supper, plans were laid for morning.

The night was cold and very beautiful. For the first time we noticed a full moon, which gave the high peaks about us a rare, ethereal glory, but the night was too cold to admire for long our superb surroundings. In the morning, the weather was partially clear, though thick, dark clouds appeared to the east. This was unusual, for generally the clouds appeared in the west and south. We wondered if the long anticipated break in our good weather were upon us. Fortunately, about 9 o'clock the west wind sprang up and for several hours we could see the battle of the winds with great rolling masses of mist sweeping over Windy Gap, there to be met by a stronger wind from Kashmir which drove them back into Turkestan. The sun warmed the rocks and the day became very comfortable.

Soon Petzoldt and I had passed our high point reached the day before and were well on our way up the famous Black Pyramid which caps Abruzzi ridge. This was to be the crux of the climb for, ever since our first examination of it, we felt that the last thousand feet leading onto the great snow shoulder was by far the most difficult and inaccessible stretch of all. We were very excited, but the severity of the rock work kept our minds completely on the business at hand. Petzoldt again skillfully anticipated the best route several minutes before we reached it, and by noon we came to a steep snow gully which we had studied from below and up which Paul had predicted our route would lead to the top of the Pyramid.

For an exhausting half hour we kicked steps up the narrowing gully, and were finally forced to traverse out to the right onto perilous-looking slopes. More pitons were used, their protection being very welcome. A slip on these slopes would have landed us in Camp I after a rapid but by no means comfortable journey. Shortly after noon we shook hands at the top of the Black Pyramid at an altitude of approximately 24,500 feet. Abruzzi ridge had been conquered and we had found a route to the snow fields of the 25,000-foot shoulder.

The exhilaration of that moment was not due entirely to our altitude. Most of the Karakoram was in view before us. Far to the southwest the white cone of Nanga Parbat rose high above the snow peaks about it. Broad Peak, graceful as ever, seemed near enough to touch across the glacier below. Masherbrum, farther to the west, was clear and beautiful. We wondered whether its summit had been reached by our friends on the British party. Still we had no view into the Shaksgam to the north. That was to come later.

After a restful cigarette, which seemed especially welcome at these high altitudes, we turned again to our task. Above us was a steep, high slope spotted with patches of powder snow. To our left a brief rock ridge fell away into nothing, and on the right, above a great cliff, was a small slope leading to a broken icefall which came from the 25,000-foot shoulder. The last seemed the easiest and safest route, and we began to cut steps for a horizontal traverse toward the icefall. The pure green ice fell away sharply to an awful abyss below, for it lay at an angle of 45°. It is possible that this ice could have been formed by wind or pressure, but in the face of existing theories we think it more likely that melting of the snow must take place even as high as 24,500 feet. An hour's work was needed to cut some 80 steps, and to drive two ice pitons to secure our passage; we then landed in the middle of a great icefall formed of blocks and towers of firmly packed snow tumbled from the summit of K2. We puzzled a way through this maze to find ourselves on a 30° snow slope with clear sailing ahead. Up this we plodded, going slower and slower, and being reminded more and more of our advanced altitude. Around 3 o'clock we emerged at the top of the snow slope 300 feet below the long-sought 25,347-foot point.

Here at last was one landmark whose altitude we knew precisely from previous triangulations, and which had been the focal point of our eyes for many weeks. Alas, the summit was still out of sight above us. Between us and the face of the cone stretched another small slope whose gentle curve hid the final rock pyramid from our anxious gaze. It was too late to go farther, so Paul took photographs of our magnificent surroundings as we turned back toward Camp VI. When we arrived, we found the support party stubbornly, though not comfortably, established in three precariously pitched tents. They too had their tale to tell, for they had carried 35-pound loads up from Camp V over the loose stones below. The Sherpas and Bates and House had labored all afternoon in this restricted space, chopping away rocks frozen in the ice and building up braced but sloping platforms for the two other tents.

We now felt further removed from the common world than ever before, for our tiny campsite clung insecurely to the steep slabs, and the nearest level ground which we could see was some 7,000 feet below us on the Godwin-Austen Glacier. Life at home, with its complications, petty annoyances, hopes and struggles, seemed futile and very, very far away. And yet our thoughts were frequently with our friends and families. We all felt that could we only be home for a few days, our energies and enthusiasm would be greatly strengthened, and we could attack the last few thousand feet with renewed vigor. Our nearest contact with home consisted of letters which we could be writing, but, alas, never seemed to do.

After dinner came a council of war, by far the most serious and decisive of the many we had had. With us in Camp VI we had perhaps 10 days of food and fuel. Several camps below were well stocked, so that we could retreat without taking food or tents with us. Above us we were certain at least two more camps would be necessary were we to reach the summit. This meant that each camp would need at least 7 days of food, and several days must be consumed in establishing them. Our margin of safety was getting very slim. Should we push on higher as fast as possible, hoping that our brilliant weather would continue? Or should we play the conservative game and retreat in full marching order? The latter was undoubtedly the wiser move, but somehow, having worked so long and gone so far, we felt that a small chance must be taken.

The big question was the weather. If we were sure the good weather would continue, we would be quite safe to go higher for two more camps, returning only when our food was almost exhausted. With good weather and without mishap, we felt that we could reach the summit. On the other hand, if a storm should break in two or three days, we would have no alternative but to wait until the weather cleared again.

The mere thought of climbing down in storm over our route, which had been difficult enough under perfect conditions, was horrifying. In storm or even after fresh snow, we would be in serious trouble on House's Chimney, on Petzoldt's Gendarme, and on the slopes below Camp III. The long delays required for safe assurance of each climber would mean certain frostbite if we retreated in a storm. No, there was no alternative. We must go down in good weather.

Therefore, we must either turn back before the storm broke or else be prepared to wait until the storm had exhausted its fury. That there was to be a storm in the near future seemed probable. We had had two weeks of almost uninterrupted clear weather at a time in the season when all authorities agreed the weather was bound to change, and for the last two days the cloud bank over Turkestan had grown ominously larger. A storm was certainly to be expected, but how severe it would be was a question that time alone could solve. All our previous storms had lasted only three to five days, but the French Expedition in 1936 had lain in their tents for two solid weeks of snow and wind. It was becoming increasingly evident that we could advance at most but one camp higher.

Our first objective had been the establishment of a safe and direct route to the summit. Our second objective far overshadowed the first—to bring the entire party home unscathed. We felt that in reaching the great snow field below the summit cone we had well completed our first objective. Abruzzi ridge, though far from an easy route, was a direct one, and, if discretion was used, a safe way to the summit.

After several hours of discussion, we finally decided that we would still be within our margin of safety if two men were established as high as possible with three days of food, with the understanding that they would return immediately should bad weather threaten. Those two could climb in one day as high on the summit cone as time and strength would allow before returning to Camp VI and beginning the retreat. It was a difficult decision. We all felt its gravity but agreed that it was the only one which could be made, a compromise between our vaulting ambitions and safety.

Who then were to be the two chosen? The whole group had made plans as a committee; each man was in perfect condition, and each man equally able to carry the burden of the final climb. But Petzoldt and I had reconnoitered the route, and the few extra days of high altitude had presumably acclimatized us slightly better. Accordingly House and Bates volunteered to establish camp for us, and return to Camp VI while we two went higher. No one slept soundly that night, for we all realized that our adventure was drawing to a close, and that the high goal which we had set ourselves was to be unattained.

On the morning of the 20th we had again perfect weather, confirming our decision of the previous evening. Above us the sky was a dark inky blue, a sky of very high altitude. Far to the west a tiny cloud bank kissed the top of Nanga Parbat. There was no wind—our weather was still holding. Four loads were made, one for each sahib, for the Sherpas, we felt, had reached the limits of their climbing ability. Just before we left, the indomitable Pasang begged to be taken, and we could not resist his smile or his spirit, so our loads were lightened to make a fifth pack. We did not consider the other two Sherpas, stalwart though they had been, capable of going higher over the increasingly difficult route. We left them to drowse in the sun.

House and Petzoldt started first on one rope, while Bates, Pasang and I followed closely. Our spirits were high, but a curious lethargy lay over the party. Perhaps it was a feeling of defeat, a regret at nearing the end of our climb, or perhaps altitude was beginning to take toll. Bates was complaining of stomach trouble, his first mishap on the entire trip. Our loads were light, under 20 pounds, but progress was very slow.

Not until afternoon did we reach the top of the snow gully with its tricky ledge leading higher to the top of the Black Pyramid, where we snatched a quick lunch, rubbing our feet, which had been numbed by the straps of our climbing irons. Attempts were made to melt some snow on the warm rocks, for we did not carry water on these climbs. The ideal combination, long since worked out, of fruit drops wrapped in snow, did not seem very satisfying to our dry mouths.

Not until 3 o'clock did the entire party reach the top of the Pyramid, and the beginning of the traverse across the 45° ice slope where Petzoldt had cut steps and fixed the pitons in the ice to secure the passage. We found that the sun had melted the ice around the iron spikes, which dangled on the rope, while water filled the holes they had occupied. If House, Bates, and Pasang were to return to Camp VI before dark, they must start at once, so they shed their loads at the beginning of the traverse. This was to be the highest point they reached, about 24,700 feet, and both Petzoldt and I realized what a sacrifice they were making by allowing us to be the two who continued the attack. But there was no time for sentimentalizing. The other three started down and, after a difficult but uneventful passage, arrived in camp just before dark. Petzoldt and I took on extra pounds and relayed the entire camp across the ice traverse, digging in our tent in the deep snow on the far side of the icefall.

The minute the setting sun left us, we became conscious of the intense cold of high altitude, a cold that seemed almost liquid and entered our very bones. We huddled into the tent and the stove was assembled, when to our horror we discovered that the match supply had been left in Camp VI. This was a catastrophe. In my pocket I found four safety matches and five strike-anywhere matches, all of dubious value. The latter, brought all the way from New York, carefully dried in the sun at many of the lower camps, had persistently failed to function well above 20,000 feet, and only with extreme care and preparatory rubbings with grease did they even glow. The safety matches, on the other hand, were made in Kashmir and were very fragile.

Petzoldt struck the first one. It fizzled—and went out. I tried one of the safety matches. It broke off at the head. Petzoldt, in desperation, seized a strike-anywhere match and struck it almost casually. It burst into flame and the stove was lighted.

Only six matches were left, so after supper we melted a great supply of water for the morning. The pot then was wrapped in all our clothing and put under our feet, a device which we had before found effective in preventing water from freezing. We cursed ourselves for forgetting to bring extra matches, and my diary notes say, "This neglect must have been an evidence of altitude effect." Everything else was complete, and as we snuggled into our warm sleepers, each of us wondered about the coming morning.

"I think the weather looks settled," said Paul.

"I'm sure of it," I replied, feeling all the while that the clouds had looked rather ominous, and wondering if he had the same doubts.

"If only the wind holds off, the cold won't be too bad."

We each thought for a moment about numb fingers and toes on other mornings before the sun reached us.

"Are those matches safe?" from Paul.

"They're here in my sleeper."

"We'd be out of luck with no matches."

Silence.

"Well, tomorrow's the big day. Let's get some sleep."

In the morning we did not stir until the rising sun warmed the tent. It was a perfect day. Three matches were used before one finally lighted our stove and assured us of a warm breakfast. Three matches remained.

We left our tent in order for the return of the two exhausted climbers we were sure to be that evening, and finally donned our climbing irons in the cold, windless morning. Our four Shetland sweaters, flannel shirts and the windproof suits with two pairs of light wool mittens and ski gauntlets barely sufficed to keep us from frostbite, even though there was no wind.

Separated by 60 feet of light alpine rope, we began the final stage of the climb. Two hours of steady effort brought us to the point reached two days before, where we rested and took more photographs of the inimitable scenery below. The cloud bank over Turkestan had vanished, but the west wind was still holding its own. Nanga Parbat was clear and we seemed assured of at least one more beautiful day.

Above the shoulder, we were again forced to the east, where we struggled up gentle snow slopes of peculiarly variable consistency. For 100 feet the sharp spikes of our climbing irons barely dented the icy crust. Over the next stretch we waded up to our knees in powder snow, and then came patches of frost feathers. These strange structures are formed by winds of high velocity and low temperature which pile masses of fine powder snow into fantastic drifts, some of them hundreds of feet long, three or four feet deep, and several feet wide. When one steps on these drifts, a great piece many yards long may break off and slide away; consequently one must approach them with circumspection.

On the whole, however, we found the going not too difficult, but gradually, as we were forced more and more toward the east, the snow became deeper and more powdery in the lee of the true shoulder. Progress grew more labored. Soon we came to the foot of a veritable cliff 50–60 feet high, the upper lip of a great crack in the snowfield. It was hopeless to attack this, so we continued along to the east, finally finding a steep narrow snow bridge which led to the upper level.

This was very shaky, and only after some difficulty were we able safely to reach the higher slope, where we floundered in soft powder snow up to our hips. The altitude was beginning to tell. Petzoldt was feeling strong and moving rapidly, but I had a curious weakness in my legs, so that every upward step was an effort requiring several breaths. And yet my mind seemed very clear and active. By 1 o'clock we had reached the top of the great snow field; barely 300 yards away across a gently sloping snow shoulder rose the final cone.

At first glance it seemed difficult, but more detailed inspection convinced us that it was a direct route from the snow field to the summit. Between us and the base of the summit pyramid, however, lay several hundred yards of snow shoulder covered with ice fragments which clearly were remnants of avalanches coming from the great ice cliffs below the summit. We had seen from below such masses of ice break off, and were we to be caught by such a fall, there would be no question of our fate. The distance over which we would be exposed was quite small, however, and there were no difficulties to prevent us from crossing rapidly. Still, it was a hazard, and one which future expeditions must bear in mind. We lunched briefly and rested with almost the whole of the Karakoram well below us. Then we took off the rope and coiled it to dry in the sun while we went a little farther.

Petzoldt, being the fresher, started off sturdily and in a few minutes was out of danger from icefall at the base of the summit cone. I could see him ahead of me working steadily upward, pausing now and then to take bearings. My progress was ludicrously slow. Every inch I gained in altitude was an effort. My legs were so weak I was forced to rest every five or six steps, and soon fatigue made me forget all danger from above. I struggled on—why I do not know, for it was foolish to try to gain a few more feet, and yet something within drove me to go as high as I possibly could. Various thoughts flashed through my mind. Had I ever been so tired before? Would I be less tired with another day of acclimatization at this altitude? Could Bob or Bill have done better?

At last, at the base of the final cone, I could go no farther. Petzoldt was 150 feet above me, working on the rock, as I sat down against a huge boulder. I had reached my limit. Soon I turned back and staggered down to where we had left the rope on the outer end of the shoulder, well beyond reach of avalanches. There I lay in the sun and rested. Petzoldt had stopped and was working in the rocks.

After 15 or 20 minutes of complete rest I counted my pulse. It was 135, whereas normally at sea level it is 50. I thought of all sorts of notes to write in the little book I carried, but somehow had not the mental energy to put them down. Mingled with a deep and heartfelt regret at abandoning the attack, when success seemed within our grasp, was a sense of relief that at last the hard struggle was over and we were free to return to Base Camp and home, with the realization of our job incomplete but nevertheless well done. I tried to look ahead years into the future so as to cement firmly in my mind recollections of these great moments on our mighty peak. There were other emotions too deep to be expressed. I felt that all my previous life had reached a climax in these last hours of intense struggle against nature, and yet nature had been very indulgent. She had scarcely bothered to turn against us the full force of her elements. Indeed, she had favored us with perfect weather and not too difficult conditions, preferring to let our puny bodies exhaust themselves in the rarefied atmosphere. How small indeed we were to struggle so desperately to reach one point on the earth's surface, a point which had been so real a goal to us for many months! I believe in those minutes at 26,000 feet on K2, I reached depths of feeling which I can never reach again.

My musings were interrupted by a shout from Petzoldt who struggled down and collapsed beside me. He too was very tired, though much fresher than I. We had come up from Camp V very rapidly. There had been only three nights of acclimatization above that camp, and we had been working almost continuously under difficult conditions for the past two weeks. He told me after a brief rest that he had found at the very base of the summit pyramid a large flat space which he felt would be an ideal site for a final camp. From what he had seen of the rocks above this platform the climbing would not be so difficult as the Black Pyramid at the top of Abruzzi ridge. He had spent some time in examining it, and was convinced, as was I, that a direct and not too difficult way led from our resting place directly to the top of the mountain. At a little over 26,000 feet he had fixed his camera in the rocks and with the point of his ice ax tripped the shutter and taken a self-portrait, which later turned out to be excellent.

There was no question but that our work was done, and we turned to descend at 4 o'clock with mingled emotions. The whole world was deathly still; not even the clatter of rock falls broke the calm. All the peaks about us seemed breathlessly awaiting our descent. We trudged down to Camp VII in a deepening twilight. About us the mountains turned first pink, then lavender, then purple. We reached camp safely, exhausted and cold, but curiously content.

Our first thought was tea. With infinite care we waxed one of the matches, dried it as much as possible, and struck it. It fizzled and went out. A safety match broke off at the head. Paul in a gesture of bravado struck our last one. It lit and we were assured of our warm supper. Too tired for much talk, we melted water for the morning, snuggled in our sleeping bags, and drowsed off to a dreamless sleep.

from In the Throne Room of the
Mountain Gods
by Galen Rowell

The 1938 and 1953 American expeditions to K2 set high standards of comradeship. But when Americans returned to the mountain in 1975, vicious feuding among party members helped keep the group low on the mountain. Photographer and climber Galen Rowell (born in 1940), with the help of expedition members who contributed diary entries, offered a brutally honest account of the party's woes. In the Throne Room of the Mountain Gods *helped to usher in an era of tell-all expedition books.*

O
n June 16, I climbed to Camp II with Lou, Wick, Rob, and Steve. Jim and Dianne stayed below to help with the lower end of the winching system up to Savoia Pass. The two Freds were in base camp with Leif, both very subdued after a wild confrontation with the rest of the team. I sympathized fully with their emotions about the expedition, but not with their threats to go home. During the approach, both Freds had been more upset than anyone about the porters' failure to honor their contract when the going got rough. Now, to my way of thinking, they were doing exactly the same thing. We owed it to each other, even if we were no longer friends, to stick together long enough to make a serious attempt on the mountain. Otherwise, many man-years of effort and hope would have been spent in vain.

The Freds believed that the Whittakers and Wickwire formed a conspiracy in Seattle to place themselves on the summit to the exclusion of others. I didn't believe it. The kinds of partnerships that are often called conspiracies are usually nothing more than expressions of mutual self-interest. Wick and Lou *seemed* as if they were involved in a conspiracy because each was individually motivated toward the same goal: being first on the summit. Jim recognized them as the winners of a self-styled competition. But if an agreement on the summit team existed before-hand, why had Wick and Lou pushed so hard to prove themselves? If a conspiracy had really existed, why didn't they just take it easy, waiting for Jim to pull them out of a hat after we prepared the lower camps?

Each of us had a slightly different interpretation of the Freds' revolt. Unfortunately, Fred Dunham did not keep a diary, but what follows are the descriptions that the other team members recorded at the time.

Lou Whittaker:
Big crisis today! Last night the Freds talked 'til midnight and today Stanley says he has *quit* the expedition. Feels he has no say in anything and that Jim and Wick and myself are run-ning the expedition without letting anyone else have a vote. They were both very quiet yesterday after a ribbing that they got when they laughed because Wick and I were turned back from Camp II because of snow. Jim said usually when some-one tries to do what we all want, like try to climb the moun-tain, failure would not be something to delight in. . . . The Freds have been so negative on everything—the country, the coolies, the HAPs, Manzoor, and now the rest of the team. I think a fear of the mountain may have them both stymied.

Dunham said he would carry tomorrow but Stanley may not. . . . He is really in a pout right now like a five-year-old—hard to sympathize with. . . . I didn't think I was being too strong with the Freds, but Wick said we (Jim and I) can tend to bulldoze through problems and can come on very strong.

Rob Schaller:
Two days ago we had a real crisis with the two Freds, both suddenly admitting to being alienated by the Big Three and

not feeling a part of the expedition. Stanley believes there is a conspiracy to get the Big Three on the top and we are only coolies to accomplish that purpose. He seems to have transferred his hostilities toward the Baltis to the rest of us. . . . Stanley talks seriously of leaving and I talk with him for hours but to little avail.

Dianne Roberts:
I haven't been able to sort out the thing with the Freds in my own mind. A few days ago they began being deliberately uncommunicative after going to Camp II with Lou and Wick. Then in an odd series of conversations they revealed first to Galen and Steve, then to Wick and Jim, that they were totally pissed off with the way things were going, that they felt cut off and ignored by the others, that their opinions were being laughed at and a lot of other paranoid bullshit including the accusation that Jim, Wick, and Lou were involved in a conspiracy (hatched in Seattle) to get the three of them to the summit of K2 by employing the forced labor of the rest of the team. Whew. It came as a shock to everyone—both in its content and in its intensity, but it did serve as a catalyst to bring out feelings that have been brewing for weeks. The rest of us (except Leif) sat at Camp I talking about it for most of one afternoon and the next morning. Galen got into it a lot, trying to justify, or at least explain the Freds' outburst in terms of the "autocratic/dictatorial" running of the expedition all along the way. Hell—all kinds of accusations were flung about with rare abandon. But not too much of it made any sense—except the clear revelation that our group has been divided in half all along, with neither half understanding the other since the beginning.

Jim Whittaker:
Stanley is really running off at the mouth. Claims he is going

to quit the expedition—that Lou, Wick, and I have a pact, made in Seattle, that the three of us are going to reach the summit of K2 and he is just going to carry for us. Claims no one else will get a chance. He says that I am a dictator, Wick is ignoring everyone else but Lou and I and to hell with everyone.

Manzoor Hussain [in a letter written after the expedition]: Fighting and quarrels had started between Freds and Lou and Wick. . . . In fact the team had started breaking itself into four sections right from the beginning. Fred Dunham and Fred Stanley formed one section (the extremist left). Lou Whittaker and Jim Wickwire, another (whom everybody called the most ambitious for the peak). Steve Marts, Rob Schaller, Galen Rowell and Leif Patterson formed the third section (the moderate ones). . . . Jim Whittaker and Dianne Roberts formed the fourth section, isolated from whatever was happening in the expedition. Fred Stanley had a bitter quarrel with Jim Whittaker and thought he was amongst foes rather than friends.

Leif Patterson:
The fifteenth opens with a tremendous crisis. Dunham is disgusted with the way things have been going. Stanley wants to quit. They have some poignant reasons. Feel pretty bad, as if expedition is falling apart. . . . Last night Galen had a long talk with the Freds. Very late in the morning some of the party sets off without resolution of the dispute. . . . My line with all I talk to in the team is that we need each other, that we must be honest toward each other. Imagine then, that same evening, just before Rob arrives in Camp I, a radio conversation with Wick in the same camp. Wick instructs Manzoor to send a telegram to Wick's wife, censuring Joanne [Rob's fiancée] for giving personal information about Rob

to newspapers—and threatening Joanne with later court action. Why isn't Rob notified? Why isn't telegram sent directly to Joanne? Where does this information about releases come from up here? This is intrigue behind each others' backs, a real shock to me.

On morning of June 16th, Fred Stanley cuts in on the radio to have it out with Jim Whittaker. He inquires about the telegram, which cannot now be hidden from Rob. Whittaker refuses any discussion. Fred is bitter. But the net result is that the telegram is called off—a good thing.

[After a carry to Camp I] Fred Stanley and I . . . had a talk . . . got along fine. Fred is very strong and very conscientious. Why won't the upper echelons in our team recognize his fine qualities? Fred is deeply disappointed. He came to climb with Wick and Dunham as much as to scale K2—and what has he got from Wick?

Fred loves to needle Whittaker. It is not the right approach. I have a plan: if Camp III gets established, I want the two Freds and myself to take the lead in putting in Camp IV, provided only our health will hold.

My lungs are not clear. . . . This is such a messed-up trip: my own sickness would mean little in a good team of first-rate friends. But the team is an unhappy one. It is nearly split apart from inner tensions. It is my lot to help pull together, unify, and without sufficient health I cannot succeed in that. I believe that you do not remedy a disastrous confidence crisis merely by talking it over. That is a first step. But the crisis was precipitated by cumulative *actions* in the first place, and actions cannot be eradicated by words, only by other actions. I believe we can still overcome difficulties and unify our team by actions which will allow each individual recognition for his efforts, and by honesty. The Wick-Lou summit consideration should be dissolved. Wick should do his job as deputy leader, which would first and foremost be to mend his relations with his close friends: the two Freds and Rob. The summit must be there to tempt all of us, not only a couple of gung-hos. The illness afflicting us as a team is already dangerously far advanced.

Jim Wickwire:

A major new crisis has hit the expedition: the possible defection of the two Freds. The problem has been brooding for some time. Both have felt they have had little involvement in expedition decision-making, that any ideas or comments they have about what should be done are not listened to or are rejected out of hand. Fred Dunham has been in deep gloom since the Manzoor radio incident of the tenth. Last night after dinner Fred D. unloaded to Galen and Steve how unhappy he was that "his friend Jim Wickwire had been distant," and that he was fed up with constantly being put down by Jim. Last night, I could hear both of them talking in subdued voices far into the night. Something serious was up and was confirmed by Galen's relation of his discussion the previous evening with Dunham. Apparently, Stanley felt the same way and there was talk of their leaving the expedition.

I could not accept the assertion that the entire problem was one of a clash of personalities. Granted, Jim has come on a trifle strong at times; Lou, too, but I believe . . . that both of them are intimidated by the mountain and by the time and distance from persons they care a great deal for.

After breakfast, Jim and I went to their tent to talk with them. Jim led off, saying that his principal objective was to get up the mountain and that everything he had done had been directed toward that end. That to reach the summit every person on the team was important and if he stepped on their toes he was sorry. Fred S. remarkably responded: "Nice pep talk, but I don't believe a word you said." I angrily interjected, "That's completely unfair." And so it went, in a very unsatisfactory way, for a few minutes with Jim there and then for another half hour with them alone. . . . Finally I walked away. Just before leaving for Camp I, talked briefly to Fred Dunham, who said he would continue to work for the expedition because of what he felt was an obligation to those persons who had made contributions at his behest. During the discussion with both Freds, I conceded I wanted to get to the top of K2, that was why I was here, and if I didn't make it to the top, I wanted to leave here with no regrets and knowing that I had given everything to the effort of getting there. Curiously, Fred Stanley said that the reason he came on the expedition was because of Fred's and my presence. That's nice, but not a sufficient reason for coming all the way to Pakistan and K2. . . .

Spent the entire afternoon in our tent discussing pros and cons of what to do. Galen, Jim, Dianne, Lou, and Steve. Nothing conclusive, except maybe to offer them the route-finding to Camp III. To me this is an admission we have been wrong. I don't think we have. At least to the extent they think. . . .

Rob . . . spent nearly four hours with the Freds in their tent that afternoon. No startling new allegations. They feel the expedition is divided into two camps: Jim, Lou, and I in one; everyone else in the other. They thought it would be poetic justice if Steve Marts and a Balti got to the summit and none of us did. Or, better yet, and here is a real twist, both Whittakers get to the summit and I don't. These are my friends? . . .

Motivation on any Himalayan expedition is the name of the game. If you don't have a lot of it, you won't put up with what you have to go through to reach the high summit you are striving for. I admit to having very strong motivation for climbing K2. I make no apologies for it. The Whittakers have it. They should not have to make apologies for it. Rob and Leif—and I think Galen—also have it. But the Freds don't. That's why I resent and refute the notion this is all some giant putdown of them by us. Of course there have been and will continue to be personality clashes, but to hang it all on that is utter bullshit.

But in the last analysis, I am spending four months in Pakistan because I want to reach the summit of my dream mountain. For various reasons the Freds (particularly Stanley) are opting out. Lou has the same dream I do, and—if the route goes, and if we stay strong—we will go to the summit together. And if we don't, it will not be because we haven't given the effort of our lives.

(Next morning) Things have really gone to hell vis-à-vis Stanley. At 8:00 a.m. he came on the radio and wanted to know the basis for the telegram to Mary Lou. Rob and Steve were in the tent for breakfast, and I hadn't yet told Rob about the telegram, mainly because I was reluctant to compromise Steve as the source. Stanley was insistent, so in Rob's presence, I explained the genesis of the telegram. Rob nodded in understanding. Stanley charged that I had stabbed Rob in the back. There followed one of the most irrational, hate-filled diatribes I have ever heard, directed at Jim and me. He yelled that there was a conspiracy among Jim, Lou, and me to put the three of us on the summit to the exclusion of all the others. . . . There had been discussions about who was strongest in the team . . .—Lou, Jim, and me—but absolutely no pact to put all three of us on the summit. We had simply looked around and concluded that we had greater motivation than the others, except perhaps for Leif and Rob. . . .

A few minutes ago Galen said that on the approach march the other five felt alienated from Jim, Lou, and me, as though we had formed a group with its own ambitions for the summit—that we had not been warm and compatible on the approach. Compatibility is a two-way street, and he would place the entire burden on us to walk the full length of the street. To me, the whole thing is a commentary on the insecurity of the others, an indication of their need to be wet-nursed. I was happy on the approach just to be here in this great country. Why should I have sought out those who did not share my feelings as opposed to one who did—Lou? Friendship is mutuality, not sitting back waiting for your "friend" to come minister to you.

Fred Stanley:
Last evening when I got to camp with Steve, the porters and Manzoor welcomed us, untying our rope and carrying our packs to our tents. A kind of warm glow came over me. I got into my sweater and down vest and wind shirt, got my cup out, and headed for the cook tent. . . . Dinner was ready. I was feeling pretty good and somewhere into the conversation I mentioned that Fred and I could hardly contain ourselves at the irony of Wick and Lou starting out for Camp II the previous *afternoon* and then returning fifteen minutes later (in a snowstorm) after all their noise and valorous talk. That is, I started to mention it and Jim jumped on me, shouting me out, saying how the two Freds were happy about their failures . . . how we're always happy when something goes wrong, how we were happy when he didn't make Camp I from base camp in 45 minutes as he had bragged he would (this I knew nothing of), etc. I just shut up and slowly finished my dinner. . . .

I am really at a low ebb. I have lost all enthusiasm for the expedition, wishing there was some way out without leaving the rest in the lurch. Each person in this small group counts a lot. The talk this morning is to have Wick and Lou return to the lead with Rob and Galen going to II to set up the winch system. I left earlier when the talk turned to the virtues of the first two fixing the route or not, to finish my cocoa and pancakes in peace away from the sound of the Whittakers' voices drowning out Galen's and even Fred's, I think. . . . Lou and Jim can always shout a little more than the other guy is willing to, knowing it's no use to argue with them, or they can attack him personally, saying his knowledge of fixed lines in Yosemite is of no use here, etc. Jim asked Fred—it sounded like a challenge to me—if he had any objections to Wick and Lou going into the lead again. I really don't give a shit. I was even hoping I would wake up good and sick this morning so I could just have an excuse to lie about—maybe even go down. If I had Alex Bertulis's address I would send him a letter telling him how lucky he was to get off this thing when he did even as he did. A blackballing by Whittaker raises him a notch in my eyes. And I know damn well no one besides Wick, Lou, and perhaps Jim have a chance for the summit. . . .

Wick is sitting on the fence, I think, wanting to stay in good with Jim and Lou, certain that Lou as the leader's brother and he as deputy leader will be the ones for the summit. . . . I hope it's a picket fence and he gets one up the ass. . . .

Jim sent a couple of telegrams . . . saying how we were gouged on approach but how nice things are going now. . . .

Fred just came in from what he called a psychotherapy session with Galen and Steve. He said they talked over some of the same feelings we've all had. Galen says he's just going to enjoy the company of others and work toward the success of the expedition. I tell Fred that's what I find depressing. The success of the expedition means putting a Whittaker on the summit. . . .

I've never had any great Nazi fervor about climbing K2 as perhaps Wick has. I came on the expedition for enjoyment and have had little. I can still remember Jim saying things will get better when we reach the mountain the morning Lou threatened Fred at Concordia. They've gotten worse. Galen has struck up a psychoanalysis session with the rest of the group this morning, discussing Fred and me and himself, also. I believe he's found it an opportunity to bring out his problems with the Whittakers and air them— a good catharsis for him. Lou, Wick, and everyone are getting into the act now, psychoanalyzing us. I can't hear it all, actually only a phrase or two, but I sure have to chuckle. It sounds to me like Galen's good intentions of trying to get us treated better, listened to, respected for our positions, not put down every time we open our mouths, are being shouted down.

Wick is talking vehemently. I hear noises about fragile egos, losing a few on Himalayan expeditions, crying in the tent. . . . Fred came back saying the Jims wanted to talk to us. I finally got them to understand I didn't really care to talk about it other than to say I was unhappy with personal relationships and was ready to bail out. Fred said he was ready to stay and do as he was told. . . . Jim made a pep talk and plea that he was doing things as he thought they ought to be done and was only interested in getting the expedition to the summit, and unless I was willing to talk about it there wasn't much he could do. What it boiled down to was he was begging for bodies to stay on; otherwise the expedition had had it. He finally left and Fred talked a little more with Wick, who tried to explain his position and actions, talking about safety, our supposed preoccupation with safety, technique, technical competence. . . . All I could think of was what does this have to do with the Whittakers treating people like shit?

I remembered just a minute ago that when I was a kid we used to talk about digging a hole deep enough to come out in China. What reminded me was that I just pissed a hole in the snow. . . . I'd like to jump down it and come out in Washington.

Rob came by earlier and said he tried to keep out of the morning's psychoanalysis and we talked about the situation. He said he's felt out of it—left out by the Big Three ever since Rawalpindi. . . . He seems to think as Galen, that things will get better if we five stick together, that there are or will be changes in the Whittakers. . . . Wick's aloofness to him since getting to Pakistan has hurt him. . . .

I think Wick was pretty shook this morning and I don't blame him, but I haven't laid awake the past two nights for no reason, either. When I replied "you and Fred" to his question of why did I come along on the expedition, he said that was a pretty poor reason. It was enough for me and half that reason is gone now. I don't think I've anything to prove or find out on K2. I was along for an adventure with friends.

A radio call (from Camp I) at 6:00 p.m. while we (Fred, Leif, Manzoor, and I) were finishing dinner: Wick wanted to send out a telegram to Mary Lou (his wife).

WE HAVE REPORTS JOANNE [Rob's fiancée] IS ACTING AS OFFICIAL OR UNOFFICIAL LIAISON WITH NEWS MEDIA REGARDING EXPEDITION MATTERS. SHE IS NOT AUTHORIZED TO DO SO. OUR CONTRACTUAL OBLIGATIONS TO NATIONAL GEOGRAPHIC SOCIETY AND SIERRA CLUB REQUIRE CAREFUL REVIEW BY US OF ALL INFORMATION RELEASED TO NEWS MEDIA. ALTHOUGH WE CANNOT PREVENT JOANNE FROM TALKING TO MEDIA, PLEASE ADVISE SHE FACES LEGAL ACTION IF SHE CONTINUES TO RELEASE FIRST-PERSON DIARY ACCOUNTS OR PHOTOGRAPHS TO MEDIA. OTHERWISE, EVERYTHING FINE. LOVE YOU AND MISS YOU SO.

The threat of legal action caught us by surprise and really floored us. Jim came on to Manzoor and said, "Yes, I think that's something that should be sent." I had looked out the tent door just a few minutes before to see Rob moving (in the distance) up the last slope to Camp I. Fred got on the radio and asked to speak to Jim. Jim Whittaker came on and asked, "Which Jim?" (Wick or Whittaker) and Fred said it didn't matter, he just wanted to find out the source of the rumor. Jim said he thought he'd let Fred talk to Wick, Rob was coming into camp. Wick came on, and without answering the question, said a few words and said the next radio contact would be at eight in the morning and signed off. We sat back shocked. What a stab in the back to Rob. . . . Leif said he just couldn't believe the deceit, the behind-the-back things going on in this expedition. We agreed to make sure in the morning that Rob knew of the telegram. We thought of sending another saying to Joanne this was not an expression of the whole expedition.

We talked on; Fred finally left. . . . Leif kept remarking that the five of us had the power to get the expedition running the way we wanted it. I realized that we could, on our own, stock the camps as high as we wished for as many as we wished. It's his opinion that the summit team will be chosen by expedition vote. . . . During the conversation he managed to impart to me some of his fantastic strength. Enough that I decided to stick around for awhile and start being the person I'd like to be in situations like this. . . .

After talking with all the climbers other than the Big Three, I realize they all have many of the same feelings I do, that if there come any corporate votes, it'll be 5 to 4 (corporate votes affecting me brought up by our legal eagle, Wick). . . .

I woke at seven this morning, my mind immediately in high gear—one of those situations when everything is spread before one with perfect clarity. . . . Everything I would have liked to have said to Wick and Jim the previous morning is completely sorted out in my mind now. I am looking forward to the radio contact and tell the others I would like to make it. I also prepared to do a thing I was less than proud of—recording a conversation with others when they didn't know it. Something I wanted as a personal reference. . . something I can present to Wick or Whittakers if things are said which there is going to be a question about. At eight Jim is on. I ask for Wick. He is on. I ask him if he is ready to supply the source of his rumor. In his careful lawyer's voice and words, he replies that it has only just now come to his attention that possibly first-person diary accounts of the expedition have been printed in the Seattle papers. I think he hemmed and hawed before this, saying he wanted to speak to Rob first. At some point he said that before he went further he wanted to know if I was still a member of the expedition in light of the previous day's happenings. I replied that I was still a member of the expedition until I was run out by them the way Alex was. Jim burst in on the conversation somewhere and I told him that he, Wick, and Lou were going to have to quit treating the rest of us as piles of shit into which they could kick their crampons to get a little higher on K2. I also said they should forget about any plans made in Seattle to put them on the summit first; Jim said I was bordering on insanity. Wick finally came back on the radio to speak to Manzoor and told him to cancel the telegram. Fred, Leif, and I spent a while discussing things afterwards, at least relieved by Wick's cancellation of the telegram, but not otherwise very happy.

June 21, 1975, was the solstice. But there was no summer at base camp. Nothing was green. No birds chirped, no insects buzzed. It had been snowing steadily for three days, and the camp took on the appearance of a deserted outpost in the Arctic.

My life seemed as empty and as barren as the landscape. My bronchitis had developed into pneumonia, and I was trying to bide the time until I was well again. I realized that this dark day was the twenty-first anniversary of Mario Puchoz's death on K2, officially from pneumonia. That scared me, but I tried cheering myself by remembering that Puchoz had probably died of pulmonary edema, misdiagnosed as pneumonia. My only contact with the doctor was by radio. Rob, Steve, Wick, and Lou were waiting out the storm in Camp II, unable to descend because of blizzard conditions and avalanche danger. Rob prescribed Keflex, a strong antibiotic, and kept trying to boost my morale by suggesting that I probably just had the flu. But I was only too aware that my symptoms were the same as Leif's when he had pneumonia. I had come down with bronchitis, and then suddenly succumbed to great weakness and fever. I tried to sleep sitting up because I couldn't breathe well lying down. Every night I sat half awake under the strange delusion that I had two heads attached to the same body. At the height of his illness, Leif had a somewhat similar vision of being in two bodies.

The two Freds were also in base camp. Stanley had some sort of stomach ailment and Dunham had a very bad cough. Their behavior resembled that of unskilled laborers who believe they have no chance of advancement in their jobs. When they were healthy they were willing to work, but not too hard and not too long. If they felt sick, as they did that day, they simply took sick leave.

Those in the high camps were constantly insinuating that the Freds were fudging, and that they could have gone up on the mountain if only they had had the desire. The Freds overheard many of these thinly veiled sarcasms and were reinforced in the belief that the Big Four's only concern for their welfare had to do with their ability to shuttle loads. The attitude of those up high was, "If I had a cough or a stomachache it wouldn't stop me from going on the mountain," and it was sincere.

Feeling under the weather might not have prevented *them* from climbing to higher altitudes. But the Freds valued their health and safety far more than the glory of reaching the summit. Maybe, as some had suggested, they really did not belong on K2. But this attitude implied that we had cornered the market on the one right way to climb a mountain, and I didn't buy that notion at all. Moral considerations aside, the Freds had definitely lost interest in the climb by this time, and this might not have happened if they had been treated differently. Dunham no longer took the expedition seriously and called it "the highest Boy Scout Jamboree in history."

The week before, I had been in agreement with the Whittakers and Wickwire. I thought the Freds were letting the expedition down by threatening to quit. After all, I had taken more abuse from the Big Four than anyone else had, yet I was sticking with it. I was prepared to work hard at high altitude day after day in order to establish the route for whomever would go to the summit. I had geared myself to suffer all manner of discomfort and discontent. I was ready to be away from base camp for a month or more, ready to sleep in camps that grew increasingly colder and smaller, ready to feel my breathing change from an automatic reflex to a consciously controlled effort, ready to temporarily deprive myself of tiny luxuries of human existence that even the poorest street dweller of Calcutta might take for granted.

I was ready to climb the mountain, but I was not prepared for what would soon happen to me. Because of the Freds' illness, Lou had developed an eagle eye for malingerers. I became an unfortunate victim of circumstances.

Still recovering from bronchitis, I had arrived at Savoia Pass on the afternoon of June 16 with Lou, Wick, Rob, and Steve. This was the same day that Fred Stanley had challenged Jim over the radio. The five of us were on our way to Camp II, and most of our camp gear was on a sled below the ice face, where Jim and Dianne were waiting for us to set up the winch that Stanley had hauled up to the pass. The winch was designed to be mounted on an absolutely flat surface, and positioning it on an angular rock so that the base was tight and flush while the long handle could be cranked with considerable force was very difficult. After an hour's work I was able to temporarily jury-rig the winch with nylon hold-down straps going all over the place. We hauled up a single load of gear shortly before dark.

For five people we had five sleeping bags and several days of food, but only two tents and one stove. The small two-man tents were designed with a low and narrow profile for stability in high winds. Inside, two were too many and three were crammed like sardines in a can. Lou and Wick, the two broadest men, took one tent while Rob, Steve, and I squeezed into the other. Since Lou and Wick had the most room, they offered to cook for all of us. Melting enough snow for five men over one tiny stove took hours. In pitch darkness at 9:30 p.m. Lou passed us enough water to rehydrate our freeze-dried dinners. After eating I asked if we could melt more for drinking and filling our bottles. The stove had been turned off and they did not intend to relight it. I resigned myself to passing the night with no water—no great hardship at sea level. At high elevation, however, a person loses considerable water just by normal breathing, since hot, humid, exhaled air contains far more moisture than cold, dry, inhaled air.

By midnight I had not slept a wink. My mouth felt as if I were trying to swallow a ball of cotton. Finally I could stand it no longer, and I crawled over my companions to the tent door. I opened it and plunged my lips into the soft powder snow. It was strange to be consumed by thirst and yet, like an ocean sailor, surrounded by a form of water that I could not drink. At a temperature near zero, the light powder snow provided only a few teaspoons of moisture before my mouth grew so cold that snow stuck to my lips. I returned to my bag and lay awake. Water was so near and yet so far. Like a drug addict deprived of a fix, my every thought was directed toward one substance, and I longed for the dawn as I never had before.

June 17 broke clear, and after what seemed an eternity the stove was lit and my body and mind were renewed by water. But it was not enough. I felt very weak and told the others that I could not join them on the route to Camp III. Rob and Steve opted to stay behind with me.

Together we would try to remount the winch and haul up more tents, stoves, and food.

Lou and Wick set off on the ridge above Camp II. When they neared their old high point, Wick led up a fifty-five-degree snow gully to a perch where he could see most of the corniced north side of the pass. The snow ramp that Wick and Lou had seen from the plane was nowhere to be found. Unless a narrow, hidden traverse existed higher up, the route to Camp III would have to go directly along the crest of the pinnacled ridge itself. Sadly disappointed, the two men returned to Camp II and helped us with the winching. By evening we had hauled several hundred pounds of new supplies into camp.

Rob talked over the radio to Fred Dunham in base camp, who complained about a severe cough. Rob prescribed the usual Empirin with codeine. After the radio transmission we discussed the irony of the Freds having slight ailments and feeling depressed because they did not want to be on the mountain, while Leif had a major illness and felt depressed because he wanted to be working on the mountain with us.

Each of us realized that the next day would be a critical one. We would have to find a route over which thousands of pounds of supplies could be moved to the higher camps, even though we knew that the ridge was composed of steep rock gendarmes coated with unstable snow and ice. Going over the top would be something like traversing a mile of the Manhattan skyline *after* it had been relocated to a spot at 20,000 feet elevation where storms raged more than half the time. When we got past the ridge, there would still be a vertical mile of unclimbed, unexplored ridge between us and the summit.

On the morning of the eighteenth I dragged myself into the roomy three-man tent where breakfast was being prepared. As soon as I sat down I announced, "I can't go with you today."

"Why not this time?" Lou asked with a tone of suspicion.

"Because I feel very sick. I've got a headache, muscular pains and chills, I feel extremely weak, and my eyes are sensitive to light."

"I've got the same symptoms," Lou answered, "and I'm going to climb this mountain. If you wanted to climb K2 as much as we do, you wouldn't stay back for every little thing. I thought you were shaping up, but now I see you're no better than the Freds. I think you're just scared of the mountain."

Lou's diatribe seemed unreal to me. As if in a dream, I felt too sick and sluggish to argue. I repeated that I felt very weak and feverish and I could not go on. While the others ate breakfast and packed equipment, I curled up in a corner of the tent and lay silent. Finally, I returned to the small tent and crawled back into my sleeping bag.

Lou had implied that anyone who stayed behind was scared of the mountain. It was a challenge I could not meet. I knew that I should descend to base camp, but I felt too weak to go by myself. All four of my companions were packing up for an attempt on the ridge. Soon I would be alone.

Rob poked his head into the tent, turned around to make sure that he wasn't overheard, and told me, "I think you made the right decision. If you still feel sick tonight you should go down. I'll go down with you if necessary. Today is a perfect day that we don't want to miss." I knew this was true. The team had been trying for more than a week to push the route past the gendarmes.

"I'll be okay here," I replied. "I hope you guys make it. Lou is wrong about me. I'd like to be up there with you today and I want to climb this mountain."

"I know," Rob said as he backed out of the tent. Behind him the others were profiled against the skyline, walking out of camp on snow that squeaked with the cold. Rob shouldered his pack and stepped briskly to catch them. In a minute they were gone.

Throughout the morning my illness increased. I tried to write in my diary, but felt too weak to put down anything more than the date and temperature. When I stepped outside to urinate, I fell dizzily to my knees.

Just before noon I heard footsteps coming into camp. Peering through the tent door, I caught a glimpse of Lou and rolled back onto my stomach. I did not think Lou would believe that I was really sick, and I planned to wait for Rob. His credibility as a doctor might convince the others that I should be taken down. But the figure that walked into camp was not Lou. I had seen Jim, who had decided to carry a load alone from Camp I. Haltingly, I told Jim about some of my symptoms, expecting another lecture about chickening out. Instead, even before I finished describing my sickness Jim said, "You should go down and I'll help you."

I descended the ice face under my own power, but I was so weak by the time we reached the easy slopes below that I had to support myself on two ski poles and slowly lurch along one step at a time. I rested for a long time at Camp I before donning skis for the three downhill miles to base camp.

Meanwhile, the others were fixing ropes up the ridge. Wick led up several hundred feet of steep, hard ice to a point just below the first gendarme where the upper Northwest Ridge came into view. The climbing up high looked fine, but the area directly in front of Wick on the lower ridge looked more difficult than ever. The route going directly up was very tough, but beyond the top of the first gendarme the horizontal traversing would be even more difficult, especially for those with heavy loads trying to follow on fixed ropes.

That evening a five-day storm moved in. No one moved from Camp II because of the obvious avalanche danger and white-out conditions. For the first time, Wick voiced aloud the possibility that our attempt on the mountain might fail. Still, he adamantly insisted that he would not leave until the expedition had "given everything we have to put forth."

In base camp my temperature was over 101° for three straight days. It was hard for me to imagine what those days would have been like stormbound in a tiny tent at 20,500 feet. Jim may very well have saved my life.

On the night of June 20 I wrote this entry in my diary:

> Perhaps one of the biggest flaws in expedition mountaineering is that it can sometimes promote a ruthless brand of militant enthusiasm that runs roughshod over friendships, health, safety, and reason. For a time, in the

face of storms, avalanches, and extreme altitudes, climbers in the militant rut must consider themselves immortal. Perhaps they never consciously think about immortality, but with their minds and bodies they act out a role as if they were immune from death. They seek that one memory of standing for a few moments above everyone else, and in order to get there they constantly try to elevate themselves and lower others. It doesn't have to be so.

Base camp was a somber place inhabited by the sick and the dispirited. The Freds' spirits sunk to a new low after they discussed avalanche hazards over the radio with Wick and Lou and received only skeptical replies. Lou and Wick believed that Stanley had an abnormal fear of avalanches as a result of being buried by a big one in 1974 in the Soviet Pamir Range, where he climbed with Pete Schoening's expedition. Stanley saw his caution as intelligent, not neurotic, and claimed that Lou and Wick wouldn't listen to reason. "What it boils down to is that campsites they have picked as safe I would place a short distance away in what I consider a safer place because of my experience. Both Lou and Wick said the slope to Savoia Pass was a good one even after the wind caused sloughs. Now it's avalanched several times. Lou said the slope above the pass was a safe one. Later it slid over the anchor points, and we lost some items we had cached there."

Leif had proved to be very different from the somewhat meek and submissive man we judged him to be during the early stages of the expedition. We all knew that he had a tremendous drive to climb mountains, but we had seen him absorb direct insults without reacting in his own defense. At that time Stanley thought that Leif might be a little naive. I believed Leif to be too modest and gentle for his own good. But after all our weeks of discord and conflict, Leif emerged as the man with the greatest strength of character among us. When humility was a virtue, he had it. When a backbone was needed, his became unbendable. He was the only member of the climbing team to be fully accepted by both of the opposing factions.

On June 21 Leif visited Jim in Camp I to discuss what he termed the "fanaticism" of the lead climbers. The statements on this subject in his diary had been growing increasingly strong, until they culminated in, "Are they willing to go over dead bodies?" Instead of holding his emotions inside until they burst, as the Freds did, Leif brought them into the open as tactfully as possible. Jim agreed that a problem existed and that changes should be made, although he held a far more benevolent view of the men who had so far forged every step of new ground on the ridge. Jim was definitely becoming more mellow and he showed a new awareness of how critical his own decisions were in healing the breach in our social order.

When Leif returned he and I had long pleasant discussions about the arts, science, and life for two evenings running. I had sorely missed this sort of unobstructed conversation on the trip; it had always developed during the normal course of other expeditions I had been on. When our conversation touched on our own expedition, however, we held back, afraid to reveal too much of ourselves to each other. We hid many of our true feelings and weighed each other's words for emotional content on a delicately balanced scale. On this subject we reserved our deepest feelings for our inanimate diaries. One night, for instance, Leif wrote, "What is this adventure about? Where is the beauty when I can't share it? Life is love and love is sharing. For sharing is the detection of universal unity. . . . The thought haunts me that not the ridge of K2, but our own disunity will defeat us."

Another week passed, one day blending into another while I passively waited out my illness. The first storm had lasted for five days. After Jim, Lou, Wick, Leif, and Steve made another attempt on the ridge, a new storm began, forcing them once again to sit it out in Camp II. Their second try on the ridge had not been encouraging. They had left late, at 9:30 a.m., climbed to the old high point, and covered only a hundred vertical feet of new terrain before the worsening weather forced them to descend. Wick led all that day, and he judged the last part to be the most difficult climbing encountered on the expedition to date.

That evening, Wick, Jim, and Lou discussed the odds of climbing the mountain. Wick's diary entry reflected the doubts that were beginning to surface:

Jim Wickwire:

It was the first time I've heard Jim openly talk about failure. So many things have gone against us . . . I still think we have a chance, but we need some big breaks-absence of poor weather, sickness, and continued route problems low on the mountain. If we don't climb K2, which now is surely a possibility, if not a probability, I will say it again: I want to walk away from this mountain with no regrets, knowing I have given the effort to reach its high summit all that I had to give. Even now, with nothing more, the expedition, despite all the problems and frustrations, has been a richly rewarding experience: the new friendship with Lou (at the cost of hurting old friendships); the challenge of climbing on steep rock, ice, and snow at 21,000 feet—these are enormously satisfying. K2 is one hell of a mountain and just to have been on its flanks is a rare privilege.

from The Last Step

by Rick Ridgeway

The sixth American expedition to K2, led by Jim Whittaker, attempted a new route on the mountain in 1978. Thwarted by poor snow conditions, Jim Wickwire and Louis Reichardt crossed over to the Abruzzi Ridge to finish their climb. Wickwire lingered on the summit. He hadn't appeared at high camp by the next morning, when Rick Ridgeway (born in 1949) and John Roskelley left the camp for their own summit attempt.

September 7. Summit pyramid, The Narrow Couloir, about 27,000 feet. 7:30 a.m.

thought, *Check that it is a solid hold, frozen in the blue ice. O.K., looks good. Lift your leg, high—it's difficult to lift your leg with the first layer of angora wool underwear, the two layers of pile wool over that, followed by the nylon jumpsuit. Kind of binds. There. Now place your crampons carefully on the rock. Put your axe through the shoulder strap on your pack, get it out of the way. You need both hands for these next moves. Dust snow from the handholds, look for edges on the rock. Keep your balance, move slowly, make each move count. Do not waste energy because you have none to spare. Altitude about twenty-seven thousand feet. You can go on oxygen once above this steep section.*

John was only a few feet above me when we started through the narrows of the couloir, and I looked directly into the teeth of his crampons. Only his front points were on the ice and rock so that the remaining sharpened steel points—ten on the bottom of each boot— poised above me like an executioner's axe. I did not want John to slip.

I waited for him to make the several moves necessary to pass the steep bottleneck; then he was above the difficulties and it was my turn. I found two good handholds, and using my arms to balance, I leg-pressed my body up, moved my hands to higher holds, and lifted the next foot. Between my legs I could see the couloir fall away steeply to the Abruzzi Shoulder, to Camp VI, and ten thousand feet below that, to the Godwin-Austen Glacier.

Remember, I told myself, you cannot make a mistake. You have no rope.

Wind continued in gusts, lifting spindrift in swirls—small snow devils—backlighted by morning sun. The wind seemed to be lessening, however, and the sky, cloudless and clear to crystal visibility, boded a magnificent summit day—if Wickwire were in good shape.

It was about seven-thirty. I wondered, Where will we find Wickwire? Did he make it down this far before bivouacking, or was he still higher? What if he tried last night to climb down. It was black. This is very steep climbing, he would have been solo, very tired; he could have fallen. We would never learn what became of him.

Dark thoughts, fuzzy scenarios, disjointed images, dreams from a high-altitude opium den. I thought, I feel no emotion. Wick may be dead, he may be above me frozen, he may be ten thousand feet below me, crumbled on the glacier, yet I feel nothing. Last night there was alarm, there was that feeling of possible tragedy, of possible loss, that feeling of emptiness. Now I feel nothing. I recognize that Wick may be in trouble. Beyond that, no other feelings, no other thoughts except how to make the next move up this steep couloir.

I must breathe evenly, coordinate my breathing to my footwork. That will save energy. I must move with precision. There is a beauty in what I do, isn't there. Despite the extreme altitude, the weight of this oxygen bottle, I can still be coordinated, I can still move with grace and economy. I can still dance.

I have two more moves, and then I will be out of the couloir. Lift the leg, carefully place the crampon, test the handholds, pressure the leg muscles, move up. Always up, one more step higher, one more step toward the top. I am above the gully. Where to from here? There will still be some kind of traverse to turn the ice cliff above me that will lead to the snow gully and eventually to the summit snowfield. How far is John? Look up, I should see him now, he should be just around the corner. There he is, but wait. I stare at the scene before me mesmerized; I am not prepared for what I see: Twisting swirls of ground spindrift. Rainbow red, blue, and violet flashes—refractions of a million crystal eyes and the fathomless indigo of rarefied sky. Brilliant white. Ice cliffs, shining with wet, sensuous smoothness. Extreme altitude and vertigo. A feeling of no time: no beginning, no end. Frozen in the scene two figures. One, below the other, blue-suited and moving slowly—John. The second, standing above, no apparent movement, legs slightly spread, arms down, a scarecrow figure yet also godlike, still not moving—frozen solid? Jim Wickwire.

I watched John climb the last few feet to Wick, who stood, not moving, in his scarecrow stance. Was Wick alive? Motionless, he stood staring down at us. Then he raised his arm—a greeting. He was alive; he had survived. I could see they were talking to each other.

I looked down to the snow and ice in front of me to concentrate on the climbing until I reached the more level stance where Wick and John were resting. As I neared, I could hear their conversation:

"I was on a small flat spot a little below the summit. Pretty cold."

"Frostbite?"

"I think so. It's hard to tell."

"Can you make it down the rest of the way by yourself?"

"Yeah. I'm doing O.K. I've got the hard part behind—that traverse over here to the gully."

Wick indicated with his ice axe. I climbed up and joined the conversation. Wick looked haggard, of course, ice in his beard, eyes sunken and tired but still with a sparkle, a determination. It looked to us as if he had suffered no serious damage, but it was impossible for us, or for Wick, for that matter, to then realize the extent of his injuries. We continued to talk, joking, making light of an ordeal John and I—emotions obscured in the anesthesia of twenty-seven thousand feet—could in no way share.

"Good luck, you guys. I'll see you back in Camp Six."

"Be careful, Wick. You still have the couloir to get down. Move slow."

"Don't worry. I'll be O.K."

Wick climbed past us, and John patted him affectionately on his cap. A simple gesture, and neither John nor I had any way of knowing it brought Wick close to tears. It was the first human contact in fourteen hours—fourteen hours of which he had counted each minute. It was a small gesture of affection of one human for another that Wick, for the rest of his life, would not forget. Wick climbed slowly to the top of the gully, turned inward, and began his descent.

Watching him, I thought, Not now Wick, not after what you've been through. Not after victory. Be careful, go slow, make no mistakes.

Wick's movements were mechanical and stiff, like the Tin Man of Oz with no oil. There was no way, without rope, we could assist him. We only crossed our fingers.

John called to him, "Wick, when we get back remind me to enroll you in my climbing school. You could use a few lessons."

Wick looked up and smiled that open but closed-teeth smile that meant he felt confident. I knew he could make it, and John and I turned to our next task—the summit.

"Let's go on oxygen from here up," I said.

We looked at our next climbing obstacle—a steep rock and ice traverse—and it seemed like a good idea to cross it with the benefit of oxygen. We unshouldered our packs, carefully balancing them on the steep slope. John removed his bottle and pushed it into the snow, then set his regulator and mask alongside. He then strapped on his pack.

"What are you doing?"

"Leaving the oxygen. I'm going without it."

I paused, looked at my own twenty-pound apparatus, and considered the option.

"There's no way I'm hauling that thing to the top," he said, pointing to the bottle. "I know I can get up without it."

I suspected John was right; *he* could get to the top, but I was less certain about myself. True, Lou had made it without oxygen, but I considered both him and John physically stronger than me. I did not want to risk getting this close and not being able to make it because of a last-minute decision to leave my oxygen—especially since I had carried it all that way. To leave the bottle, jammed into the snow at twenty-seven thousand feet, with an untapped 3,900 psi supply of pure oxygen, seemed absurd.

"I'm going to use mine."

"O.K."

John waited while I removed the regulator—carefully wrapped in plastic to protect against moisture—screwed it on the bottle, and opened the valve. Full pressure—no leaks. Next I fitted a cloth skullcap to which straps from the aviator-type mask would fit. I had to shoulder the pack, bottle inside, then secure the second-stage selector valve to a drawstring I had earlier sewn on my parka. I had practiced this procedure many times, in the lower camps waiting out storms, adjusting the straps and snaps, checking the regulator, with soapy water, for leaks, making certain I would arrive at the point where I would begin using oxygen with a problem-free apparatus.

But even after all that, something was wrong. My mask would not seal around my face. Its straps seemed to lead to the snaps on my skullcap at the wrong angle, and without a tight fit I would leak valuable oxygen. John watched with growing impatience as I removed the skullcap and refitted it. Again, the mask pulled askew. Again, I removed the skullcap. John lost patience.

"I'm going. See you up there."

"I'll be along as soon as I get this thing straightened out."

John started the traverse, obviously finding it easier without the weight of his oxygen. He moved across the snow laced with rocks, crossing legs and placing his crampons on rock with expert precision, movements automated by subconscious accumulation of years of experience. He held his axe with one hand on the shaft, the other on the adze, placing the pick in the ice between the rocks. He reminded me of the old sepia photographs of Armand Charlet, the great French alpinist famous for ballet precision when climbing ice. Below John's feet the rock and ice angled abruptly, disappearing to empty space, and all I could see was the zebra stripes of the glacier about two miles down. John moved in perfect balance, made more dramatic because he had no rope. Not bad, I thought, for over twenty-seven thousand feet.

I continued to hassle with my oxygen apparatus. John disappeared around a corner, and my frustration mounted. I once again removed the mask, and the skullcap, and studied them. I rerouted the fastening straps through loops on the mask and fitted the skullcap at a different angle. It was worse, the mask dropping hopelessly from my face. I tried a different lacing, but it too failed. My fingers were freezing. The more I studied the puzzle, the more it bewildered me.

I thought, *Damn it, this is crazy. I had that thing adjusted days ago. Everything was ready. Now study it, Ridgeway; think. Imagine what my IQ score would be right now. Even a half-wit chimpanzee could do better than this. John's probably halfway up the snow gully by now, on his way to the summit snowfield. How long have I been fiddling with the contraption? Five minutes? Twenty minutes? This is like being loaded on dope. Can't think right. Don't even know how much time has passed. Too bad my watch broke. Don't let my mind wander; focus on this problem. O.K. It's simple: It worked before, when I tested it in the tent, so therefore it has to work now. Try putting the strap through the other loop, around the nose piece on the mask, then back through the bottom loop. That doesn't look right, either. John must be halfway to the top by now. If I don't hurry, I'll never make it. He climbs faster than I do anyway. Maybe I'll just end up staying here all day, fiddling with this mask, while he climbs to the summit. The thought of that chimpanzee comes to mind again. Remember a picture I once saw of a chimp wearing eyeglasses, sitting and staring confoundedly at a book. The same thought now, only it's me, Rick Ridgeway, sitting just like the chimp, staring confoundedly at my oxygen mask. O.K., now don't let my mind wander; focus on this mask. Let's see, what else can I do?*

Try to climb K2 without oxygen?

Can I do it?

I had been performing satisfactorily up to that point, without oxygen, carrying the dead weight of the cylinder. Without that hindrance it would be even easier. But there were over a thousand feet to go. What would it be like at twenty-eight thousand? Would it be possible for me? I considered the danger of pulmonary edema. If that happened, there would be no hope. My lungs would fill with blood, and I would die.

I had to make some decision fast. I was quickly losing body temperature, starting to shiver. I needed to move to regain warmth. The wind was still dropping, but even the direct sun failed to warm. I looked again at my regulator, and the chance that I could correctly adjust the straps seemed remote.

What about brain damage? I knew there was that risk; it was a real concern. Brain cells do not replace themselves; cerebral damage from hypoxia is a clinical fact. I had another whimsical thought: If I had any brains to begin with, I wouldn't be up here at over twenty-seven thousand feet on K2 freezing to death, so what have I got to lose?

I chuckled at the thought.

I realized I was getting dingy.

I was very, very cold.

I set the mask and regulator in the snow, removed the bottle from the pack. Putting on the near-empty pack, I grabbed my axe and started across the traverse. I would climb without oxygen, and I would put every ounce of energy remaining in my body into reaching the summit. I thought, I might just be able to make it.

September 7. Summit pyramid, about 28,000 feet. 2:30 p.m.

There are only two hundred more feet at the most even though I'm not sure I can lift my foot and then the next foot and the next until I get to the top. Not after coming this far. Not this close.

So up goes my boot and crampon. There, that's better, now breathe a few times, and think about that next step. This will be over soon, and the sooner I lift the next foot, the sooner it will be over. Keep thinking: I've come this far, I have to make it.

I can't lift the foot. I can't move up any higher. Have to rest, have to rest, have to rest.

No. I cannot.

John is ahead of me. Look up at him. See, he's still moving, and moving faster than me. He has been breaking most of the trail. I can't let him do all the work. I have to do my share. So lift my foot and catch up and help break trail. There. That's better. Now think about the next foot.

When will it end?

John is stopping to rest. He is hunkering over his is axe, head down, facing the slope. I must catch him. If I can make ten more steps I can reach him, and then rest, but not before. That is it: Ten steps, then rest. O.K., now up with the foot, breathe, breathe, breathe, and another step. No good, can't make it. Have to stop for a minute; getting dizzy again. John is still resting. Only four or five steps and I can rest too. Lift a foot. Now only three more steps, now one more step and I can rest. Careful, don't collapse, don't slide down the slope. Rest on my axe.

"You O.K.?"

"Slow. Hard to breathe. Forcing each step. Sorry I'm not breaking more trail."

"Can you lead a little?"

"I'll try. Need to rest first."

"We're close—maybe a hundred fifty feet."

"If that is the summit. If not, if it is farther behind the ridge, don't know if I can make it . . ."

"Don't worry, we've got it now."

John is right. We have it now, keep remembering that. We are too close not to make it.

I must get up; I must move on. This will soon be over. No more getting up at 3:00 a.m., no more freezing in predawn starts. I can sit in a hot bath and feel the steaming water on my skin. Never again for the rest of my life will I take a bath and not think of this moment I wanted to soak in steaming water, so get going and soon I can have that bath.

Lift a foot.

Carefully place my crampons. This surface is irregular, small crescent patterns in the ice, and my ankles hurt from twisting to the angle of the slope.

Lift a foot.

Noise and voices. Like there are many people around me, like on a crowded train with everyone talking. Echoes, noises, voices. A din like a million voices. But that's crazy, there is no one around.

Lift a foot.

Fingers are so hard. There is no doubt this time they are frozen. It's strange, like my fingers are made of a foreign material. Must be what artificial limbs are like. It's my right hand, mostly, because that is the hand I've been holding my axe in. I should switch hands. But then my left hand would freeze, and since my right is already frozen, why freeze my left too. Does that make sense? I guess so, keep the axe in my right hand.

Lift a foot.

Look at the slope, scimitar-shaped, arching upward brilliant white against purple sky. The left side of the summit slope drops away, and I can see a steep rock ridge joining the summit slope near the top. Is that the finish to Bonington's route? It would be too hard to climb that the way I feel now. Could anyone do it? Maybe a future generation of climbers? Poor Nick Estcourt, down there somewhere buried in ice.

Lift a foot.

How nice it would be to sit on a warm beach. A tropical beach with white sand and palm trees. It's easy to imagine, look there, in front of me, I can even see a palm tree now, in the sand, growing there, in the snow. Lift a foot.

John is just behind me. I've been leading now for some time, but I've only come, what?—twenty feet since I rested. It seems so far, though. There is a slightly offset edge in the ice surface—a convenient mark—about another twenty feet in front. Focus on it. Begin stepping until I get there. Think of nothing else.

Lift a foot.

Breathe, breathe, breathe, gasp hard, even then I can't get enough air. Lift a foot, another, another, keep going to the mark.

It's close. Keep going.

Getting dizzy, head pounding, noises—the voices, the voices. Keep going, force it out from somewhere, somehow force out the will to step, to lift the foot, the mark is close, one more step.

I made it.

Breathe, breathe, breathe. Getting dizzy again, spinning, can't get enough air. *Can't breathe fast enough. Don't panic, keep control, breathe fast. Feel like I'm drowning, will my lungs explode?—don't panic. Lean on my axe. Breathe fast. There, the dizziness is starting to go away, but the voices, the voices.*

"You O.K.?"

"Have to rest. Tried to go too fast. Hallucinating."

"I'll take the lead."

Rest while John climbs. He is stronger than I am. How can he do it? He is doing most of the step-kicking. I can't do my share. Not enough strength. But we are close now. Maybe fifty feet to the summit ridge. Hope to God the summit is close behind the ridge. If it's farther . . .

Get up, follow John. It's so much easier following in his steps. Sections of the ice are hard and it doesn't matter who leads, but sometimes the crust breaks, and that is when John's job is hardest.

Lift a foot.

It's not bad the first few steps after I've rested. But then each one starts getting harder. My body is screaming for oxygen. Each step harder, need to breathe more. The farther away from the last rest, the harder, but I can't rest again. Not now.

Lift a foot.

So close. Soon it will be over. John is maybe fifteen feet ahead, now maybe twenty. He is climbing faster. He is making the last steps to the summit ridge. His head is even with the ridge, now he is on it.

What does he see? How far is the summit? He isn't saying anything. Is it farther behind? Do we still have more to go? How can I do it?

Lift a foot.

Catch up to John. He is resting on the top of the ridge. Close now, only a few more feet. He isn't saying anything. But I can't talk to him because I have to breathe fast.

Stop. He is ten feet away. Look at him. He is looking down at me. Breathe a few times so I can talk.

"Can you see it? How far? How far to the top?"

John is looking at me. Now he is smiling. Is it good news?

"Fifty feet. A fifty-foot walk up a gentle slope and we're on the summit."

September 7. The summit of K2, 28,250 feet. 3:30 p.m.

No wind. No clouds. Cerulean sky, brilliant sun, and at once a feeling of warmth through the thick parka, and also a strange cold. Nothing quite real, the feeling of dream. Below, a world falling in all directions. Snow peaks too numerous to identify, and glaciers traveling to distant horizon. Quiet, but an inner noise, a ringing in the ear. A thought: As an old man I will often recall this moment; I must try to remember it. It must be important. But there is failure to feel much emotion. The only feeling is absolute fatigue.

We were on the summit. We had made the last few steps together, arm in arm. From the summit ridge it was an easy walk to the highest point, but just short of it John had stopped.

"It may be corniced. Summits usually are. I'm not going up there."

He spoke with much finality. Neither of us seemed to remember Lou and Wick had been there the day before and had reported no cornice. But we were beyond remembering, beyond rational thinking, operating only on instinct. I thought, It may be corniced, but we've come too far not to reach the very pinnacle.

I volunteered to belly-crawl up to the highest point. John stood back, holding my ankles. I eased up to the edge, and peered over. There was solid snow under me, and the south face dropped down so steeply, about twelve thousand feet, I had a euphoric sense of flying. John crawled up behind me, and together we sat on top, holding each other, too exhausted to speak.

I told myself several times, Remember this moment. Remember what it is like. Later in my life, years from now, I will look back, many times, on this scene; this day will stand above all.

But I could not appreciate it. I was only thankful at the moment to rest, to breathe and lessen the dizziness, and if I felt anything akin to elation, it was from the realization I no longer had to go up. This was it; there was no higher place to climb.

We rested. The sky was calm; at 28,250 feet there was no breath of wind, and the sun shone through cloudless atmosphere. We could see to the curve of the earth. To the north and east, two distant peaks somewhere in the wild vastness of Chinese Turkestan; to the west the peaks of Hunza, Shangri-La, the secret valley, to the west and south the great Karakoram—a turbulent sea of endless summits and glaciers. Away to the south the singular Nanga Parbat. Closer, the Gasherbrums, and below us the summit of Broad Peak, a flat, wide strip like an airplane landing field. Broad Peak, the first eight-thousand-meter peak to be climbed without oxygen in 1957, and now, in 1978, we, also without oxygen, looked down on its summit. To the east the brown hills of Sinkiang, and far, far off, at places distant and mysterious, occasional glacier-covered summits.

Twenty feet below the summit, toward the northwest, there was a flat rock bench, and we climbed down to rest. The rock was warm and I lay back and my breathing eased and I closed my eyes and drifted to half consciousness. I had few coherent thoughts, just images of boots and crampons and snow and endless steps. I opened my eyes.

I thought, Remember where I am. I am on the second highest point on earth. I must remember that. Think how hard I have worked to get here.

I had the idea that to better remember the summit I would take some of it with me. I got out of my climbing hammer and started pounding on the rock. John looked over.

"What are you doing?"

"Souvenirs. Take a few pieces of rock back. Christmas isn't far off, and they'll make great presents."

"Good idea."

Soon John and I were sitting on the rock beating on it with our hammers, prying small chips of stone.

"We should take some photographs, too," John said.

"Yeah, I forgot about that."

I lay back on the rock, propped on one arm, while John took my photograph.

"We've been up here almost an hour," he said.

"An hour?"

"We should take a couple of pics on the summit and head down."

We climbed back to the high point on the snow ridge and took a few photographs of one another. I recalled the way summit photographs normally looked: The climber stands, ice axe above head in victory, chest puffed out, flags waving like a sale at a used car lot. That was not at all how I felt. I had no feeling of having conquered anything. I thought of something Barry Bishop said after he climbed Everest: "There are no conquerors—only survivors." It was true. We were two small humans on top of an awesome mountain that was indifferent to our climb. I stood on the high point, dropped my arms, and held the axe across my waist. I could not wave my arms; I could not grin in victory; I could only stare across the empty space below me. John took the photo, and we began our descent.

September 7. Camp VI Abruzzi. 25,750 feet. About 5:00 p.m.

Hard as he tried, Wick could not sleep. He had arrived back in Camp VI, after passing John and me on our way to the top, about nine that morning, and was greeted with warm drinks and warm hugs by his summit companion. Lou was much relieved to see that Wick had weathered his ordeal, apparently suffering only a few frostbitten fingers and toes. Lou had been uncomfortable with his decision to leave Wick on the summit, although at the time it seemed the logical thing to do: Lou had been, without parka, extremely cold, it had been very late in the day, Wick had said he intended to leave the summit just behind Lou. Nevertheless Lou knew if Wick had had any major problem on his bivouac—if he had not been able to survive the night—he would have had to live with his decision the rest of his life. It was with that thought heavy on his soul that Lou had seen Wick's weathered face appear that morning in the tent door.

Other than an hour spent shoveling drifted snow off the tent walls, and a few more minutes lowering Lou into a crevasse (Wick holding Lou's ankles) to retrieve an ice axe he had somehow dropped, they passed the day in sleeping bags. They were languid, physically spent, but not able to sleep—only to lie in an indolent dreaminess as the hours melted together. It was about five when John arrived, an hour ahead of my much slower descent.

They offered John hot lemonade, which he drank with enthusiasm. John crawled in the tent he and I shared, and in the last twilight I arrived. It had taken all my inner resources to make the last steps to Camp VI. Just above camp, I had slipped, sliding about twenty feet before digging my axe into the hard snow. I had barely acknowledged the mishap that normally would have caused sharp self-reprimand to be more careful; as it was, I was so exhausted I hardly recognized the ease with which such a slip could have resulted in fatality.

When I arrived Lou and Wick had more hot lemonade. I savored first the feeling of the mug on my hard fingers (the ends were too numb to feel even the hot liquid), and then the tangy, steaming drink washing my mouth, heating my throat, then my stomach, and finally spreading to my body. Other than rest, and a fuzzy hope to soon be off the mountain—to be safe in Base Camp with this ordeal behind—hot liquid was the only desire left to me.

Finishing the hot lemonade, I made my way to our neighboring tent and crawled in to join John. Light had disappeared, and the stars were sharp in clear, black sky. I wanted badly only to find my sleeping bag and crawl in. Nothing else mattered.

"Why don't you sleep in the Denali," John offered. "I'll take the McKinley tonight."

The Denali is a warmer and consequently heavier bag than the less substantial McKinley model. John and I had chosen to take the lighter bag, intending originally to use it for bivouac on the direct finish, but since plans had altered we were then sleeping one in the warm bag and one in the much colder bag. For three nights I had used the light bag, and for three nights I had been cold. John's offering to switch bags agreed with my desire to get warm as fast as possible. Also, since for three nights there had been only an hour, or two hours at the most, in which we had been able to *try* to sleep, the thought of a night with no

1:30 wake-up, combined with warm bag, seemed a full and just reward for the day's effort.

"Thanks, buddy," I said.

It took several minutes to remove my boots. My breathing was heavy and labored; it seemed the congestion my lungs suffered on Everest was returning, and for a moment I thought it could be pulmonary edema. I considered the symptoms: There was no gurgling in my lungs—the telltale of edema—and consequently I supposed I most likely had a bronchial congestion compounding the already difficult task of breathing at such high altitudes. With my boots off, I removed my parka and jumpsuit, and clothed only in wool underwear, I quickly slipped into the thick down bag before my shivering became more violent. For several minutes I lay fetus-style, shaking, but slowly gaining warmth and slowing my breathing. There were no thoughts in my mind.

"We should drink more liquid," John said.

I did not acknowledge. He was right, of course, but there was no way I had the energy necessary to start the stove and melt the snow to prepare drinks.

"I'll get the stove going," he said.

"Thanks, John. I'm too out of gas to help."

I thought, And only yesterday I was upset at John because I thought he wasn't doing his share digging the tent platform. It's so easy to lose patience under the strain of altitude.

Warmth slowly returned to my body, and my shivering stopped. I lay listening to the stove hissing, feeling pleasure from the Pavlovian recognition that we would soon have hot brews. John was fiddling with another stove, apparently changing fuel cartridges, but I paid no attention. I was thankful he had the discipline necessary to melt snow; I knew even with a major dredging for possible remaining energy I could not help him. I was so exhausted it took over a full second to respond to the deep, airsucking explosion.

"Out of the tent," John screamed.

I opened my eyes. Flames were everywhere, covering everything. My hair was burning, the tent walls were burning, and my sleeping bag was in flames. The stove had exploded. I had an instant flash—a panic—of being burned alive, and then I felt the claustrophobia from not being able to breathe. The next second I had only one, dominant thought: Escape the tent. Which entrance? I could see the shape of John's body already half out the main door; that left me to bolt through the opposite end, the vestibule. In a continuous motion I slipped out of my bag and through the drawstring back entrance of our flaming tent.

Outside I could see John already reaching through the gaping holes in the tent walls to save boots and climbing clothing—the loss of which would jeopardize our ability to descend. I pulled my bag out—still burning. It was nearly destroyed, and without thinking I threw it down the slope. It appeared to have been the major fuel to the fire, and with the emergency under control John and I turned to see the bag, still aflame, roll hundreds of feet down the Abruzzi Shoulder and disappear over the ten-thousand-foot drop to the glacier. It reminded me of when as a child I watched the firefall display in Yosemite.

"You guys O.K.?" Lou yelled.

"Yeah, but the tent's gone. Some of the other gear is probably damaged too, but we won't know until morning."

I was again starting to shiver. Our predicament seemed ludicrous: There I was, in only my wool underwear, exhausted, at night at 25,750 feet with the temperature about thirty below zero, dehydrated and coughing and barely able to breathe, with only one pair of wool socks on my feet—now rapidly freezing—staring at the charred remains of our tent, where only moments before I had been cuddled blissfully in a warm bag. And it had been my night for the Denali bag, too. It didn't seem fair.

"Rick's bag burned up," John reported to Lou and Wick. There was no response from them as they realized the import of this information.

"There's no choice," he continued. "We're going to have to crawl in with you guys."

Two days before when Lou and Wick had, with Terry, established Camp VI Abruzzi, the three had sandwiched into the tent designed to house, with no luxury, two people. It was a difficult night. Now, with our physical condition further deteriorated, Wick and Lou contemplated the nearly uncontemplable thought of four in the tent.

"It might not be possible to fit us all in here," Wick said.

"No choice," John replied. "Otherwise we'll freeze with only one bag—the McKinley at that."

John rummaged in the remains of our tent for the reasonably undamaged McKinley bag, and I found my parka. That was enough goosedown to get us through the night, and since we would be packed so tightly in the other tent, being short one bag might cause discomfort but not injury. Pulling out our remaining bag, John handed it to me.

"You'd better get in this," he said. "It looks like you're pretty cold."

Despite my now uncontrollable shaking, I felt a warm camaraderie for my summit partner who was willing to give up his sleeping bag that he had all rights to claim. With some feeling of humbleness at his gesture, I accepted the offer.

"Thanks, pal. That's nice."

I crawled in first, squeezing against Wick, who was sandwiched against the tent wall. I bent my limbs and torso trying to dovetail with the shape of Wick's contorted figure. John crawled in. It was impossible not to overlap limbs and torsos. We squirmed, trying to find a reasonably comfortable position for everyone.

"I've got to move my shoulder."

"Wait, then. I've got to move my arm first."

"Then I'll have to move mine, too. Hold on, my leg is jammed."

Eventually we reached, at least for a while, equilibrium. It was immensely uncomfortable. My head was under Wick's arm; my chest jammed against John's back. Again, the claustrophobic feeling returned. My lungs were congesting, and I breathed faster—gasping rapidly—to get enough oxygen. I had the feeling of drowning. Phlegm stuck in my throat, and I thought I might black out. Panic. In desperation, I forced my torso out the tent door, upsetting the bodies interlocked like pieces of a puzzle, and hung my head outside, gasping. The others squirmed to regain positions.

"You O.K., Rick?" Wick asked. "Think it might be edema?"

"Don't know. Congestion. Can't breathe. Coughing up junk."

I was getting worried. I was starting to cough up hard nodules covered with blood. My lungs ached; my body cried for water.

"Any water left?"

"No," Wick said. "We'll have to wait till morning."

I squirmed back inside, and again we jockeyed about, unavoidably elbowing and kneeing each other. Eventually we regained temporary equilibrium. No one could sleep. We lay quiet, wishing the hours speed through the night. John, without bag, was cold but complained little. He was in a very contorted position, too, and he tried to force the discomfort from his mind. But it was no good. Sometime in the middle of the night he could no longer stand it.

"I've got to change," he said.

"What?"

"I've got to move to the other side of the tent. This is killing me, and I'm freezing."

John started to crawl over me to trade places with Wick. There was a jumble of arms and legs and down gear, and the panic of claustrophobia returned. Again, I could not breathe. With two bodies draped over me, I struggled to sit up and get my head higher to clear phlegm from my throat. I tried to get my head out the tent door.

"What the hell. Wait a minute, Ridgeway."

"Can't breathe. Got to get out."

"Can't you guys get in one place and stay there?" Lou complained, losing patience.

I hung my head out the tent, gasping, and then John and I changed positions. The tiny tent stretched and bulged as bodies pressured against the sides. John found a position that at least he could force himself to maintain. I stayed half out the door, coughing nasty stuff out of my lungs. My head and shoulders were getting cold, and my thirst was awful. I told myself over and over, be patient. The night will end. We can start the stove in the morning and make a gallon of lemonade. A full, complete U.S. gallon. Be patient.

Despite my difficulty breathing, the cold forced me back in the tent. I tried to lie still, to overcome my claustrophobia, to not think about my dehydration, to wait patiently for the dawn. It was our fourth night without sleep, our fourth night in the death zone. I began counting the hundreds of minutes until dawn, when we could crawl out and stretch and make drinks and then begin our escape. I only hoped I could find strength to get down; I hoped whatever was causing the blood I coughed up became no worse. I didn't want to burden the others who I knew would be taxed to their limits getting themselves down. Of the four of us, it seemed I was in the worst shape. In the cold predawn I thought how four of us had reached the summit, how the expedition was now a success, but also how much room was left for mistake, how easy it would be to quickly trade that victory for tragedy.

September 8. Camp VI, 25,750 feet. About 11:00 a.m.

On the warm insulating pad spread on the floor of the tent, with full sun shining through the large holes in the burned-out tent walls, I lay half-conscious. I was dressed in wool underwear, in which I had passed the dreadful night, and my jumpsuit. My head lay on my parka, and on my feet I had only one boot. The other was next to my hand, tongue pulled open, but at the last minute I had lost the desire necessary to continue dressing, and had collapsed on my parka. That the day was relentlessly passing—that it was nearly noon—and we were still not prepared to begin our long descent, seemed in no way important.

I was consumed by total torpor; my mind and body melted in the warm sun. John lay next to me, apparently asleep. We were surrounded by the wreckage of our charred tent. Luckily, the gear needed for our descent had not burned, but it had taken some time to sort the debris, and the job was not yet finished. Wick and Lou had managed, meanwhile, to melt snow for nearly two liters of water, and I had drunk my ration with religious thanksgiving. Wick and Lou were presumably also asleep, or, like me, half-conscious; there was no voice from their tent.

Earlier that morning, waiting for the sun to heat the air sufficiently for us to crawl wearily from our tomblike tent, we had acknowledged the importance of descending rapidly, given our deteriorating condition and the uncertainty of how long the good weather would hold. We made plans to drop that day to Camp IV, and then the following day to Camp II, or perhaps even to Camp I. It would depend, in part, on where the others were positioned to assist our descent; their help breaking trail down would speed our escape.

Now, despite acknowledging the importance of rapid descent, we told ourselves that if we left before noon, there still would be sufficient time to get to Camp IV. It was not sound thinking, but rather giving in to our greater need for rest.

The sun shone on my face and I felt my skin burn. My lips were already cracked and bleeding, my neck peeling, and I knew I should apply protection lotion, but I had not the energy to search it out; I simply let the sun burn. My breathing seemed more regular, and my coughing and the choking phlegm also decreased. I thought I should try again to put on the other boot, but I could not bring myself to the task. I dozed, warm in bright sun, thankful for the absence of wind, and I dreamed of faraway places and of tropical sun.

"We'd better get moving soon. It's almost noon."

It was Lou's voice, and it sounded as though he and Wick were preparing to get under way. Lifting one hand, I pushed my goggles over my eyes, then dropped the hand. I opened my eyes. John was not moving. I wondered if I could find the energy to fit my other boot. I knew I must; I knew we had to start down. But the langour was all-consuming. I felt drugged.

I finally mustered the will to sit up and slowly lace my boot. I found my crampons and fitted them over the thick, insulated overboot.

"Time to go?" John asked.

"Yeah, we'd better get under way, I guess."

John sat up wearily and started lacing his crampons. I was still very thirsty and longed for another drink, but there was no time to melt snow. We would have to wait until evening, at Camp IV. With crampons fitted, I forced myself to stand and shake off the lassitude. I located my pack and sorted what to take and what to leave. Extra pile pants—leave. Camera—take. Extra mittens—leave. Sack of summit rocks—take. Stove and cookware—leave. I found the oxygen regulator I had picked up yesterday on the descent. It cost six hundred dollars. It also weighed several pounds—leave.

With packs shouldered, we wearily stepped out of camp, leaving behind the tents and miscellaneous gear to the gods of the mountain and also, no doubt, to the goraks who would most likely fly even that high to scavenge our jetsam. The sky was limpid and cloudless, and we descended with the summits of Broad Peak and the Gasherbrums to our right. The valley of Godwin-Austen was formed of ice and rock walls, and the flutings on the ice faces were furrows in a vertical field of whiteness. One face was cut by a sharp line marking the fracture of a slab avalanche. I thought of Nick Estcourt.

The descent was slow and mindless and required little care until we arrived at a steep drop of hard ice before the corner marking the beginning of the traverse to the snow dome on which Camp V was situated. We faced into the ice and carefully downclimbed, kicking our front points and placing the picks of our ice axes. We were all conscious of not wearing a rope. We were conscious of our exhaustion, and the need to keep reminding ourselves to be careful, to keep telling ourselves that after all we had been through it would be unthinkable to face tragedy. With these thoughts, we inched down the ice. When I made the final move to the more secure and less steep snow, I realized the last hard section of unroped climbing was behind me, and I was that much closer to safety.

It was easier hiking the remaining distance to Camp V, but we were reminded, nevertheless, that we still held space on the roulette wheel. We traversed a fifty-yard-wide swath of avalanche debris from a big serac that had broken from the hanging glacier sometime during the last few days. We picked our way through the jumble of ice blocks knowing had we been there during the avalanche there would have been no chance of survival.

We were at a crawl. John led, breaking through the soft snow. Lou followed, then Wick, and finally me. I was slowest. We came to a small rise that we knew was the back of the snow dome. Camp V was a hundred feet farther. At the tents Wick turned around, and with dismay he watched me trying to make the last uphill distance to camp. I could not walk. I was on hands and knees, crawling.

"John, look at Ridgeway," Wick said. "Can you believe that. He's crawling."

"Don't worry," John said. "He's come this far. He'll make it."

From Wick's Journal

September 8. Camp V. Difficulty in writing. Fingers frostbitten. Back at Camp V with Lou, John, and Rick. Getting down today from Camp VI was an ordeal. We walked like zombies—like sleepwalkers—during the three hours it took us. We were to have descended to Camp IV this afternoon, but Rick and I both suffer frostbite, and we did not want to risk further damage by descending the shaded face below Camp V. We are all exhausted, but John and Lou have more strength than Rick and me. Details later as I am absolutely without strength.

September 10. Camp III. Storm. A new, violent storm has hit us following the long Indian summer that enabled us to climb K2 and retreat this far, but our attempts to now descend to Camp I are frustrated. We have not been able to locate the fixed ropes below Camp III. They are buried somewhere in deep snow. We need them as guidelines down the mountain. There is no visibility. John and Terry are out trying to locate the rope now.

Yesterday was long. We descended from Camp V to here with a brief stop at Camp IV to brew up. Still very weak. John, with more energy than the rest of us, led down, following the trail Terry and Cherie had made the day before. We arrived late afternoon. Warm greetings from the Bechs, waiting for us in Camp III (everyone else was in Camp I). Drinks, rehydration.

1:20 p.m. John and Terry just returned. No luck on the rope. Appears we are pinned here at least until tomorrow. Jim and Rob (on the radio in Camp I) were strong in urging us to come down. We told them impossible in these conditions. They worried we are deteriorating physically and mentally. Actually we are recovering strength compared to what we went through above. But we need to get off the mountain to ultimately recover. Jim and Rob seem pessimistic about the projected length of the new storm. Seven days. Tomorrow, notwithstanding the weather, we will descend with or without the fixed ropes. We'll get down tomorrow. We must.

September 11. The slopes below Camp III. 22,500 feet.
About 10:00 a.m.

Bitter cold wind out of the east. Mist and cloud. My companions just visible although less than a rope length distant. Spindrift carrying rapidly across my legs. Feet buried in deep,white powder. Exhaustion; the continuing task to force on, to make new steps. My body deteriorated, skinny with loss of muscle tissue. Sore lungs, difficulty breathing. Fingers now turning gray and black. The longing, the desire, for it all to end.

I thought, if only the weather had lasted one more day, we would now be off the mountain. As it was, we had been forced to hole up one day in Camp III, and now despite the continuing storm, we were pushing down. We had never located the fixed rope just below Camp III; and therefore we needed a climbing rope. Terry and I had spent several hours yesterday climbing back toward Camp IV and cutting two lengths out of the fixed rope (that line was not buried because no snow accumulated on the much steeper knife-edge ridge). With that line we had roped up, and we were now feeling our way down, scouting through the thick, blowing clouds, probing our memories to identify familiar landmarks. We must get down.

It had been a feeling of warm homecoming to find Terry and Cherie waiting, in Camp III, for our arrival. There was a mug of hot cocoa when we entered camp, and many embraces. To have someone simply to melt snow for brew water was great assistance, and Terry's and Cherie's faces held much sympathy for our haggard condition.

Actually, our condition seemed improved from the two previous days; yesterday's convalescence in Camp III was welcome rest. Wick and I were easily the worst, and it had been mostly up to John, with help from Lou, to break trail down to Camp IV and then across to Camp III. During the two nights since we had begun our descent, I had slept on oxygen, and the gas had improved my lung congestion remarkably. Breathing was easier, although still painful. My fingers were turning mottled gray and black, but I think the oxygen also mitigated the damage of the frostbite. And I had had a nasty abcess—which smelled of infection and made each step across the traverse a trial—that Cherie had nursed in Camp III: it was now less painful. It had been an embarrassment to ask her to clean the infection—more because of the wound's septicity than from my nakedness. But she had dismissed my concern with a nurse's indulgent laugh, and her ministrations gave me a warmness toward both her and Terry who, despite their disappointments, and their own weakened condition, had stayed high on the mountain to assist our descent.

Wick now seemed in worse shape. He had used no oxygen during sleep, and that morning he awoke with pain in his left side and difficulty breathing. He said it felt like broken ribs, but since he had not fallen, or bashed himself, Cherie thought it was more likely pneumonia. It was hard with Wick to judge whether the pain was serious, because he was stoical and not given to complaint.

We were in two teams, Lou, Wick, and John on one rope, leading and cutting a swath through the deep snow, and Terry and Cherie and me following on another rope. No one spoke. We silently trod downward, each of us alone with our thoughts. Lower on the ridge, at Camp II, there had been less snowfall, and we easily recovered the fixed rope. Untying from our climbing rope, we each descended at our own pace, and I chose to go last. I realized it was my last trip down the ropes; I was leaving places filled with so many memories, with so much emotion, that I wanted the time alone.

While I waited for the others to open distance down the ropes, I rested in one of the abandoned tents, nibbling what snacks I could find in the rifled food bags: a pepperoni stick, a few Corn Nuts, a piece of beef jerky. The beef jerky caused me to remember an incident from the Everest expedition two years earlier. Just before leaving for Nepal, we discovered our shipping invoice listed forty-five pounds of beef jerky. It is against the law to import beef products into Nepal, and with no time to retype the entire 240-page invoice, we had the idea simply to erase all the f's in beef and retype in t's, so we were importing forty-five pounds of beet jerky.

The thought brought a grin. Memories. Everest, K2—all behind, all memories. I crawled out of the tent, secured my brake system to the rope, and began the dramatic descent to the glacier, slowly rappelling rope length after rope length. I thought how Lou and I had fixed these ropes so many weeks before (I could count the time in months, too). The cloud cover had in some places opened to blue sky.

At the steepest place in the descent I stopped, secured the rope, and hung off it, silently studying the geography. Across the back of the glacier the familiar features of Skyang Kangri were colored subtle pastels of green and purple and light browns. The rock face divided into two monolithic intrusions, one light gray stone, a source of sun, of things positive, the Yang; the other dark stone, the color of earth and moon, the Yin. Both sides were cut with long linear dikes of still other stone, knife-sharp in contrast. Snow from the latest storm delicately laced the rock walls. The mountain rose boldly against a sky piebald of grays and browns, with patches of cerulean blue. Skyang Kangri's northeast ridge descended to Windy Gap, the pass to Shaksgam, and over the pass I could see the needle summits of lesser peaks, the last disturbance of the Karakoram before giving way to the endless brown hills of China. Memories.

I thought, My companions will be arriving in Camp I by now. There will be the joy of reunion, the hugs, the congratulations, the tears. The relief. Yes, there will be much relief.

I looked up the ropes, up the snow gully, then down to the glacier. It was time to go. The others would be concerned if I did not arrive soon. But I had to wait a few more minutes before releasing the rope and continuing my rappel. It was the thought of the relief, that we had done it. We were all down alive. It was behind us, we had climbed to the summit, and now we were all down alive. We had been climbing on K2 for sixty-seven days. We were all going to make it. That was the relief. That was what caused the tears coming down my cheeks, tears I had to wipe away before continuing into camp. I didn't want my companions to see me in tears.

Bad Summer on K2
by Jon Krakauer

K2 claimed 13 lives in 1986, more than the total of 12 deaths that had occurred on the mountain in all previous years. Jon Krakauer's attempt to account for the carnage foreshadowed his first-hand description of the Everest disaster a decade later.

I n the northernmost corner of Pakistan, in the heart of the Karakoram Range, is a forty-mile tongue of rubble-covered ice called the Baltoro Glacier, above which rise six of the seventeen highest mountains on the planet. In June, 1986, there were 150 tents pitched at the head of the Baltoro, sheltering expeditions from ten nations. Most of the men and women living in those tents, whose ranks included some of the world's most ambitious and highly regarded climbers, had their sights set on a single mountain: K2.

At 28,268 feet, the summit of K2 is some 800 feet lower than Mt. Everest, but its sharper, more graceful proportions make it a more striking mountain—and a much harder one to climb. Indeed, of the fourteen mountains in the world higher than eight thousand meters, K2 has the highest failure rate. By 1985 only nine of the twenty-six expeditions that had attempted the peak had succeeded, putting a total of thirty-nine people on the summit—at a cost of twelve lives. In 1986 the government of Pakistan granted an unprecedented number of climbing permits for K2, and by the end of the summer an additional twenty-seven climbers had made it to the top. But for every two people who summited, one would die—thirteen deaths in all, more than doubling the number of fatalities in the preceding eighty-four years. The toll would raise some thorny questions about the recent course of Himalayan climbing, a course some people believe has become unjustifiably reckless. The new modus operandi leaves so little margin for error that climbers now commonly begin their ascents with the understanding that if things go wrong, the bond between ropemates—a bond that was until recently held to be sacrosanct—may be discarded in favor of a policy of every man for himself.

The present direction of high-altitude mountaineering was set, it is generally agreed, in the summer of 1975, when Reinhold Messner and Peter Habeler pioneered a new route up a 26,470-foot neighbor of K2's called Hidden Peak without bottled oxyen, a support team, fixed ropes, a chain of preestablished camps, or any of the other siege tactics that had traditionally been de rigueur in the Himalaya. Messner pointedly termed this bold new approach "climbing by fair means," implying that it was cheating to get to the top of a mountain by any other way.

In a single stroke, Messner and Habeler significantly upped the ante in a game that did not lack for high stakes and long odds to begin with. When Messner first announced that he would climb an 8,000-meter Himalayan peak in the same manner that climbers tackled routes in the Tetons and Alps, most of the world's foremost climbers labeled the plan impossible and suicidal. After Messner and Habeler succeeded, anyone with designs on usurping Messner's throne—and more than a few of the men and women camped beneath K2 in 1986 had such designs—was left with little choice but to attack the highest mountains in the world by equally "fair" and incautious means.

The most coveted prize on K2 was its striking South Pillar, huge and unclimbed, a "last great problem" that Messner had nicknamed "the Magic Line." Soaring two vertical miles from glacier to summit, it demanded more steep, technical climbing at extreme altitude than anything previously done in the Himalaya.

There were four teams attempting the Magic Line in 1986, including an American party under the leadership of a thirty-five-year-old Oregonian named John Smolich. Early on June 21, a bright, cloudless morning, Smolich and partner Alan Pennington were climbing an easy approach gully at the base of the route when, far above them, the sun loosened a truck-size rock from the ice, sending it careering down the mountainside. As soon as the boulder struck the top of the gully, a fifteen-foot-deep fracture line shot across the low-angled snowfield, initiating a massive avalanche that engulfed Smolich and Pennington in a matter of seconds. Climbers who witnessed the slide quickly located and dug out Pennington, but not quickly enough to save his life. Smolich's body, buried under thousands of tons of frozen debris, was never found.

The surviving members of the American team called off their climb and went home, but the other expeditions on the mountain regarded the tragedy as a freak accident—simply a matter of being at the wrong place at the wrong time—and continued their own efforts without pause.

Indeed, on June 23, two Basques—Mari Abrego and Josema Casimaro—and four members of a French-Polish expedition—Maurice and Liliane Barrard, Wanda Rutkiewicz, and Michel Parmentier—reached the summit of K2 via the mountain's easiest route, the Abruzzi Spur. Liliane Barrard and Rutkiewicz thereby became the first women to stand on top of K2, and, more impressive still, they did so without using bottled oxygen.

All six climbers, however, were forced by darkness to bivouac high on the exposed side of the summit pyramid, and by morning the clear, cold skies that had prevailed for the previous week had given way to an intense storm. During the ensuing descent the Barrards—both very experienced Himalayan climbers with other 8,000-meter summits under their belts—dropped behind and never reappeared. Parmentier guessed they had fallen or been swept away by an avalanche, but he nonetheless stopped to wait for them in a high camp on the off chance that they might show up, while Rutkiewicz and the Basques, whose noses and fingertips had begun to turn black from frostbite, continued down.

That night—June 24—the storm worsened. Waking to a complete whiteout and horrible winds, Parmentier radioed base camp by walkie-talkie that he was descending, but with the fixed ropes and all traces of his companions' footprints buried by fresh snow, he soon became lost on the broad, featureless south shoulder of K2. He staggered around in the blizzard at 26,000 feet with no idea where to go, muttering "grande vice, grande vice" (huge emptiness), as climbers in base camp tried to guide him down over the radio by their recollections of the route.

"I could hear the desperation and fatigue in his voice as he went back and forth in the storm, looking for some clue to the descent," says Alan Burgess, a member of a British expedition. "Finally Parmentier found a dome of ice with a urine stain on it, and we remembered it. By this insignificant landmark we could guide him down the rest of the route by voice. He was very lucky."

On July 5, four Italians, a Czech, two Swiss, and a Frenchman, Benoit Chamoux, reached the summit via the Abruzzi route. Chamoux's ascent was done in a single twenty-four-hour push from base camp, an extraordinary athletic feat, especially considering that just two weeks before, the Frenchman had sprinted up the neighboring slopes of 26,400-foot Broad Peak in seventeen hours.

Even more extraordinary, though, were the deeds underway on K2's south face: a two-mile-high expanse of steep, ice-plastered rock, avalanche gullies, and tenuously hanging glaciers delineated on one side by the Abruzzi Spur and on the other by the Magic Line. On July 4, the Poles, Jerzy Kukuczka, thirty-eight, and Tadeusz Piotrowski, forty-six, started up the center of this unclimbed wall in light, impeccably pure style, bent on pushing the limits of Himalayan climbing to a whole new plane.

Kukuczka was the heir apparent to Messner's unofficial title as the world's greatest high-altitude alpinist. When he arrived at the base of K2, Kukuczka was nipping at Messner's heels in the race to climb all fourteen 8,000-meter peaks; he had already bagged ten of them, an accomplishment that was especially impressive considering the expense of mounting Himalayan expeditions and the pathetic rate of exchange for Polish *zlotys*. To fund their expeditions, Kukuczka and his Polish comrades had been routinely forced to smuggle vodka, rugs, running shoes, and other unlikely commodities that could be bartered for hard currency.

Just before sunset on July 8, after a lot of extreme technical climbing and four brutal bivouacs (the last two of which were without tent, sleeping bags, food, or water), Kukuczka and Piotrowski struggled to the summit of K2 in a howling storm. They immediately began to descend the Abruzzi Spur. Two days later, with the two climbers totally strung out and still battling their way down through the blizzard unroped, Piotrowski—who, because of numb fingers, had been unable to properly tighten his crampon straps that morning—stepped on a patch of steel-hard ice and lost a crampon. He stumbled, righted himself, then lost the other crampon. An attempt to self-arrest wrenched his ice axe out of his hands, and he was soon hurtling down the steepening slope out of control. Kukuczka could do nothing but watch as his partner bounced off some rocks, then disappeared into the mists.

By now the summer's death toll was beginning to give pause to most of the climbers still on the mountain, but for many the lure of the summit proved stronger. Kukuczka himself departed immediately for Nepal to attempt his twelfth 8,000-meter peak and gain ground on Messner in the race to knock off all fourteen. (The effort would prove to be in vain when Messner reached the summits of Makalu and Lhotse the following autumn, to claim the fourteen-summit crown.)

Shortly after Kukuczka returned to base camp to tell his troubling tale, the thirty-eight-year-old Italian solo climber Renatto Casarotto set out on his third attempt that summer to climb the Magic Line alone. This attempt, he had promised his wife, Goretta, would be his last. Solo ascents of difficult new routes on Fitzroy, Mt. McKinley, and other major peaks in South America and the Alps had given Casarotto a heroic, damn-the-torpedoes reputation, but the Italian was in fact a very cautious, very calculating climber. On July 16, a thousand feet below the summit and not liking the look of the weather, he prudently abandoned his attempt and descended the entire South Pillar to the glacier at its base.

As Casarotto made his way across the final stretch of glacier before base camp, climbers watching through binoculars from the camp saw him pause in front of a narrow crevasse that blocked his path and prepare to hop across it. To their horror, as he did so the soft snow at the edge of the crevasse gave way and Casarotto suddenly disappeared, plunging 130 feet into the bowels of the glacier. Alive but badly injured in a pool of ice water at the bottom of the crevasse, he pulled his walkie-talkie out of his pack and called Goretta. At base camp, she heard her husband's voice whispering over the radio, "Goretta, I have fallen. I am dying. Please send help. Quickly!"

A multinational rescue party immediately set out, reaching the crevasse in the last light of the day. A pulley system was soon rigged, and Casarotto, still conscious, was hauled to the surface of the ice. He stood upright, took a few steps, then lay down on his rucksack and died.

The only expedition on K2 to make no effort to conform to Messnerian ethics was a mammoth, nationally sponsored team from South Korea. Indeed, the Koreans didn't care how they got to the top of K2, just so long as they got someone from their team there, and then got him back down again in one piece. To that end, they employed 450 porters to haul a small mountain of gear and supplies to base camp, and then methodically proceeded to string miles of fixed rope and a chain of well-stocked camps up the Abruzzi Spur.

Late in the day on August 3, in perfect weather, three Koreans reached the summit using bottled oxygen. After starting their descent, they were overtaken by two exhausted Poles and a Czech who, using conventional siege tactics but no oxygen, had just succeeded in making the first ascent of the route on which Casarotto and the two Americans had perished—

Messner's coveted Magic Line. As both parties descended together into the night, a famous Polish alpinist named Wojciech Wroz—his attention dulled by hypoxia and fatigue—inadvertently rappeled off the end of a fixed rope in the dark—the seventh casualty of the season. The next day, Muhammed Ali, a Pakistani porter ferrying loads near the base of the mountain, became victim number eight when he was hit by a falling rock.

Most of the Europeans and Americans on the Baltoro that summer had initially disparaged the ponderous, dated methods by which the Koreans made their way up the Abruzzi Spur. But as the season wore on and the mountain prevailed, a number of these climbers quietly abandoned their previously ballyhooed principles and made free use of the ladder of ropes and tents the Koreans had erected on the Abruzzi.

Seven men and women from Poland, Austria, and Britain succumbed to this temptation after their original expeditions packed it in, and decided to loosely join forces on the Abruzzi. As the Koreans prepared to make their final assault, the ad hoc group made its way up the lower flanks of the mountain. Although this multinational "team" ascended at different speeds and were widely scattered over the route, all five men and both women had reached Camp IV at 26,250 feet—the highest camp—the evening before the Koreans mounted their successful summit bid.

While the Koreans made their way to the top in the flawless weather of July 3, the Austro-Anglo-Polish team remained in their tents at Camp IV, having decided to wait a day to make their own push for the summit. The reasons for this decision are not entirely clear; whatever the explanation, by the time the European team finally started up the summit tower on the morning of the fourth, the weather was about to change. "There were great plumes of clouds blowing in from the south over Chogolisa," says Jim Curran, a British climber and filmmaker who was down at base camp at the time. "It became obvious that major bad weather was on the way. Everyone must have been aware that they were taking a great risk by pressing on, but I think when the summit of K2 is within your reach, you might be inclined to take a few more chances than you normally would. It was, in retrospect, a mistake."

Thirty-four-year-old Alan Rouse, one of England's most accomplished climbers, and Dobroslawa Wolf, a thirty-year-old Polish woman, were the first to start up the summit pyramid, but Wolf quickly tired and dropped back. Rouse continued, however, taking on the exhausting work of breaking trail by himself for most of the day until, at three-thirty in the afternoon, just below the top, he was finally caught by Austrians Willi Bauer, forty-four, and Alfred Imitzer, forty. About 4 p.m. the three men reached the summit, and Rouse, the first Englishman to reach the top of K2, commemorated the event by hanging a Union Jack from two oxygen cylinders the Koreans had left. During the threesome's descent, five hundred feet below the summit, they saw Wolf asleep in the snow, and after a heated discussion Rouse persuaded her that she should turn around and go down with him.

Soon thereafter, Rouse also met two other members of the team on their way up, Austrian Kurt Diemberger and Englishwoman Julie Tullis. The fifty-four-year-old Diemberger was a celebrity in western Europe, a legendary *Bergsteiger* whose career spanned two generations. He had been a partner of the notorious Herman Buhl, and had climbed five 8,000-meter peaks. Tullis, forty-seven, was both a protegée and extremely close friend of Diemberger's, and though she didn't possess a great deal of Himalayan experience, she was very determined, very strong, and had been to the top of Broad Peak with Diemberger in 1984. Climbing K2 together was a dream that had consumed the two of them for years.

Because of the late hour and the rapidly deteriorating weather, Rouse, Bauer, and Imitzer all tried to persuade Diemberger and Tullis to forego the summit and head down. They mulled this advice over, but, as Diemberger later told a British newspaper, "I was convinced it was better to try it finally after all these years. And Julie, too, said, 'Yes, I think we should go on.' There was a risk; but climbing is about justifiable risks." At 7 p.m., when Diemberger and Tullis got to the summit, that risk indeed appeared to have been justified. They hugged each other and Tullis gushed, "Kurt, our dream is finally fulfilled: K2 is now ours!" They stayed on top about ten minutes, snapped a few pictures, and then, as the gloaming faded into the cold, bitter blackness of the night, turned to go down, joined by fifty feet of rope.

Almost immediately after leaving the summit, Tullis, who was above Diemberger, slipped. "For a fraction of a second," says Diemberger, "I thought I could hold us, but then we both started sliding down the steep slope, which led to a huge ice cliff. I thought, 'My God, this is it. This is the end.'" At the foot of the mountain during the ascent from base camp, they had come across the body of Liliane Barrard, where it had landed following her ten-thousand-foot fall from the upper slopes of the peak three weeks earlier, and the image of Barrard's broken form now flashed into Diemberger's mind. "The same thing," he mused with despair, "is happening to us."

But somehow, miraculously, they managed to stop their slide before shooting over the edge of the ice cliff. Then, fearing another fall in the dark, instead of continuing down they simply hacked out a shallow hollow in the snow and spent the remainder of the night there, above 27,000 feet, shivering together in the open. In the morning the storm was upon them in earnest, Tullis had developed frostbite on her nose and fingers, and she was having problems with her eyesight—possibly indicating the onset of cerebral edema—but the two climbers had survived the night. By noon, when they reached the tents of Camp IV and the company of their five fellow climbers, they thought the worst was behind them.

As the day progressed, the storm worsened, generating prodigious amounts of snow, winds in excess of 100 miles per hour, and subzero temperatures. The tent Diemberger and Tullis were in collapsed under the brunt of the storm, so he crowded into Rouse's and Wolf's tent, and she moved into the tent of Bauer, Imitzer, and Hannes Wieser, an Austrian who hadn't gone to the summit.

Sometime during the night of August 6, while the storm continued to build, the combined effects of the cold, the altitude, and the ordeal of Tullis's fall and forced bivouac caught up to her, and she died. In the morning, when Diemberger learned of her death he was shattered. Later that day, the six survivors used up the last of their food and—even more ominously—the last of their fuel, without which they couldn't melt snow for water.

Over the next three days, as their blood thickened and their strength drained away, Diemberger says they "reached the stage where it is hard to tell dreams from reality." Diemberger, drifting in and out of bizarre hallucinatory episodes, watched Rouse go downhill much faster than the rest of them and eventually sink into a state of constant delirium, apparently paying the price for the energy and fluid he expended breaking trail by himself on the summit day. Rouse, recalls Diemberger, "could speak only of water. But there wasn't any, not even a drop. And the snow that we were trying to eat was so cold and dry that it barely melted in our mouths."

On the morning of August 10, after five days of unabated storm, the temperature dropped to minus-twenty degrees Fahrenheit, and the gale continued to blow as hard as ever, but the snow stopped falling and the sky cleared. Those who were still able to think clearly realized that if they didn't make their move right then, they weren't going to have enough strength left to make a move at all.

Diemberger, Wolf, Imitzer, Bauer, and Wieser immediately started down. They believed they had no chance of getting Rouse down in his semicomatose condition, so they made him as comfortable as they could and left him in his tent. No one harbored any illusions that they would see him again. The five conscious survivors, in fact, were in such bad shape themselves that the descent quickly deteriorated into a case of everyone for himself.

Within a few hundred feet of leaving camp, Wieser and Imitzer collapsed from the effort of struggling through the waist-deep snow. "We tried in vain to stir them," Diemberger says. "Only Alfred reacted at all, weakly. He murmured that he couldn't see anything." Wieser and Imitzer were left where they lay, and with Bauer breaking trail, the other three kept fighting their way down. A few hours later Wolf dropped behind and did not reappear, and the team was down to two.

Bauer and Diemberger made it to Camp III at 24,000 feet, only to find that it had been destroyed by an avalanche. They pressed on toward Camp II, at 21,000 feet, where, after dark, they arrived to find food, fuel, and shelter.

By this time, according to Jim Curran, everyone at base camp had "totally given up hope for the climbers still on the mountain." They were incredulous, therefore, when, as it was getting dark on the following evening, "we saw this figure stumbling slowly down the moraine toward camp, looking like an apparition."

The apparition was Bauer—horribly frostbitten, barely alive, too exhausted and dehydrated to even speak. Eventually he managed to convey that Diemberger, too, was still alive somewhere above, and Curran and two Polish climbers immediately set out to look for him. They found Diemberger at midnight moving at a crawl down the fixed ropes between Camp II and Camp I and spent all the next day getting him to base camp, from where, on August 16, he and Bauer were evacuated by helicopter to face months in hospitals and multiple amputations of their fingers and toes.

When garbled word of this final disaster reached Europe, it became headline news. Initially, particularly in England, the once-popular Diemberger was vilified by the media for leaving Rouse to die at Camp IV, especially after Rouse, instead of beating a safe and hasty retreat from the high camp on August 5, had waited, apparently, for Diemberger and Tullis to make it down from their overnight ordeal on the summit pyramid.

Curran insists that such criticism is unjustified. Rouse and the others, he believes, stayed at Camp IV on August 5 not primarily to wait for Diemberger and Tullis, but because they "must have been incredibly tired from the day before, and the storm would have made it extremely difficult to find the route from Camp IV to Camp III. The area around Camp IV, remember, is nearly featureless, and everyone was aware that Michel Parmentier had nearly gotten lost trying to find his way down from there in similar conditions."

And when the descent was finally begun from Camp IV, says Curran, "there was absolutely no way that either Diemberger or Willi Bauer could have gotten Rouse off the mountain alive. They were both nearly dead themselves. It was an unimaginably desperate situation; I don't think it's possible to pass judgment about it from afar."

Still, it's difficult to resist the temptation to compare the turn of events in 1986 to a strikingly similar predicament eight K2 climbers found themselves in thirty-three years earlier, at very nearly the same place on the mountain. The climbers, part of an American expedition led by Dr. Charles Houston, were camped at 25,000 feet on the then-unclimbed Abruzzi route, preparing to make a push for the summit when they were hit by a blizzard of unusual severity that kept them pinned in their tents for nine days. Toward the end of this storm, a young climber named Art Gilkey came down with a deadly ailment called thrombophlebitis, a clotting of the veins brought on by altitude and dehydration.

Gilkey's seven companions, in no great shape themselves, though considerably better off than Diemberger and company, realized that Gilkey stood almost no chance of surviving, and that trying to save him would endanger them all. Nevertheless, says Houston, "So strong had become the bonds between them that none thought of leaving him and saving themselves—it was not to be dreamed of, even though he would probably die of his illness." In the course of being lowered down the mountain, Gilkey was swept to his death by an avalanche, but one can't help but be impressed by how his companions stuck by him to the bitter end, even though in doing so they were all very nearly killed.

It can be argued that the decision not to abandon Gilkey in 1953 was the height of heroism—or that it was a foolishly sentimental act, that had an avalanche not fortuitously taken Gilkey off his teammates' hands, their chivalrous gesture would have resulted in eight deaths instead of one. Viewed in that light, the decision by those who survived K2 in 1986 to leave terminally weakened partners seems not cold-hearted or cowardly, but rather eminently sensible.

But if the actions of Diemberger and Bauer appear to be justified, larger, more troubling questions remain. It is natural in any sport to seek ever-greater challenges; what is to be made of a sport in which to do so also means taking ever-greater risks? Should a civilized society continue to condone, much less celebrate, an activity in which there appears to be a growing acceptance of death as a likely outcome?

For as long as people have been climbing in the Himalaya, a significant percentage of them have been dying there as well, but the carnage on K2 in 1986 was something else again. A recent and very comprehensive analysis of the data shows that, from the beginning of Himalayan climbing through 1985, approximately one out of every thirty people who has attempted an 8,000-meter peak has not come back from it alive; on K2 last summer that figure was, alarmingly, almost one out of five.

It is hard not to attribute that worrisome statistic at least in part to Reinhold Messner's remarkable string of Himalayan feats over the past decade and a half. Messner's brilliance has, perhaps, distorted the judgment of some of those who would compete with him; the bold new ground Messner broke may have given unwarranted confidence to many climbers who lack the uncanny "mountain sense" that's kept Messner alive all these years. A handful of alpinists from France and Poland may have what it takes to stay at the table in the high-roller's game that Messner launched, but some men and women seem to have lost sight of the fact that the losers in such games tend to lose very big.

Curran cautions that one can't make generalizations about why so many people died in the Karakoram last summer. He points out that "people got killed climbing with fixed ropes and without fixed ropes; people got killed at the top of the mountain and the bottom; old people got killed and young people got killed."

Curran goes on to say, however, that "if anything was common to most of the deaths it was that a lot of people were very ambitious and had a lot to gain by climbing K2—and a lot to lose as well. Casarotto, the Austrians, Al Rouse, the Barrards were all—the word that comes to mind is overambitious. I think if you're going to try alpine-style ascents of 8,000-meter peaks you've got to leave yourself room to fail."

Too many people on K2 that summer, it would appear, did not.

from Snow in the Kingdom:
My Storm Years on Everest
by Ed Webster

Ed Webster (born in 1956) and three companions in 1988 climbed Everest's forbidding Kangshung Face—without oxygen or Sherpa support. Three of the team went for the summit after emerging from the Face onto the South Col, but only British climber Stephen Venables made it. After a brutal night in the open, he rejoined Americans Webster and Robert Anderson for their descent down the Kangshung.

Standing outside the Japanese tent at 27,500 feet, it was imperative that we descend to our own tents, sleeping bags, and stoves at the South Col as quickly as possible to rewarm and rehydrate our tired, parched bodies. As yet, I hadn't begun to consider how difficult it would be to retrace our route down the East Face, but it was clear we had pushed ourselves to the limits of our endurance. Roping together on our seven-millimeter rope, we descended to the Col. Robert went first, guiding Stephen, who was very wobbly-legged, while I came last, wondering if I could hold the rope if someone slipped. Luckily, the terrain quickly eased, and soon we were back on the flat, frozen, windswept desert of the South Col.

Stumbling back to our two tents at Camp 3, the full realization of how extended we were began to sink in. At this extreme altitude, 25,900 feet, there was absolutely no chance of being rescued. Helicopters do not fly above 20,000 feet, and while there were several expeditions on the mountain's Nepalese side, none were close enough to lend assistance; none of them even knew we were here. We were three people very much alone, utterly exhausted, with virtually no possibility of any outside support. A full 8,000 feet below—in Tibet—Mimi, Joe, and Paul, we hoped, awaited our return at Advanced Base.

When Stephen and Robert paused to rest, I hiked ahead, still unaware of the extent of my frostbite injuries, and pulled out my Nikon to photograph them walking towards me. I took two portraits of my half-frozen companions. In the first image, Stephen leaned in fatigue against Robert, but in frame number thirty seven, Stephen stood alone, his ice ax raised in victory. It was a particularly proud moment.

I do not remember very much about the rest of that day. Oxygen deprivation, our overwhelming fatigue, and the lack of food, water, and sleep combined to make us incredibly lethargic. We began to act out our lives in super slow motion. I know that we lay down and rested in the tents at the Col, that we took our suits off and crawled willingly into the luscious warmth of our sleeping bags, and that we then made a brew of tea, only because somehow I took pictures of these things, too.

I dimly recall taking off my overmitts and liner gloves and inspecting my fingers. Grey in color, cold, numb, and woody feeling, the fingertips of my left hand, I noted, appeared considerably worse than those of the right. Fretting over what to do, I finally decided to rewarm them in our tiny pot of hot tea water. Stephen did the same with his frozen left toes. While we knew that rewarming frozen tissue should only be done when all chance of refreezing the injured tissue had passed, we were positive we'd have relatively little trouble descending the East face. What could possibly be worse than the nightmare we'd just survived? We calculated that in two days' time at the most, we'd be safely in expedition doctor Mimi's care at Advanced Base.

Then we collapsed, dead tired, and slept. If we knew that we should have tried to descend to Camp 2 that day, we never discussed it. Careful, rational observations no longer seemed of much importance.

Subconsciously, I think we did know that spending this third day above 8,000 meters was dangerous, perhaps even deadly, but our bodies craved only sleep and rest. The summit push had taxed us almost beyond human limits. We were ready to go home; the question was, could we still get there?

Time crept by. I blinked awake from the depths of sleep and peered at the luminous dial of my watch. It was 2:30—but in the morning or the night? I no longer knew. My mind could not think. What day was it? Where were we? We're on the South Col on Mount Everest. . . . After the long agonizing night huddled in the Japanese tent, it felt so deliciously warm to be snug inside my sleeping bag. . . . Couldn't we just lay here a little longer, please? I didn't want to move, so I fell back asleep, for the rest of that day and night.

With no food left, the next morning our physical and mental condition went from bad to worse, and hopes for an easy, rapid descent faded. Today was our fourth above 8,000 meters without oxygen . . . our bodies would not respond to signals from the brain . . . we could barely move . . . every effort verged on a superhuman struggle. Stephen's and my last gas canister had run out yesterday, but luckily Robert's stove was still going. Stephen and I lay in our bags, inert, unable to make a single effort to prepare to descend, and waited hours for Robert to deliver us a single, half-filled pot of hot water, our breakfast. We were a pathetic sight, unmotivated, listless, and slowly dying, at times completely uninterested in doing anything to save ourselves from what would certainly happen should we fail to act. I began to realize we were engaged in the fight of our lives.

The two tents at Camp 3 on the Col were too heavy to carry. We would abandon them here, and bivouac in the open in our sleeping bags at Camp 2. At Camp 1 were two tents and a food cache. I also discarded my wonderfully warm down bibs. Then, trying to cut out even more weight, and reasoning that my wool mittens would be easier to rappel with, I left behind my heavily insulated overmitts. In retrospect, another costly error.

I crawled outside the tent, alternately lying and sitting in the snow until the final, most awkward task of fastening crampons to boots was accomplished. But could I stand? I glanced over at Robert, laying flat on his back in his tent, boots protruding out the entrance like a dead man's. Yet every so often he would come to life, sit up, and fiddle with his crampons before collapsing again . . . Stephen was also preparing to go, and lay prone on the ground, corpselike, in front of our tent. I pulled out my auto-camera to take a picture of him, and he waved at me half-heartedly to prove that he was still alive.

Yes, I could stand up, with difficulty. Shuffling to the east side of the Col, I carefully stepped down the initial, steep slope and plunged into waist-deep, fresh powder snow. Good for skiing, but not very easy to walk through! Afternoon storms the past two days had done the damage; additional snow had been blown over the Col onto the leeward side by the powerful winds. Conditions in the upper part of the snow bowl were about as bad as they could have been. The avalanche danger was extremely high. To make matters worse, thick monsoon clouds smothered my view.

We had no choice but to continue to Camp 2. Earlier in the expedition we'd discussed the possibility that we might descend into Nepal, into the Western Cwm, if conditions warranted. And while that escape might have been justified now that the snow conditions were so bad, several steps down the East face were several steps too many to reverse. I continued stumble-stepping down the slope in the whiteout, plunging each boot deep into the powder, my ears straining for the slightest sound of the snow settling or cracking. I was listening and waiting for disaster.

"What's it like down there?" yelled a voice from above. It was Robert. I could see him silhouetted on the rim of the South Col 500 feet above.

"Dangerous! Whatever you do, don't glissade," I shouted back. "Don't slide down the slope. Follow my tracks!"

Only minutes later, I shook my head in disbelief. Far to my left, Robert was now almost level with me! A small, lonely figure, he stood in the center of the huge snowfield directly below the Col. How did he get there so fast?

"What are you doing!?" I shouted over.

"I glissaded. It looked fine," Robert mumbled. "I guess I got going kind of fast. Uh . . . I dropped both of my ice axes too. Could I borrow your extra ski pole?" He now spoke with greater alarm; he had fallen about 300 feet.

Stephen left Camp 3 ten minutes after Robert, so he did not see Robert's fall. When Stephen reached the Col's edge, he saw only Robert's initial toboggan-slide dent in the snow. Below him, Robert and I had already been swallowed by the clouds. Stephen also decided—unwisely— to glissade. He also lost control and took a dangerous fall.

Robert and Stephen had each lost their ice axes. As a result, during the remainder of our descent of Everest's Kangshung Face, I was the only one with an ice ax. Robert used my spare ski pole, and Stephen now carried nothing in his hands for safety or support, neither ice ax nor ski pole.

I continued wading down the soft snow slope, peering through the enshrouding mists, hoping and praying that somehow I could still find the way to Camp 2—which after my teammates' falls felt very far away. I made each plowing, plunging step through the deep fluffy powder with the greatest effort, my strength flowing from a hitherto-untapped reservoir deep within me. I was thankful this new supply existed, but how long would it last?

Unexpectedly, I heard a dull muffled roar break loose above me as multiplying sound waves raced downhill through the grey curtain of cloud. An avalanche! Fortunately it was not heading directly for me, but had originated above me, to my left. Then, to my horror, I realized that the roar of falling snow came from the huge unstable snow slope where I had last seen Robert. My stomach tightened into a fierce sick knot.

The curtain of mist was so dense that I could not actually see the avalanche. I could only hear the falling debris, now well to my left, now below me, as multiple thousands of tons of snow and ice—carrying one human body—erupted over the edge of the immense Lhotse ice cliffs. I pictured Robert standing in the center of the snowfield as the billowing white tidal wave overwhelmed him, carrying him down and down, tumbling over the abyss to his death.

Turning back downhill, breathing hoarsely, I began walking again. Only Stephen and I remained. Robert was gone. How would we tell the others that Robert had died on the descent? I didn't know. My breath came in spasms. Stephen and I had to survive this climb. We couldn't give in to the mountain. No, we could not die.

Minutes later I glanced back up to confirm my worst fears. Only one dot, a small black figure against the white snow, was following in my footsteps. Not two dots; just one.

Adrenaline carried me down the next several hundred feet. Stopping to take a rest, I turned around . . . and there were two dots now, not one! I counted them twice and then a third time to make sure my eyes weren't deceiving me. Robert had not died in the avalanche! I felt a surge of happiness knowing he was still alive, but I shook my head in disbelief, wondering how my brain had tricked me. Had I hallucinated again?

I still thought we could reach the Flying Wing and the snow platform at Camp 2 before nightfall. Carefully, I stepped across a partially hidden bergschrund, trying to remember at what level we had diagonalled across the bottom of the tremendous snow basin below the South Col. After descending vertically several hundred more feet, I slowly angled to my left. We'd made a long traverse uphill to the left from the right-hand end of the Flying Wing; I now had to reverse this section. Unfortunately, since our ascent, the snow conditions had completely changed. Now I was wading through thigh-deep unconsolidated powder, ripe for an avalanche of massive proportions.

As I began to cross the snowfield, I was aware that it was heavily laden. It could fracture at any second, without warning. Traversing almost horizontally to cross it, I also knew I was breaking a cardinal rule of mountaineering—traversing directly across an avalanche slope—but here there was absolutely no alternative.

If the slope avalanched, as I had every belief it would, I would be swept into one of many waiting and deep crevasses, or sent tumbling into the Witches' Cauldron at the base of Lhotse, 7,000 vertical feet below. There would be no escaping death if the slope gave way, but maybe the others would survive. Maybe the snow would fracture below them and only I would be swept away. They might be spared. I made each footstep as softly as possible, my heavy boots sinking into the fresh-fallen snow.

I reached the far right-hand side of the snowfield above the right end of the Flying Wing, and hunched over with relief. The next obstacle, a large bergschrund, was a deep crevasse formed by the detached uphill side of the Flying Wing snow block. I knew this potentially lethal gap was immediately below me. On the way up, we'd crossed it via a fragile snowbridge, but where?

As I stumbled towards the bergschrund, an alarming thought found its away into my brain. Why weren't we now roped together for safety? In fact, where was our climbing rope? I didn't have it. Neither, I thought, did Robert or Stephen. Before leaving the South Col, we hadn't discussed if we should tie into the rope or not, presumably because during the summit climb we'd each become accustomed to climbing solo and unroped. No doubt we assumed we wouldn't need to rope up below the South Col either. Only months later, looking at a photo I'd taken, did I discover the missing rope. It lay coiled in the snow in front of Stephen's and my tent on the Col. Quite simply, we'd forgotten it.

Confused by the thick clouds, I could see about fifty feet, far enough to discern the Flying Wing's jagged upper lip extending far to the left. Then, materialising out of the cloud appeared an apparition. It was a tiny orange flag, the highest of our bamboo wands, which I'd placed four days earlier to mark the route over the crevasse. I stumbled forward through the snow and grabbed the wand; it was real! Carefully I tiptoed downhill towards the bridged bergschrund. I couldn't tell if the snowbridge was solid enough to support my weight, so I jumped across.

After landing on the far side, I hear a whoompf behind me—the sound of snow collapsing and falling into unknown depths. A black hole identified the the place where the bridge had given way, five feet left of where I stood. There the crevasse was much wider. The others would see the black hole and know to be careful.

Camp 2 was almost in sight. I descended the next snow slope, circled around the overhanging ice cliff at the right end of the Flying Wing, and waded over to our platform. At dusk, I cleared loose snow from where we had tented on the way up. Then I found four or five extra fuel cartridges hanging in a stuff sack suspended from ice screws pounded into the Wing.

Robert straggled in next. We threw out our sleeping bags and lit the stove for a brew. Stephen appeared as darkness fell. Robert produced some tubes of Japanese instant coffee and milk he'd found two days earlier, which we drank. Unfortunately, we hadn't cached any sugar, extra tea bags or soup here. The weather then cleared, Makalu and Chomolonzo thrusting into view above the dissipating valley clouds as the cold black sky froze around us. Several more cups each of hot water quelled our thirst before we passed out, snuggled deep in our warm feathery wombs.

On the morning of May 15, we could not move from our sleeping bags for several hours. Sitting up, let alone the superhuman feat of standing upright, seemed an impossible feat of physical endurance. We talked sluggishly between naps, or passed out collectively. Twice Stephen tried to melt snow for drinking water, but the hot stove melted into the snow—and when we fell asleep, the stove tipped over, spilling the hard-won liquid. Well, it didn't really matter, did it? Did anything much matter? There didn't seem to be any rush to do anything, certainly not to descend. We had plenty of time. The sun was out, and the daytime temperature grew increasingly hot. The problem, in fact, loomed with stark undeniable reality: if we didn't leave the Flying Wing, we were going to die here.

Never noticeably hot-blooded, I became increasingly angry at our situation. I felt the extreme nearness of my own death. Overcome by lethargy, Stephen and Robert lay asleep in their sleeping bags, but for some reason I was slightly more alert. I didn't know why. While fiddling awkwardly with the stove cannister with my frostbitten fingertips, turning the on-off key and fumbling with the lighter to ignite the burner, I felt boiling surges of anger well up inside me. I shouted at Robert and Stephen that we had to keep going, that we had to move, that we had to act. We couldn't just lie here and die.

I suppose I recognized I'd assumed the temporary role of leader, but it was leadership by default. I didn't want this duty. I was much more comfortable with a shared democratic leadership, but I also knew I couldn't hold out much longer. Another day without food, perhaps two at the most, and I thought I might be finished. So if it was my turn to lead us today through the fray, then so be it. If through my anger and outrage at my impending death I could help rouse Stephen and Robert, then so much the better.

All three of us had been frostbitten on the summit day on May 12 and during our forced bivouacs that night, but Stephen' and Robert's injuries didn't appear as severe as mine. Miraculously, Stephen's hands and fingers hadn't been injured at all during his 28,600-foot bivouac—thanks to Eric Shipton's competent care and a yak driver's fire; more hallucinations, Stephen explained—but the end of his nose, left exposed to the wind, was frostbitten and now had turned a mottled ashen grey. Because of the extra-insulating layer of the super-gaitors Stephen and I wore over our mountaineering boots, neither of us had removed our boots yet, so we could only guess the condition of our toes. The toes of his left foot, Stephen mentioned, were numb. Nine of Robert's fingertips, like mine, were covered with bulging black frostbite blisters, and the toes of Robert's left foot also felt very cold, he said.

As the morning waned, the weather turned cloudy, holding off the midday heat as we tried to prepare to descend. We'd leave by 11 o'clock, we agreed, before our departure time slipped to 12 noon, then one, two, and three o'clock. Try as we might, we could not pack our belongings, or clip on our crampons, or stand up, the most demanding challenge of all. Every exertion had to be willed by a tremendous effort commanded from our oxygen-and-energy-deprived brains. As Robert later phrased it, "We possessed the collective energy of a mouse." We talked little. Had Joe and Mimi and Paul seen us descending? Should we signal to them? Stephen thought they might have seen our head-lamps last night, but if they hadn't, surely they would be looking through the telescope at Advanced Base today.

Hours slipped away. . . . A third attempt at brewing hot water succeeded. Then Stephen discovered a packet of instant potato flakes and some freeze-dried shrimp and clam chowder he suggested we eat. The mention of food nauseated me. I declined, but he and Robert ate some mashed potato.

A single thought kept circling through my mind: "I must get to Advanced Base so Mimi can take care of me." My fingertips were looking increasingly ghastly; my frostbite blisters were growing bigger. After first propping myself up on one elbow, I succeeded in sitting up with a great effort. Two hours later, after collapsing repeatedly, I had stuffed my sleeping bag. I continued to urge Robert and Stephen to descend. When I left camp at 3:45 p.m., they were still fastening their crampons. It would be dark at six.

Almost as soon as I departed, the sky congealed into a bleak grey sheet. Snow-laden monsoon clouds thickened around and above me, blending evenly with Everest's undulating snow slopes and ice cliffs. At least the clouds masked the sun's heat, but soon it was snowing again. Visibility diminished to forty feet. The waist-deep snow was enveloping, somehow comforting. To sit down for a long rest would be so easy. Unconscious of any danger, I slid unexpectedly down a thirty-foot ice slab which had been concealed by two feet of powder snow. Landing on a powdery cushion, I brushed myself off and began angling to my right down a snow ramp leading into the maze of crevasses we'd threaded through on the ascent. Nervously, I scanned my surroundings. Near the ramp's base, I knew I needed to turn sharply left above one of the largest crevasses. The turn was unmarked; we'd been conserving our remaining bamboo marker wands.

My fatigue was growing. I tripped over a short icy step. A second later, I had the unpleasant realization that I was sliding down the mountain headfirst on my back. Instinctively, I clutched at my ice ax, jabbed the metal pick into the snow, pivoted my body uphill, jabbed my boots and crampon points into the snow—and stopped—all in several seconds. Trembling with fear, I ferociously kicked my crampon points into the hard ice buried beneath the top snow layer, and reestablished myself on the slope.

One hundred feet lower, a gaping crevasse leered up at me, its fathomless blue void waiting to swallow me. I looked up. Stephen and Robert were descending; I could see their ghostly figures through the mist and lightly-falling snow. This was insanity! It would be dark in an hour. What did we think we were doing, descending this late in the day? It would be better to return to Camp 2, use our remaining fuel to brew hot water, get a good night's sleep, and descend early tomorrow morning. We had wasted the entire day.

"This is crazy! I just missed falling into a huge crevasse!" I shouted up to Robert. Minutes later, he slumped beside me. Then Stephen joined us.

"Stephen, I nearly killed myself. We've got to climb back up to Camp 2, otherwise we'll be sleeping out in a snowdrift!"

It became apparent we had no option but to retrace our steps back up to the Flying Wing. To continue descending in such poor visibility, unroped, surrounded by crevasses, would have been suicidal. Stephen eventually agreed with me; Robert was too tired to care. Accepting our fate, we willed ourselves uphill towards camp. What took us one hour to descend took three killing hours to reverse.

Just below camp, we were stopped by the thirty-foot, sixty-degree ice slab we'd slid over on the way down. With only one ice ax for three, I was wondering how we would negotiate this section. Comically, Stephen and I balanced up on our front points side-by-side, each holding onto the ice ax between us. Then, while I swung the ax until the pick lodged, Stephen hung on tight to my wind jacket; then, precariously balanced, we climbed up the ice together. After repeating this procedure several times, we reached easier angled snow.

Robert looked up questioningly from below. "Don't forget to leave me that ax!" he instructed.

"I'll leave it for you here, partway up," I said, climbing down a move and slamming the pick firmly into the ice. The only problem was that the ax was still two body lengths above him.

"How am I supposed to climb up to it?" he asked

I wasn't sure, but Robert was inventive. He'd figure something out!

Stephen and I continued to camp. It was pitch-dark by the time all three of us resettled under the Flying Wing's ice canopy. We collapsed, having eaten virtually nothing in two days. I made a brew of hot water, and we shared several meagre grit-filled mouthfuls. We absolutely had to get an early start in the morning. My strength was dwindling and our chances for escape were almost gone.

The sun rose gold over Tibet. Feeling the sun's warmth penetrate into my sleeping bag, I peeked outside to see towering Makalu resplendent in the early light. Snug in my bag, I was deliciously warm. I could have stayed there forever. That was the problem. I struggled to prepare to leave, making two brews of hot water, and inevitably knocking over the stove once or twice. Every action was made with a fragile economy of effort and in the slowest possible motion. Stephen and Robert were awake, too, but hardly stirred. I hounded them.

"Stephen," I half-joked, "you're not going to be famous unless you get down alive."

We talked about the mountaineers who had perished on K2 two years earlier, in 1986. Trapped in a storm at 25,900 feet on the Abruzzi Spur, they ran out of food and fuel. Some died in their sleeping bags; others while making a last-ditch effort to descend the mountain. Among the dead were two of Britain's best mountaineers, Alan Rouse and Julie Tullis. We did not want to die as they had.

I remembered yesterday's ordeal of stuffing my sleeping bag, so I decided to abandon both my sleeping bag and my parka. By carrying the minimum amount of weight, I hoped to increase my chances for living. But by abandoning my survival gear, I irrevocably committed myself to descending to Advanced Base Camp in a single day. If I failed, I'd be stranded tonight without a sleeping bag or any warm clothing. I dressed in my capilene expedition underwear, my one-piece pile suit, a pile jacket, hat, and wool mittens. In my pack, I carried half a quart of water, my two cameras, and the rolls of Kodak film I had taken at the South Col and above.

Again, I left first, departing from the Flying Wing at 24,500 feet at 10 a.m. Glancing over my shoulder occasionally, I didn't see Robert or Stephen for a couple of hours. This was a battle for our lives. We could encourage each other, we could lend moral support, but we could not carry each other down Everest. Ultimately, the willpower to survive was an individual commodity. Robert later told me that when he left Camp 2 that morning, he tried to get Stephen moving, but Stephen hadn't budged from his sleeping bag. Would he lay there and die? Robert hadn't known the answer, but eventually Stephen did force himself to stand up and follow us.

Soon I reached the ice step where I'd stumbled and self-arrested the previous afternoon. Sitting down in the soft snow, resting, I decided I'd gone too far right yesterday. I gambled instead on traversing left around a steep snow rib to look for a big crevasse I remembered vividly from our ascent to Camp 2 six days ago. But how much the mountain had changed! It was nearly impossible to recognize landmarks because of the tremendous amount of new snow and the smothering clouds.

Using every route-finding skill I'd learned in twenty years of climbing, I stood up and began breaking trail through the crevasses in the blizzard. I excavated a trench to my left through a deep snowbank, climbed down a steep fifteen-foot incline, and saw several crevasses in front of me. None of them looked familiar. Cautiously, I waded towards them, holding my ice ax at the ready in case I fell in. A snowbridge spanned the first crevasse; gingerly I stepped onto it and pooled enough energy to jump over the weak-looking midsection. Breathing easier once I reached the far side, I jumped a second crevasse and plowed straight ahead, thinking that maybe I knew the direction of our route to Camp 1. I moved ahead slowly, cautiously, and prayed that a higher power would guide me.

Then, through the cloud, I caught another glimpse of orange. By sheer luck, I'd found the next bamboo wand! We were on our route. The wand also gave me a solid connection with a not-so-distant past. I stopped in my tracks. Paul, Mimi, Joe, Pasang, and Kasang were waiting for us below. We were not completely alone. Finding that slender stem of bamboo shook me from my dream world and gave me new incentive to return to Earth.

Still there was no sign of Stephen and Robert, but I was convinced my partners were alive and would soon be coming. Even though they'd been far from energetic when I left camp this morning, I never once imagined or thought that they were dead or in trouble. We already had survived so much together that I began to think we would all probably live. Death was still a possibility, but it no longer seemed as likely as it had yesterday, although we still had more than 5,000 feet to descend.

I set off downhill toward the next landmarks, Stephen's Ice Pitch and the next big crevasse. Halfway down the slope, I located another wand, fallen over and half-buried by the new snow. "Keep going," I chanted under my breath, my optimism growing. "Keep going . . . keep going . . . keep going . . . keep going. . . ."

The clouds were as thick as ocean fog; I could have sliced them with a knife. Downhill through this misty uncertainty was the only direction my legs would carry me. As I plunge-stepped down the smooth snow slope, my sixth sense prickled with awareness. An avalanche trap! The gently-curving slope was smothered in three feet of new-fallen snow. Had the powder had time to bond with the old layers beneath? I kicked at the snow with my boots. The adhesion seemed vaguely secure. I continued. What choice did I have? I vowed with every stumbling step toward safety that if I lived through this climb I would never, ever, do another route that was this dangerous.

What I would have given to be transported virtually anywhere else from the hell of this frozen world! I imagined warm, white sandy beaches; sunny Colorado; the normal everyday things in life: going for a walk, eating dinner with friends. Things I'd too often taken for granted. As soon as I escaped from this mountain, I would revel in the mundane.

My strength faltered. My arms began to feel light and buoyant, my legs leaden. I breathed from the hollow pit of my empty stomach. From my breath came the energy to move, but my motions became jerky and slow, one foot placed barely in front of the other as I pushed through the snow like a human plow, moving closer toward salvation and release from this wretched cage. I couldn't recognize any landmarks, but I knew I must be getting near the steep incline of Stephen's Ice Pitch.

My mind began to falter. Just keep moving, I told myself. Don't dare stop or you'll never get going again. Pace yourself, don't hurry. You don't have the strength to hurry! Don't even think, just let your legs move. Walk, walk slowly. Breathe, breathe slowly. Slowly, breathe—breathe, slowly. . . .

I heard a shout. Robert was 100 yards above me.

My companions were alive! Once more, I began my halting awkward movements down the slope. I saw the next crevasse, 150 feet lower. It was wide and unfathomably deep. One slip and you'd disappear without a trace.

The snow slope was church-roof steep and tilted straight into the crevasse. I began to traverse left across it toward the snowbridge we'd used to cross the gap on our ascent. The snow was bottomless. Each footstep collapsed into the one below it. Then I realized I'd descended too far. I would have to climb back up and make a higher diagonal traverse. I began retracing my steps, and yelled at Robert to go left earlier than I had.

"Left?" he responded weakly. I nodded, too exhausted to speak. I'd eaten nothing in more than two days, and had consumed only a few cups of tea and a bowl of noodle soup in more than four days. I thought the climb back up those hundred feet would kill me. Moving against gravity at that altitude, and in our condition, was a torment beyond comprehension.

A second stumbling figure appeared through the mist and cloud. Stephen. So you're alive, too! Good for you.

We'd reached Stephen's Ice Pitch, now buried beneath several feet of powder snow. Angling left, we carefully plowed a trench down the slope. Passing Robert, Stephen and I tip-toed across the snowbridge and began the final slog towards the top of our fixed ropes still another thousand feet below.

Again, I went in front, breaking trail. The snowbridge was a solid landmark. We were definitely on route, and I felt a new burst of energy. We'd placed far too few wands to mark this section, however, and I followed my instincts down short ridges and small snowfields that characterized this portion of the route, relieved that the worst of the avalanche danger was at last behind us.

Eyes shifted nervously from side to side, searching for the correct route. Here? There? Maybe that way. Legs faltered, stopped, then started. Energy? What was energy? Air was food. My muscles felt almost useless, but with every downhill step I began to gain invisible nourishment from the increasing amounts of oxygen in the atmosphere.

Move legs, move! You've got to keep moving! I remembered Fritz Wiessner's words, and chanted them over and over in a solemn incantation:

"Sometimes you've got to fight it."

"You've just got to fight it." Rest. Breathe.

"Sometimes you've got to fight it."

"You've got to fight it." A few more staggering steps.

"You've got to fight it."

"You've just got to fight it."

My breath became labored. Stay in control, Ed! Left foot, right foot, step. Good!

"You've got to fight it."

"You've got to fight it."

I found another bamboo wand at the start of a snowy prow. I walked to the end of the plank where it was corniced and overhung on both sides. We must have climbed up one side. I returned to the wand. Stephen and I walked to the end of the ridge for a second look.

"I think we went this way," he said with surprising conviction, and started to descend a steep snow trough. Suddenly, there was a loud crack, a whoosh, and Stephen was caught in a small avalanche. Riding atop the wave of falling snow, he flew down a fifty-foot cliff and landed in a huge mound of soft snow on the flat terrace below. Springing up out of the drift like a hippo jumping out of a mudhole, Stephen shouted cheerfully, "Yes, that's definitely the right way!"

Shaking my head in disbelief, I walked back to the wand. A shorter trough led down to the left. I took several steps. I was also avalanched, but only fell twenty feet. We continued. Stephen broke trail. We could no longer see Robert, but Stephen assured me he had seen him coming.

Then I noticed Stephen had stopped. I joined him.

"Don't you think we should try over there?" I suggested, motioning to our right down the next snow slope.

"What?" said Stephen, seemingly perplexed.

"Well, it looks better that way to me," I said.

"Ed! We're at the fixed ropes!" he blurted, pointing to a piece of orange eight-millimeter diameter rope emerging from the snow.

My gaze settled fondly on the orange rope. I couldn't believe it. We were going to live! I reached over, embraced Stephen in a bear hug and shook him in celebration. All we had to do was rappel 3,000 feet to the glacier. Maybe we could still get to Advanced Base Camp tonight. Before starting down the ropes, we saw Robert some distance above us.

"You okay?" I shouted.

"See you at Camp 1!" he yelled, adding that he was fine, just slow.

"No! We're going to Advanced Base no matter what!" I shouted. Robert waved back, and we began to descend. We dug our harnesses and figure 8 descenders out from under three feet of new snow (we'd cached them here to save carrying the extra weight any higher), and I strapped on my harness and immediately began racing down the ropes, hurrying from one anchor to the next. I'd been so concerned with staying alive that until I started rappelling, I hadn't given my stiff, wooden fingers much attention. It took a while to get used to holding the rope, and for the first time I began to realize that my fingers, especially those of my left hand, were very, very cold. I now began to worry. My fingers were not mending as I had hoped; in fact, they felt much worse.

Laboriously, I ripped the fixed ropes out from under the mantle of snow. I felt a surge of relief seeing that the Jaws of Doom crevasse had not widened or collapsed. The ropes across the Tyrolean traverse were intact, just stretched tighter than ever! I continued down to the terrace above the Webster Wall. There, the rope disappeared into the snow, so I unclipped from the rappel rope and walked without a belay to the edge of the seventy-five-foot overhanging cliff. The pink eleven millimeter rope down the Webster Wall was buried deeply, but by stamping out a platform and carefully peering over, I just caught a glimpse of it hanging free down the wall.

I dug the rope out of the snow and rappelled to Camp 1. It was 5:30 p.m. when Stephen joined me. We had a short discussion about whether we should continue, or remain here for the night. What little body warmth I still possessed was rapidly seeping out of me. Since I no longer had a sleeping bag or parka, at all costs I had to keep moving, to generate heat and stay warm.

When we'd left Camp 1 almost nine days ago on our way to the summit, we'd collapsed the tents on purpose. They were now buried beneath several feet of snow. I hardly recognized the campsite. Stephen pointed out a large trough created by an icefall of recent vintage, directly over the place where our tents had been pitched. It would have taken us an hour of hard work to excavate the tents, and since the descent from Camp 1 to Advanced Base took two hours in good conditions, I lobbied strongly to continue. Reluctantly, Stephen agreed.

I started down the snow slope below camp. The fixed rope here was also completely buried. All our nine-and eleven-millimeter static fixed ropes were white in color (we'd gotten a discount on the price!) and virtually impossible to detect against a white snow slope. Now where was that damned rope? Gingerly, I climbed as far down as I dared, unroped, and began digging with my ice ax. Below loomed the 2,000-

foot drop straight into Big Al Gully. As I continued to chop at the snow, suddenly I heard a pronounced crack—and the slope avalanched just above me. Two feet of silky snow cascaded through my legs into the fearsome abyss. I gripped my ice ax with a burst of adrenaline. I did not fall.

"Oh, there's the rope," I said, spotting it at the base of the avalanche fracture. Stephen volunteered to go first, and we rappelled to the bottom of Paul's Ice Pitch, with Stephen digging out each rope length from under the snow. It was a peaceful evening, the weather was clearing, and I remember being nostalgic rappelling past the Greyhound Bus— the first Cauliflower Tower—thinking fondly that I'd never see it so close up again.

Once more, we were about to be caught on the mountain in the dark. I became increasingly worried and told myself to stay calm and in control. We'd soon be down. Paul, Mimi, and Joe would take care of us. It was getting dark, no stopping it, and we had to deal with the situation like we'd dealt with the rest of this hellish descent: as best as we could.

As darkness fell, we discovered neither of our headlamps would work. Then Stephen fumbled and dropped his spare headlamp bulb. When Stephen couldn't pull up the next section of fixed rope, I rappelled down and joined him at the bottom of Paul's Ice Pitch. Taking my ice ax, he rappelled down and chopped each rope length free, inch by inch, from beneath a two-inch thick layer of water ice that had frozen over the ropes in the last week. It was painstaking work—and one poorly-aimed blow could cut the rope. I hadn't thought our situation could worsen, but it had. I shivered so hard my limbs trembled. All I could hear was Stephen's chopping, then the much-anticipated "Right!" or "Off!" which meant he'd reached the next anchor and it was my turn to descend.

Then the toe bail of my right crampon came unclipped. The crampon dangled uselessly below my boot, still strapped, however, around my ankle. With frostbitten fingers, I couldn't fix it. Rappelling down the fixed ropes in the dark with frozen fingers, no headlamp, and only one crampon became an endless nightmare. Often the rope was so badly iced we couldn't pull up enough slack to clip our figure-of-eight descender in for a proper rappel. The painful alternative was a wrist rappel, clipping into the rappel rope with a sling and carabiner from one's harness, then wrapping the icy rope around your wrists and forearms for friction. Gripping the rope as tightly as I could with my useless fingers, I began sliding down the rope. Several times I couldn't hold on any longer. Then I let go, fell, slid, and bounced down the slope until my safety sling from my harness to the fixed rope was stopped by the next anchor. I hoped and prayed a stupid mistake wouldn't kill me this close to safety.

Stephen led the entire descent down the buttress. We were more dead than alive when we reached the Kangshung Glacier at about one or two in the morning. Finding our short length of eleven-millimeter rope stashed at the resting rock, we roped up. The recent warm weather and monsoon clouds hadn't allowed the glacier surface to freeze at night, and the crust was now in about the worst possible condition. Instead of well-frozen snow, which would support our weight, a thin, breakable skin masked a mush of unstable-depth hoar, loosely-packed snow resembling large Styrofoam pellets. When the crust broke, as it did about every thirty feet, it was like plunging into a jar of marbles with both feet. Extricating oneself was extremely difficult, especially in our weakened state.

We tried to keep our sense of humor about the situation. This, too, became impossible. Hopefulness and grim determination gave way to anger and sudden outbursts. I slipped back into my old habit, getting increasingly upset at Venables for moving too quickly, for pulling the rope tight and yanking me off my feet, while Stephen became angry with me for not moving faster to get back to camp.

About halfway to Advanced Base, Stephen began a ceaseless tirade for a hot cup of tea: "Paul! Mimi! Joe! TEA!!!" he shouted at the top of his lungs about every five minutes. I was craving a hot orange drink and Stephen wanted his bloody cup of tea. That wasn't too much to ask for, was it? We stumbled across the glacier, got lost, finally found our way through the crevasses, and inched progressively closer to camp . . . to safety . . . to warmth . . . to our friends.

"Paul! Mimi! Joe! TEA!!!"

Suddenly, I fell into another pit of unstable snow. We were roped together, standing about fifty or sixty feet apart to safeguard each other from hidden crevasses. Stephen's patience waxed thinner and thinner as I struggled to escape from this new bear trap. My right leg was stuck fast as epoxy in the hole, while my crampon, dangling uselessly beneath my boot, remained firmly rooted in the oatmeal-thick concrete.

This time, I could not get my leg out. My boot would not budge.

"Ed, can't you do something?!" Stephen protested after watching me struggle in vain for fifteen minutes.

"I'm stuck, I can't get my foot loose!" I yelled. I could tell he was at the end of his patience.

"You look like a bloody floundering bird!" he bellowed.

We were in the middle of a now-starry Everest night, barely alive, and it seemed we were never going to reach camp, even though safety was only minutes away. Stephen was angry, I was stuck, and all he wanted was a hot cup of tea. I didn't know what to do. I couldn't budge my foot. I was completely exhausted. I leaned back against the snow to catch my breath. We were so close to camp, but I couldn't escape from this damn hole! I glanced back up towards Stephen—but Stephen had gone.

After untying from his end of the climbing rope without a word, Stephen headed towards camp. I watched him disappear into the distance. Then, from the crest of the moraine ridge to my left came a sudden commotion. Other voices rang out, friends' voices, Paul's and Mimi's voices, shouting, exclaiming, and I knew we were safe. I struggled again to free my boot from its slushy prison but couldn't. Slumping backwards, I waited and looked up at the stars.

Moments later, a beam of light ran along the moraine beside me and a familiar soothing voice shouted out my name. It was Paul Teare. I'd never been so happy to hear a friend's voice, a voice which a day or two earlier I wasn't sure I'd ever hear again. I shouted his name back, and Paul bounded across the snow towards me, falling in and leaping back out like a gazelle, until he reached me and threw his arms around my shoulders and neck.

"Why didn't you let us know you were alive?" he asked.

"We tried to . . . once . . . two days ago. I stood up and flashed my headlamp from Camp 2. . . ."

"But you're okay?" Paul continued.

"No, I'm not, really. My hands are pretty bad off. They're frostbitten. My feet are all right, at least I think they are. . . ."

"I'm so glad you guys are okay!" he exclaimed. "But where's Robert?"

"He's fine, just slow. . . . He told us he would be fine. We yelled back and forth from just above the Tyrolean."

With Paul shouldering me, I pried my right boot out of the snow and we retraced his tracks back to the moraine where the walking was easier. It was 4 a.m., May 17. Minutes later, back in camp, I was greeted with a joyous welcome-home hug from Mimi. Joe was in Base Camp, sending word to the Chinese for a helicopter to come look for us. . . .

I collapsed beside Stephen inside my dome tent, grateful, so very grateful, for sleep and rest and warmth to lay down flat and rest and be warm, and drink a hot drink, even if it was grapefruit juice, to feel it trickle past my parched lips and down my scratchy sandpaper throat before memory failed me. I don't really remember what happened during the next two days. I can recall only a string of hazy dreams; Paul putting me on warm hissing oxygen, the clear plastic mask slipped over my face while Mimi tenderly soaked Stephen's and my fingers and toes in sterile warm-water baths as she fed us soup and crackers; later that morning, Kasang staring blankly at us, not understanding and very worried, and Ang Chu's brother, Sonam, crouched beside Kasang, and Sonam's body was trembling, he was so frightened and so concerned, and then Pasang's fatherly face looked down at me, smiling, his calm hand reaching out to gently hold my shoulder and reassure me everything would be all right; Robert finally returning safely that first afternoon with Joe, who had hiked out to help him, and Robert bent over outside standing in the sunshine looking quizzically into the tent at Stephen and I laying inside and looking like death, and Robert saying to us grinning that Robert grin, "So, boys, how are we feeling today?"

What I remember most is the sweet delicious sensation of being alive, of laying on the soft foam pad in my warm sleeping bag in the yellow tent, and of savoring that simple radiant joy, that great gift, of having survived. And drinking the hot grapefruit juice drink.

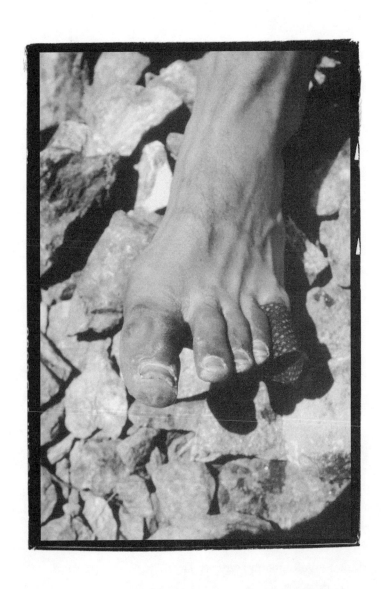

from Soldiers and Sherpas:
A Taste for Adventure
by Brummie Stokes

Frostbite is common enough on Everest attempts that it's tempting to dismiss the malady as minor. It isn't. British climber Brummie Stokes (born in 1945) and a partner survived an open-air bivouac after climbing the peak by the South Col Route in 1976, but were badly frostbitten. Stokes describes the indignities and difficulties that ensued upon his return to England.

M eanwhile there was still the frostbite to sort out. The doctors had been able to have a good look at our toes and Bronco's fingers by now, and it was clear they were eventually going to have to amputate. It only remained to decide how much should come off, and when. The answer came from Dr Michael Ward, one of the country's leading authorities on frostbite injury, who kindly agreed to come to Hereford to see us. His advice was that everything should be left alone for two months, because by that time it would be apparent which tissue was going to die off and which could be saved. That seemed fair enough to me. It just meant that we were in for a bit of an uncomfortable couple of months.

The summer of 1976 was a particularly hot one, and pretty soon, as the toes started to get blacker and to separate from the good flesh, they also began to smell terribly. They were, after all, just lumps of rotting flesh attached to the ends of our feet. After the first month, I noticed that tiny maggots were eating at the dead tissue in between the frostbite that had gone hard and the healthy flesh on my foot. A gap was appearing between the two that began to expose the bones of my by-now dead toes. I was naturally quite revolted by this and at first tried to remove them, but eventually came to realise that they were helping to get rid of all the decaying flesh and, however disturbing, ought to be left to get on with their grisly job.

Every other day the regimental medic would pop around to my quarters and take photos of my rapidly decaying feet. He wanted to ensure there would be a pictorial record of the various stages for teaching purposes in future; no opportunity is ever wasted in the SAS!

While I sat around doing very little besides waiting for the operation, I decided to learn another language to fill in some of the daylight hours. Arabic was my main foreign tongue, but as I had picked up a smattering of German on my trips to the Alps, that was what I would attempt to master next. The Education Officer from the Regiment very kindly supplied me with a series of books and tapes, from which to learn the basics. It helped take away a little of the boredom, but being still affected by the break-up of my marriage, I found myself looking forward to the evenings when friends would pop round and take me into town for a drink or a party. One of these parties was to prove a rather amusing and somewhat painful experience.

There were about twenty people in one of the flats in town which was renowned for its wild parties. This night, however, we were all sitting quietly on the floor in a circle, chatting and drinking and telling each other lies. Several of the girls were nurses from the local hospital, whom I had got to know over the years. They were a jolly crowd and good fun to be with, but nurses do have a tendency to be inquisitive and very down-to-earth, and as I was squatting on the floor with my feet stretched out in front of me, swathed in light gauze dressings to hide the discoloured toes, one of them turned to me and asked if she could have a look. She had, she said, never seen a case of frostbite before. I warned her it was not very pretty, but she didn't seem to mind, so eager to oblige and numbed by the effects of alcohol, I began carefully to discard the dressings. As the fresh air got to my feet, I noticed she reeled slightly at the smell. The other people were all looking pretty disgusted by this time, but full credit to her, my nurse hardly batted an eyelid as she knelt to study my gangrenous toes.

'For crying out loud, cover those things up!' someone shouted, as a trolley was wheeled in bearing a meal of curry.

It smelt delicious and I was hungry, but instead of helping me replace the dressings, the girl began asking about the maggots and wondered if she might be allowed to actually touch my toes so that she could know what they felt like. By now the toes were all hard and wrinkled and completely dead.

'Some women are never satisfied,' I muttered to myself, as she gently touched the dead tissue.

'Would it hurt if I squeezed them?' she enquired, and being pumped full of painkillers and booze, I told her to help herself.

The next thing I knew, a sharp pain was shooting up through my ankle and I looked down to see her fainting at my feet. She had tweaked my big toe hard and it had crumbled away in her fingers. Now it was lying, forlornly, on the carpet—although not for long. The dog saw to that. Two more girls fainted and several people were sick. It was all very embarrassing and the only good thing to come out of it was that there were not many customers for the curry. I had two helpings before falling soundly asleep on the floor.

Bronco and I had deliberately not gone to a military hospital for our treatment. We knew if we did that we were likely to be pensioned off as disabled once we'd had our operations, deemed unfit for further service. So, to avoid this, we had arranged through friends of Dick Hardie, the expedition's doctor, to have the deed done by a local surgeon at the hospital in Hereford. Frostbite was not something that is dealt with an awful lot in small market towns, especially not in the middle of summer. Because Bronco would need to have the fingers of his right hand amputated as well as all his toes, it was decided between us that it was only fair I should act as the guinea pig and have my operation first. No one was clear how much of the toes and forefeet would need to be removed in order to allow sufficient good tissue to be left

at the end of the foot to effect a healthy suture line. That was something the surgeon, a Scot, could only find out with practice and he
would have to practice on me.

The night before the operation, my friends threw a grand party for
me to say farewell to my defunct digits. Hungover the next morning, I
steered my wheelchair into the ward and presented myself to sister. She
was a charming lady who informed me that they were all expecting me,
showed me to my bed and jokingly warned me against the dangers of
her nurses taking off the rest of my toes before I got into theatre. She
had obviously heard of the escapade at the party.

The rest of that first day was spent getting to know the other patients
and staff; they all seemed very cheerful and I knew that even under the
circumstances, I was in for a pleasant stay. About twenty people turned
up to see me at visiting time, all carrying six-packs. The theory is that
alcohol is one of the best treatments for frostbite, as it dilates the blood
vessels and promotes circulation through damaged tissues. It was the
first time I have actually been encouraged to drink beer for my health.
Ward sister was a good soul and only began to remonstrate when one of
my visitors pulled out a guitar and started to play folksongs. Then, in the
interest of the other patients, as she put it, she had me transferred to a
private side ward, one which even had a fridge to keep the beer cool.

The next morning I was given a pre-med injection to calm me down
in preparation for the operation, then wheeled into theatre by one of
the nurses I knew from my party nights. I held out my arm to the anaes-
thetist, who inserted a needle which made the world go away. My head
seemed to be swaying from side to side; there was a ringing in my ears
and I fancied I saw myself hobbling along a dusty lane on crutches,
dragging my useless feet behind me. Coming towards me was the surgeon, walking his dog, and he stopped and chatted for a while.

'I don't know how much of your feet I am going to have to cut
away,' he told me, 'until we get you into the theatre. I will obviously
only take what I have to, but you must prepare yourself for the even-
tuality that you may have to spend the rest of your life on crutches or
in a wheelchair.'

My voice was full of venom as I yelled at him, 'No, no, I won't! I don't care what you say, I won't use sticks.'

'What's the matter, Mr Stokes? Come on now, wake up. Wake up for me.'

The voice of the kind ward-sister wafted into my ears from a long way off. It washed over me as I blinked open my eyes and looked into her smiling face. I realised that once again I was back in the tiny side ward and my bed. I moved my head and looked around, then putting my elbows underneath me, lifted myself up. There was a sudden searing pain all the way from my feet to my knees. The last time I felt anything as remotely painful as that was when I had been shot through the knee in Dhofar, and I was not even sure that had hurt as much as my feet hurt now.

I wanted to know how much had been taken away—or more importantly, how much I had got left. The sister explained that I still had half my feet and that the doctor was pleased with the way things had gone. I fell back against the pillow as the effect of the drug chased away the burning pain. I felt better now that it was done. I was clean again, now that the maggot-infested, black, horrible mass of gangerous flesh had been removed; and letting out a sigh, I fell back into an exhausted sleep.

It was over, though poor Bronc still had it to come. When I next awoke it was visiting time and among my visitors were my Mum and Dad, and my brothers and sister, who had travelled down from Birmingham. I could see the strain in my Mum's face and tried to put her mind at rest by telling her that everything would be all right and that before she knew it, I would be back climbing again. She attacked me verbally, as only mothers can, and told me that I must on no account climb again, that I should take up a more sedate hobby.

from Camp Six: An Account of
the 1933 Everest Expedtion
by F.S. Smythe

After three attempts on Everest in the early '20s, the British did not return until 1933. As before, they tried to climb the mountain from the North. On June 1, Frank Smythe and the young Eric Shipton set out from Camp Six on the expedition's second summit attempt, hoping to find a way through uncharted ground that loomed above. Shipton would become one of the century's great mountain explorers—but this day belonged to Smythe.

The sky was clear at daybreak. We had resolved overnight to leave at 5, but a rising wind and intense cold made this impossible. Cold we could have faced, but the addition of wind is too much for mere flesh and blood on Everest.

Matters appeared hopeless until an hour later when the wind suddenly fell to a complete calm. And it did not return. We listened expectantly for the hateful rush and tug of it, but the calm persisted.

Breakfast eaten, we extricated ourselves foot by foot from our sleeping-bags and with much labour and panting pulled on our windproof suits.

Our boots might have been carved out of stone, and they glistened and sparkled inside with the frozen moisture from our feet. I made a vain attempt to soften mine over a candle, but it was useless, and somehow or other I thrust my feet into them, pausing at intervals to beat my bare hands together, or stuff them into my pockets.

We donned every stitch of clothing we possessed. I wore a Shetland vest, a thick flannel shirt, a heavy camel-hair sweater, six light Shetland pullovers, two pairs of long Shetland pants, a pair of flannel trousers, and over all a silk-lined "Grenfell" windproof suit. A Shetland balaclava and another helmet of "Grenfell" cloth protected my head, and my feet were encased in four pairs of Shetland socks and stockings. Gloves are always a problem on Everest, and the ideal glove that is warm yet flexible and will adhere to rocks has still to be designed; in this instance, a pair of woollen fingerless gloves inside a pair of South African lambskin gloves, also fingerless, kept my hands moderately warm.

A slab of Kendal mint cake apiece sufficed for food. It was a mistake not to provide ourselves with more food, but our repugnance for it had been still further intensified during our enforced stay at Camp 6. Apart from this we carried a length of light climbing line, whilst my little "Etui" camera accompanied me as usual.*

At 7 we emerged from the tent and laced the flaps behind us. It was sadly obvious that Eric was far below his usual form. He had eaten less than I since we had arrived at the Camp, and now he complained of stomach pains, and asked me to go slowly—a request I might have made myself had he been fitter.

A shallow snow-filled gully took us diagonally upwards and across the yellow band for the best part of 100 feet. There was no difficulty, but every minute or two we had to halt and lean on our ice axes gasping for breath.

The gully petered out into a great expanse of slabs. Again there was no difficulty; advance was merely a matter of careful balance and choice of the easiest route; yet the angle as a whole on the yellow band is such that a slip would probably end in a fatal slide, especially as the climber would have little strength left to stop himself. Fortunately, our broad, lightly nailed boots gripped the sandstone well. The snow of yesterday's blizzard had been blown from many of the slabs, but here and there where it had accumulated on the shelving ledges we had to tread circumspectly.

*This, complete with one film pack, weighs one and a quarter pounds. It takes 3½ inch by 2½ inch photographs.

Though we left the camp an hour and a half later than Wyn and Waggers had done, the cold was still intense and there was little warmth in the sun which was just peeping over the north-east ridge.

The first and most lasting impression of the climber on Everest will always be the bleak and inhospitable nature of the great mountain. On the yellow band no projecting crags, ridges or buttresses stimulate the interest or the imagination; there is nothing level and the climber must tread a series of outward-shelving ledges where the rope is useless to him. Never have I seen a more utterly desolate mountainside. And above, still a weary way above, was the summit pyramid set squarely at the end of this vast rocky roof; a last tremendous challenge to our failing strength.

Traversing, and ascending slightly, we made for the foot of the first step which, from the moment we emerged from the initial gully, appeared close at hand. Its shape reminded me in some curious way of the summit of a Lake District hill which I had climbed one dewy Spring morning before breakfast to "work up an appetite." It had taken me an hour to scale 2,300 feet of turfy bracken-clad fellside, and now with eleven hours of daylight in hand I was doubtful whether we had the time or strength to climb and descend 1,600 feet. Yet, I was going better than I had expected. Exercise was loosening my cramped and stiffened limbs, and for the first time since arriving at Camp 6 I was conscious of warm blood flowing vigorously in my veins. But, unhappily, this was not the case with Eric. He was going steadily, but very slowly, and it was more than ever plain that there was something wrong with him.

Not far from the first step we crossed an almost level platform covered in small screes, a possible site for a future camp, then traversed almost horizontally. We were immediately below the step when I heard an exclamation behind me. Turning, I saw that Eric had stopped and was leaning heavily on his ice axe. Next moment he sank down into a sitting position.

Many times during the march across Tibet we had discussed what to do in the event of one man of a party of two being unable to continue, and we had agreed that unless he was exhausted and unable to return alone safely his companion should carry on alone, in which decision he would be supported by the expedition and its leader. It was an expedition maxim that no man must go on till he reached a point of complete exhaustion, and Eric was far too good a mountaineer to do this. The saving grace in high-altitude climbing is that there is a point at which a man cannot continue to ascend but can still descend relatively easily and quite safely. This is Nature's automatic safety check.*

I asked Eric whether he felt fit enough to return to camp safely. He replied unhesitatingly, "Yes," and added that he would follow slowly. This last, though I did not know it at the time, was inspired by generosity. He had no intention of proceeding further and merely said that he would to encourage me and relieve me from all anxiety as to his safety. It was another example of that good comradeship which will one day take men to the summit of Everest.

Leaving him seated on a rock I continued. I looked back after a minute or so, but he had as yet made no move.

There was never any doubt as to the best route. The crest of the north-east ridge, leading to the foot of the second step, was sharp, jagged and obviously difficult. As for the second step, now almost directly above me, it *looked* utterly impregnable, and I can only compare it to the sharp bow of a battle cruiser. Norton's route alone seemed to offer any chance of success, and it follows the yellow band beneath a sheer wall to the head of the great couloir.

*I am convinced that this automatic check rules out the possibility of a man collapsing suddenly near the summit of Everest. Such a disturbing possibility has been mentioned as the result of tests carried out by the R.A.F. in a decompression chamber. These tests revealed that at a pressure equivalent to a height of 28,000–30,000 feet many men faint suddenly and without warning. Such tests, however, are artificial inasmuch as they make no allowance for acclimatisation, and I do not believe they have any real bearing on the Everest problem. I cannot for an instant believe that under natural conditions nature acts in so arbitrary a fashion. Her processes lead slowly and unmistakably to a logical conclusion. It is only artificial conditions that she resents. Perhaps this is one of the deep-seated reasons why many Everest climbers abhor oxygen apparatus. There is something artificial, unnatural and therefore dangerous in its use on Everest. The argument that it is necessary in high flying, mines, etc., etc., cannot hold water inasmuch as such conditions are unnatural, men not being endowed with the capabilities of birds or moles, which do not, incidentally, require oxygen apparatus to sustain them.

At first there was no difficulty and a series of sloping ledges at the top of the yellow band took me round a corner and out of sight of Eric. Then came a patch of snow perhaps 30 yards wide. There was no avoiding it except by a descent of nearly 100 feet, but fortunately the snow was not the evil floury stuff I had expected, but had been well compacted by the wind; indeed, such hard snow that step-cutting was necessary.

Step-cutting at nearly 28,000 feet is a fatiguing operation, and the axe seemed unconscionably heavy and unready to do its work. In the Alps one powerful stroke with the adze would have fashioned a step, but sudden spurts of exertion are to be avoided at 28,000 feet, and I preferred the alternative of several light, short strokes. I must have looked like an old hen grubbing for worms, but even so I had to cease work and puff hard after making each step.

High altitudes promote indecision. Projecting through the snow was a rock and at first sight it seemed a good foot-hold. Then I thought it was too sloping and that I had better cut to one side of it. But I had no sooner changed my mind when I decided that perhaps after all it could be used as a foot-hold and would save me a step or two. I must have spent a minute or two turning this ridiculous little point over in my mind before doing what was the obvious thing—avoiding it. It is curious how small problems encounted during a great undertaking can assume an importance out of all proportion to their true worth.

When I had crossed the snow I again glanced back, but there was no sign of Eric following me, and I continued on my solitary way.

Contrary to accepted mountaineering practice, I found that the easiest as well as the safest method of traversing the slabs was to keep the ice axe in the outside hand as there were always little cracks and crannies to put it in. It was a third leg to me and an invaluable companion throughout the whole of the day.

Beyond the snow patch the slabs were covered here and there with loose, powdery snow. This had to be kicked or scraped away before I dared stand on the outward-sloping ledges. Progress was slow, though steady, and as I advanced and saw the final pyramid appear above the band of rocks beneath which I was traversing, there came to me for the first time that day a thrill of excitement and hope. I was going well now, better than when I had parted from Eric, and for a moment there seemed a chance of success.

The bed of the great couloir was hidden, but a subsidiary couloir and a buttress separating it from the great couloir were full in view. Both were sheltered from the wind and as a result were still heavily plastered with the snow of yesterday's blizzard. My hopes were dashed as I gazed at the buttress. It was considerably steeper than the rocks I was traversing, and snow filled every crack and was piled deeply on every sloping ledge. Was it climbable in such a condition? In the Alps perhaps, but not at 28,000 feet by a man nearing the limit of his strength. And the subsidiary couloir? Even supposing the traverse of the buttress proved practicable, what kind of snow should I find in this narrow cleft? Most likely unstable powder affording no certain footing and impeding every movement. True, it might be possible to avoid it by climbing the rocks at one side, but these, in their turn, were mostly snow-covered.

Instinctively I looked for an alternative. Could I climb directly upwards to a point above the second step and attack the final pyramid without having to continue this long, wearisome and unprofitable traverse? The wall rose above me like a sea cliff, in places it overhung, and every hold, every wrinkle and crack held its quota of snow. There was no visible break in it until the buttress where there was a gap, possibly the point reached by Norton in 1924 which might prove a feasible alternative to the subsidiary couloir. At all events direct ascent was impossible. One thing alone gave me hope: once the subsidiary couloir had been climbed and the rock band passed there seemed every reason to suppose that the principal difficulties were behind. I could see the face of the final pyramid and it did not look difficult. There was a scree slope at the base of it and higher a slope of light-coloured boulders. Energy alone would be required to surmount it. Of course, it may hold its surprises, for Everest will remain a stubborn opponent to the last; but I feel confident that once the rock band is below, the change from difficult and dangerous climbing to safe and easy climbing will inspire the climber to outlast fatigue and altitude over the remaining 600 feet to the summit.

The angle of the yellow band steepened gradually as I approached the great couloir. In general direction the ledges were parallel with the band, but they were not always continuous, and once or twice I had to retrace my steps for a yard or two and seek an alternative route. But the climbing was never difficult—it required only unfailing attention to the planting of each foot on the sloping ledges, especially when these were masked by loose snow.

Presently the bed of the great couloir became visible. It was shallow enough not to necessitate any steep descent into it, and was filled with snow, perhaps 30 to 40 feet wide, which ended beneath the rock band. Several hundred feet lower was a pitch of unknown height, beneath which the couloir widened out into a small hanging glacier, then fell steeply towards the Rongbuk glacier, a total height from my position of about 8,000 feet.

It was a savage place. Beyond was the steep and snowy buttress separating me from the subsidiary couloir, and hemming me in above was the unrelenting band of rock, and higher still the final pyramid, a weary distance away, cutting aloofly into the blue.

I approached the couloir along a ledge which bent round a steep little corner. This ledge was comfortably wide until it came to the corner, then it narrowed until it was only a few inches broad. As far as the corner it was easy going, but to turn the corner I had to edge along, my face to the mountain, in a crab-like fashion. The rocks above projected awkwardly, but it was not a place that would have caused a second's hesitation on an Alpine climb. One step only was needed to take me round the corner. This step I funked. The balance was too critical. With arms spread-eagled above me I sought for steadying hand-holds. They were not essential; balance alone should have sufficed, but I felt I could not manage without them. I could find none; every wrinkle in the rocks sloped outwards. For a few moments I stood thus like a man crucified, while my heart bumped quickly and my lungs laboured for oxygen, and there flashed through my mind the possibility of a backward topple into the couloir—an interminable slide into belated oblivion.

I retired a few yards, and apostrophised myself as a fool. I knew that the traverse was possible, and if Eric had been there I should not have hesitated. Being alone made all the difference.

I tried again, and once more found myself in the spread-eagled position but without the courage to take the one step that would have placed me in safety round the corner.

The only alternative was a ledge about 20 feet below. I was loath to lose even 20 feet of height, but there was nothing for it but to descend.

The slabs separating me from the ledge were reasonably rough, and though there were no very definite holds there were wrinkles and folds. For the rest friction should serve. Facing outwards and sitting down I lowered myself gingerly off the ledge on the palms of my hands. The friction was even better than I had hoped for, and the seat of my trousers almost sufficed by itself to maintain me in position without the additional support of the palms of my hands. There was no awkward corner in the lower ledge; it was wide and honest, and though it sloped outwards and supported a bank of snow three or four feet deep, it brought me without difficulty to the snowy bed of the couloir.

Wyn and Waggers had found the same loose, disagreeable snow in the couloir as had Norton in 1924, but I suspect that they traversed the upper ledge and so crossed higher than I. The snow at my level, as a tentative forward dig with the ice axe revealed, had been hardened by the wind and step-cutting was again necessary.

One step, then a pause to gasp, while the snow at my feet and the rocks beyond swam uncertainly before me. Then another step and another bout of gasping. The snow was very hard and the angle of the great couloir at this point fully 50°. About a dozen steps—I was across at last.

Next, how to traverse the buttress? I must climb almost straight up it for about fifty feet before continuing more or less horizontally towards the subsidiary couloir.

The rocks were steep and snow had accumulated on them untouched as yet by the wind. How had the wind swept the snow in the couloir hard and left the slabs at this side unaffected?

When these slabs are snow-free they are probably not much more

difficult than the slabs to the east of the great couloir. There are numerous ledges, and though the general angle is appreciably steeper, there
is no necessity for anything but balance climbing, and I confidently
believe no insuperable obstacle will prevent the climber from reaching
the subsidiary couloir. But now snow had accumulated deeply on the
shelving ledges and it was the worst kind of snow, soft like flour, loose
like granulated sugar and incapable of holding the feet in position. As
I probed it with my axe, I knew at once that the game was up. So far
the climbing had been more dangerous than difficult; now it was both
difficult and dangerous, a fatal combination on Everest. The only thing
I could do was to go as far as possible, always keeping one eye on the
weather and the other on the strength I should need to retreat safely.

The weather at all events was fair. In the shelter of the buttress and
the wall beyond the subsidiary couloir there was not a breath of wind
and the sun shone powerfully—too powerfully, for it seemed to sap
my strength and my resolution. I was a prisoner, struggling vainly to
escape from a vast hollow enclosed by dungeon-like walls. Wherever I
looked hostile rocks frowned down on my impotent strugglings, and
the wall above seemed almost to overhang me with its dark strata set
one upon the other, an embodiment of static, but pitiless, force. The
final pyramid was hidden; if only I were on it, away from this dismal
place with its unrelenting slabs. The climber who wins across the slabs
to the final pyramid must conquer a sickness of spirit as well as a
weariness of body.

With both arms at breast-high level I began shovelling the snow
away before me; it streamed down the couloir behind me with a soft
swishing noise. Several minutes elapsed before a sloping ledge was dis-
closed, then I heaved myself up, until first one knee, and then the
other, were on it. In this position, like a supplicant before a priest, I
had to remain while my lungs, intolerably accelerated by the effort,
heaved for oxygen. Then with another effort I stood cautiously upright.

More snow had to be cleared before I could tread a smaller ledge on
the slab above; then, to my relief, came a step unattended by this
prodigious effort of clearing away snow. But relief is short-lived on

Everest and the ledge that followed was covered several feet deep in snow bevelled into a steep bank, yet without the slightest cohesion.

Presently I had to stop, as apart from the need to rest overstressed heart and lungs, immersing my arms in the snow brought such numbness to my hands, gloved though they were, that I feared I might let slip my ice axe.

So slow and exhausting was the work of clearing the snow that I began to rely on feel alone. That is to say, when I could I trusted my foot to find holds beneath the snow rather than clear the snow away from the slabs until I could see the holds. I realised full well the danger of this, and whenever possible used my ice-axe pick as an extra support by jamming it into cracks. This last precaution undoubtedly saved me from catastrophe. There was one steeply shelving slab deeply covered with soft snow into which I sank to the knees, but my first exploring foot discovered a knob beneath it. This seemed quite firm and, reaching up with my axe, I wedged the pick of it half an inch or so into a thin crack. Then, cautiously, I raised my other foot on to the knob, at the same time transferring my entire weight to my front foot. My rear foot was joining my front foot when the knob, without any warning, suddenly broke away. For an instant, both feet slid outwards, and my weight came on the ice axe; next moment I had recovered my footing and discovered another hold. It happened so quickly that my sluggish brain had no time to register a thrill of fear; I had acted purely instinctively and the incident was over almost before I knew it had occurred. I did not even feel scared afterwards as I was climbing now in a curiously detached, impersonal frame of mind. It was almost as though one part of me stood aside and watched the other struggle on. Lack of oxygen and fatigue are responsible for this dulling of the mental faculties, but principally lack of oxygen. It is a dangerous state of mind and comparable to the mental reactions of a drunken man in charge of a car. He may believe that his judgment is unimpaired, even that he can drive more skilfully than usual; in point of fact, as statistics and the police court news reveal, he is much more prone to an accident in this condition.

Just before crossing the great couloir I had looked at my watch; it was 10 a.m. Now I looked again. An hour had passed, and I had made about fifty feet of height, not more. At least 300 feet of difficult rocks, all deeply snow-covered, remained to be climbed, before easier ground on the final pyramid was reached. Perhaps I could do another hour or two's work, but what was the use of it? I should only exhaust myself completely and not have the strength left to return.

I shovelled away the floury snow until I had made a space on which I could stand, though I did not dare to sit.

I was high up on the buttress separating the great couloir from the subsidiary couloir. Above me was the band of rock beneath which I had been, and was still, traversing. It looked impregnable except where it was breached by the subsidiary couloir, and the place already mentioned a few yards to the east of this couloir. For the rest, it is Everest's greatest defence, and stretches unbroken across the north face of the mountain. The striated limestone rocks composing it actually overhang in places, and the section above the great couloir reminded me of the well-known pitch in the Central Gully, on Lliwedd, in North Wales.

It is possible, indeed probable, that weariness and altitude distorted my judgment, but there are two things I believe to be true. Firstly, that Norton's route is practicable, and that when the "tiles," as he calls the slabs, are free of snow, they can be traversed without excessive difficulty to the subsidiary couloir, and this can be climbed on to the face of the final pyramid. Secondly, that it is not a practicable route when snow covers the slabs. But there is no doubt that even in the best conditions this part of the climb will tax a climber's powers to the uttermost. The unrelenting exposure of the slabs, dependence on the friction of boot nails for hours on end, added to the physical and mental weariness and lethargy due to altitude, will require something more than strength and skill if they are to be countered successfully. The summit was just in view over the rock band. It was only 1,000 feet above me, but an aeon of weariness separated me from it. Bastion on bastion and slab on slab, the rocks were piled in tremendous confusion, their light-yellow edges ghostlike against the deep-blue sky. From the crest a white plume of mist flowed silently away, like unending volcanic steam, but where I stood there was not a breath of wind and the sun blazed into the hollow with an intense fierceness, yet without warming the cold air. Clouds were gathering, but they were thousands of feet below me. Between them, I could see the Rongbuk glacier, a pure white in its uppermost portion, then rugged and uneven where it was resolved into a multitude of séracs and, lower still, a gigantic muddle of moraines as though all the navvies in the world had been furiously excavating to no logical purpose. Beyond it, the Rongbuk valley stretched northwards towards the golden hills of Tibet, and I could make out the Rongbuk monastery, a minute cluster of minute buildings, yet distinct in every detail through the brilliantly clear atmosphere. With this one exception, I remember no details. My position was too high, my view too vast, my brain too fatigued to register detail. There was nothing visible to challenge my elevation. The earth was so far beneath, it seemed impossible I could ever regain it. The human brain must needs be divinely inspired to comprehend such a vista, and mine was tied to a body fatigued by exertion and slowed down in all its vital processes by lack of oxygen. Somervell's description of the scene is simplest and best: "A god's view."

More by instinct than anything else, I pulled my camera out of my pocket. The photograph I took is pitifully inadequate.

I cannot enlarge on the bitterness of defeat. Those who have failed on Everest are unanimous in one thing: the relief of not having to go on outweighs all other considerations. The last 1,000 feet of Everest are not for mere flesh and blood. Whoever reaches the summit, if he does it without artificial aid, will have to rise godlike above his own frailties and his tremendous environment. Only through a Power within him and without him will he overcome a deadly fatigue and win through to success.

Descending even difficult ground at high altitudes is almost as easy as descending at an Alpine level, and within a few minutes I regained the great couloir. Recrossing it, I halted on the broad, comfortable ledge to take a photograph. It is curious that I did not remember taking this photograph or the one from my highest point until the film was developed, so I think my action at the time was more automatic than reasoned, as before starting on the expedition I told myself many times that I must take photographs whenever possible. This lends colour to a theory I have long held, that in climbing at great altitudes, when mind and body are in the grip of an insidious lethargy, it is on the subconscious, rather than the conscious, that the climber must rely to push him forwards. Therefore, it is essential that the will to reach the summit of Everest be strengthened by a prior determination to get there. Perhaps it is not too much to say that Everest will be climbed in England.

After taking this photograph it occurred to me that I ought to eat something. I was not in the least hungry, indeed the thought of food was utterly repugnant, especially as my mouth was almost dry, and my tongue leather-like, but in duty bound I pulled a slab of mint cake from my pocket.

And now I must relate the curious incident described in "Everest 1933."

After leaving Eric a strange feeling possessed me that I was accompanied by another. I have already mentioned a feeling of detachment in which it seemed as though I stood aside and watched myself. Once before, during a fall in the Dolomites, I had the same feeling, and it is not an uncommon experience with mountaineers who have a long fall. It may be that the feeling that I was accompanied was due to this, which, in its turn, was due to lack of oxygen and the mental and physical stress of climbing alone at a great altitude. I do not offer this as an explanation, but merely as a suggestion.

This "presence" was strong and friendly. In its company I could not feel lonely, neither could I come to any harm. It was always there to sustain me on my solitary climb up the snow-covered slabs. Now, as I halted and extracted some mint cake from my pocket, it was so near and so strong that instinctively I divided the mint into two halves and turned round with one half in my hand to offer it to my "companion."

It was apparent when I recrossed the couloir that I would do better to return across the yellow band by a lower route. The angle of the band west of the first step is very slightly concave, and on such slabs a degree or two in angle makes all the difference. The western end of the band terminates below in a great cut-off, a sheer precipice which carries the eye in a single bound to the Rongbuk glacier. My return route lay a few yards above and parallel to the edge of this precipice. There was no difficulty whatsoever. Care alone was needed, especially when crossing some patches of snow which, unlike those on the upper part of the band, were treacherously soft and unstable.

Very soon I found myself below the point where I had parted from Eric, but on looking up, could see no sign of him. I now had to make the choice between climbing up at least 100 feet and joining the ascending route or of traversing directly to the camp. To ascend again at this stage was utterly distasteful. I was too tired, and my legs were leaden; they would descend easily enough or traverse horizontally, but I doubt whether I could have dragged them uphill unless hard pressed. A temptation I had to resist firmly was to slant off down the yellow band by Norton and Somervell's route. This was a far easier line than the long, wearisome traverse across a series of shelving ledges to Camp 6. In two or three hours I could have reached Camp 5, even continued on down to the comfort of the arctic tent at Camp 4. Unfortunately, Eric was waiting for me at Camp 6, and if I did not turn up he would naturally assume an accident.

The climbing was simple enough at first, but presently became more difficult. Instead of the easy slabs, which had led us upwards from the camp to the foot of the first step, I found myself on a series of narrow outward-sloping ledges separated by abrupt little walls. These ledges were never continuous for long, and it was necessary when one petered out to descend to another. However, I could still afford to lose height without descending below the level of Camp 6.

This route took me across the band some distance below the place where Wyn and Waggers found the ice axe, but I did not see any further traces of Mallory and Irvine. I remember glancing down at a wide, gently sloping expanse of snow, screes and broken rocks below the band and thinking that if the ice axe indeed marked the point where they slipped, it was possible that their bodies might have come to rest there.

Some of the ledges were wider than others, and I paused to rest at intervals. It was during one of these halts that I was startled to observe an extraordinary phenomenon.

Chancing to look over the north-east shoulder, now directly in front of me, I saw two dark objects in the sky. In shape they resembled kite balloons, and my first reaction was to wonder what on earth kite balloons could be doing near Everest, a certain proof that lack of oxygen had impaired my mental faculties; but a moment later I recognised this as an absurd thought. At the same time I was very puzzled. The objects were black and silhouetted sharply against the sky, or possibly a background of cloud; my memory is not clear on this point. They were bulbous in shape, and one possessed what looked like squat, underdeveloped wings, whilst the other had a beak-like protuberance like the spout of a tea kettle. But what was most weird about them was that they distinctly pulsated with an in-and-out motion as though they possessed some horrible quality of life. One interesting point is that these pulsations were much slower than my own heart-beats; of this I am certain, and I mention it in view of a suggestion put forward afterwards that it was an optical illusion and that the apparent pulsations synchronised with my pulse-rate.

After my first reaction of "kite balloons" my brain seemed to function normally, and so interested was I that, believing them to be fantasies of my imagination, I deliberately put myself through a series of mental tests. First of all I looked away. The objects did not follow my vision, but when my gaze returned to the north-east shoulder they were still hovering there. I looked away again, and by way of a more exacting mental test identified by name a number of peaks, valleys and glaciers. I found no difficulty in Chö-oyu, Gyachung Kang, Pumori and the Rongbuk glacier, but when I again looked back the objects were in precisely the same position.

Nothing was to be gained by further examination and, tired as I was with the apparently endless succession of slabs, I decided to carry on to Camp 6. I was just starting off when a mist, forming suddenly, began to drift across the north-east shoulder. Gradually the objects disappeared behind it. Soon they were vague shadows, then, as the mist thickened, they disappeared altogether. The mist only lasted a few seconds, then melted away. I expected to see the objects again, but they were no longer there; they had disappeared as mysteriously as they came.

Was it an optical illusion or a mirage? It may be of interest to state that my height was about 27,600 feet, and that the objects were a few degrees above the north-east ridge about half-way between the position of the 1924 Camp 6 and the crest of the north-east shoulder. This gives their height as about 27,200 feet, and a line connecting me with them would have ended, not in a background of sky, but of clouds and mountains. It is possible, therefore, that imagination magnified some strange effect of mist, mountain and shadow, yet whatever they were, it was a strange and altogether uncanny experience.

The first light mist was a forerunner of other mists which quickly gathered and drifted across the mountainside, concealing familiar landmarks. It might not be easy to find Camp 6 among the wilderness of slabs in a mist, and I began to feel anxious, especially as I could not see the tent. Fortunately, however, two prominent towers on the north-east ridge, which I knew were directly above the camp, showed now and then.

In places the sandstone slabs were intersected horizontally by slippery belts of quartzite. The first intimation I had as to how slippery they were was when I lowered myself down a steep little wall on to an outward-sloping quartzite ledge. It was far more slippery than the sandstone ledges, and I did not dare trust my bootnails upon it. There was no alternative but to climb up to a sandstone ledge, and this ascent, though it cannot have been more than 20 feet, made me realise how tired I was.

Presently the two rock towers were almost immediately above me and I halted and looked round expectancy for the camp. It was still not visible. Was I above it or below it? Had my route-finding been at fault? All about me was a vast labyrinth of outward-dipping slabs. Now and then a puff of icy mist would float out of space and pass djinn-like up the mountainside to the crest of the north-east ridge where it shredded out and rushed away to join in the ceaselessly moving vapour that boiled upwards and outwards from the south-east precipice.

A few more steps. There was something familiar now about the rocks. Suddenly I came to a shallow, gently sloping gully filled with snow. There were footmarks in the snow; it was the gully immediately above the camp. Next instant I saw the little tent snugly bedded in a corner; small wonder I had not seen it before. What a relief! I let out a hoarse croak of joy and quickly scrambled down to it.

Eric was there. It scarcely needed a word on my part to tell him of my failure; he had seen enough to gauge the conditions. He had descended without difficulty and his stomach was much better. We both talked in whispers, for my mouth and throat had been dried up by the cold air. A hot drink was the first thing; I had not known how thirsty I was, for the intense desiccation of high altitudes takes the body a stage beyond the mere sensation of thirst. And the warmth of it; there was life in that drink.

We discussed plans. Now that we had failed our one desire was for comfort, and there was no comfort at Camp 6. Eric was well rested and strong enough to descend to Camp 5; I, on the other hand, felt very tired; that hour of climbing beyond the great couloir had taken it out of me more than many hours of ordinary climbing. We agreed, therefore, that Eric should descend whilst I remained at Camp 6 and descended next morning. It was not a good arrangement; men should not separate on Everest, but another miserable night wedged together in that little tent was not to be borne.

An hour later, at about 1.30 p.m., Eric left. The weather was fast deteriorating; mists had formed above and below and a rising wind was beginning to raise the powdery snow from the face of the mountain. For a few minutes I watched him methodically traversing the sloping shelf, following Jack Longland's descending route; then a corner hid him from sight and I lay back in my sleeping-bag for a much-needed rest.

For the next hour I lay semi-comatose from fatigue; I may even have slept. Then I became suddenly conscious of the tent shuddering violently in a high wind. The rest had refreshed me greatly and my brain was beginning to reassert itself over my tired body. I unlaced the tent flaps and looked outside. A blizzard was blowing; nothing was to be seen but a few yards of slabs over which the snow-laden gusts rushed and twisted. Rapidly the wind increased. I could feel the little tent rising and straining against the guy ropes, and in between the thudding and cracking of its sorely stressed cloth hear salvoes of driven snow spattering viciously against it.

Eric? I was very anxious. He must be having a horrible descent. He would do it all right; he was not one to associate with mountaineering accidents; his calm, detached confidence was a passport to safety in itself. Still, I could not rid myself of anxiety or of a succession of futile yet worrying pictures that flashed through my mind: snow and wind; wind, relentless, battering, snow-filled wind; wind as cold as death; and a lonely, toiling, ice-encrusted figure.

Towards sundown the wind fell appreciably and the clouds blew clear of Everest. Again I looked outside. Every other peak was concealed beneath a roof of clouds stretching in every direction. At that level a tempestuous wind was blowing and now and then a mass seethed upwards as though violently impelled from below and shrivelled into nothingness. The sky above was blue-green, never have I seen a colder colour, and the declining sun was entirely without warmth. Now and then little twisting devils of winddriven snow scurried past: small wonder that the Tibetan believes in a cold hell; here were its very flames licking across the slabs of Chamalung.

There was little fuel left and half of it went to cook my supper. It was 6 p.m. when I had finished. I exulted in my comfort. There were now two lots of sleeping-bags to keep me warm and I was soon snug with enough below me to defeat the sharpest stone. It did not occur to me that I was spending a night higher than any other human being; I was purely animal in my desire for warmth and comfort. Neither did I feel in the least lonely; in this respect it seemed as natural to spend a night alone in a tent at 27,400 feet as in an hotel at sea-level.

I remember nothing more until the following morning. Something heavy was pressing on me when I awoke, and I was astonished to find a snowdrift covering the lower half of my body, reaching almost to the ridge of the tent. How had it got there? Then I remembered a small hole which Eric and I had accidentally burnt in the side of the tent during our cooking operations. It was only an inch or so in diameter, yet large enough for the powdery snow to pour ceaselessly through all night like sand through an hour glass, gathering in a drift which filled nearly a quarter of the tent. There must have been a more than usually severe blizzard.*

I looked at my watch: 7 a.m.; I had slept the clock round for the first time since leaving the Base Camp, if not for the first time during the whole expedition. And I was greatly refreshed; as long as I lay without moving I felt almost as though I were at sea-level; my heart was beating slowly, steadily and rhythmically, and my brain was more active than it had been since leaving Camp 4. Perhaps I might be able to settle once and for all the vexed question of the second step before descending to Camp 4. With this idea in my mind I heaved myself up into a sitting position and began energetically to push away the snow. Instantly the familiar panting supervened, and at the same moment I was aware of the intense cold, the greatest cold I remember during the expedition. Within a few seconds sensation had left my hands and I had to push them into the sleeping-bag and put them between my thighs.

The sun had not yet reached the tent, possibly it was behind clouds, and it was useless to think of doing anything until it arrived. It struck the tent a few minutes later, and putting on my gloves I rummaged among the snow for fuel and provisions; it was some time before I found a tin, the last tin, of solid methylated and could prepare a cupful of café-au-lait. I loathed the sight of food, but I managed to force some down. Then I looked outside. One glance was sufficient: even if I had the strength or inclination (and the latter was now at a low ebb) for a reconnaissance, the appearance of the weather, to say nothing of the lack of fuel, made an immediate descent imperative. High grey clouds were stealing out of the west and overhead a formless murk was gathering in which the sun was struggling with fast diminishing power, whilst the freshly fallen snow had a dull, lifeless look. Another blizzard was brewing.

---

*The weather both at Camps 5 and 4 was very violent that night.

from K2: The Savage Mountain
by Charles S. Houston
and Robert H. Bates

When a storm trapped eight members of the 1953 American K2 expedition at 25,000 feet, climber Art Gilkey developed blood clots in his leg. An attempt to lower him down the mountain led to a fall that injured five more climbers, including team leader Charles Houston. After Gilkey disappeared—probably the victim of an avalanche—his teammates labored to save themselves, as Robert Bates recounts.

D uring the long hours of darkness we had had much to think about, and in the morning we soberly assessed our situation. Art Gilkey, who had camped here so cheerfully a few days before, was gone. Houston seemed physically able to climb but he was weak and still out of his head, had a chest injury, and couldn't reason. Whether he had internal injuries we didn't know. George Bell was an almost greater worry. His hands were covered with frostbite blisters and his feet were blotched with deeper frostbite. He wasn't sure that he could get his swollen feet into his boots again. In addition he could not see well without his glasses. Whether he and Houston could climb down, we didn't know, but we realized that we didn't have the manpower to carry them if they couldn't.

Schoening's chest seemed better during the night, but it was still a potential cause for worry. Fortunately, his hands, which he had nipped when he held the fall, had not suffered damage and did not give him trouble. Molenaar had a cracked rib and a cut on his thigh which would slow him down, but his morale was good and he was anxious to get started. Craig, too, looked exhausted, but the early morning light showed him to be obviously in better shape than he had been the evening before. Tony Streather, who with Craig and Schoening had been brewing tea for us all during the night, looked more himself than anyone did.

Craig and Streather teamed up again to cook breakfast, and though we somehow didn't feel hungry, we drank the tea, forced down the thick cereal, and made Houston eat some. There would be many problems before we reached Base Camp again, but from now on it wouldn't do to look too far ahead. The essential thing was for us to get down out of avalanche danger to Camp VI. Once there, the most treacherous climbing would be behind us, we would be close to the food cache at Camp V, and even short periods of good weather would permit the descent to lower camps.

The wind was already rising when we finished breakfast and it took an effort of will to crawl out into the raw morning, stiff and sore, and begin to pull our packs together for the descent. Houston's crampons were hard to strap on, because there was no flat place for anyone to stand or for him to put his foot. And yet they must be strapped on tightly. George Bell was having similar problems. His neck was so stiff from his cramped position in the tent that he could not straighten his head, and for dreadful minutes it seemed that he could not force his swollen and frostbitten feet into his vapor-barrier rubber boots. Fortunately most rubber will stretch, and after much pulling and straining both boots went on.

Schoening and Craig wanted to take Houston down, for he was still suffering from the concussion, and we were all very worried about how he would climb. If he stopped climbing, if he decided to act independently or if he slipped, he might bring disaster to the teammates whom he would have risked anything to save. We knew that this day's descent was the most dangerous we faced. If we could get the whole party down to Camp VI, there was a good chance that we would all get safely off the mountain. Accordingly, when everyone's crampons were on, Houston was tied carefully into the middle of Craig's and Schoening's rope and they started to climb carefully down over the snow-covered slabs. Schoening, whose ability at belaying had been established for all time, went last and anchored the rope. Those of us who were to follow on the second rope watched breathlessly as the three started down. We knew how close to exhaustion everyone was, and we worried over whether Houston would be able to climb. As we watched, he started off all right, but after going 20 feet he sat down in the middle of a steep snow patch, put his chin in his hand, and looked around as if to say, "What are we doing here?" Schoening looked perplexed. After a few moments he shook the rope and called down, "Come on, Charlie. Let's go!" And Charlie, still looking bewildered, got up and continued to climb down.

Perhaps this was a good time to have no inhibitions, for we were faced with a problem similar to climbing down a wind-swept, steeply slanted house roof, 1,700 feet long, with snow and ice covering many of the slates. The exposure was so severe that any slip would be hard to check and might pull the whole rope of men down off the mountain. We knew that we were physically exhausted and climbing under conditions that would have been extremely dangerous even when we were at our strongest. Each one of us had to climb with all the strength and skill he possessed. No one could slip.

The first rope had descended 100 yards and all were making good progress when the rest of us turned our backs on Camp VII and started to descend the relentless steep slopes. The storm clouds had risen a little, but the wind was sweeping great plumes of snow whirling across the rock slabs. Footing was dreadfully uncertain, and since Streather seemed strong, we had him go first. Next went Bell, whose uncertain step because of his missing glasses and his frostbitten hands and feet were alarming, and finally came Molenaar and I. Molenaar's leg was bothering him but he kept as sound a belay as he could on Bell, and obviously did everything he could to secure me when I moved down behind him. We had moved down only a couple of rope lengths when we saw 100 feet to our right an ice ax sticking into a snow slope at a crazy angle. Molenaar made a careful traverse across the snow to reach it. It was Houston's ax, which had disappeared in the fall, and we quickly handed it over to Bell, whose ax had also vanished in his headlong plunge down the slope. This chance find helped Bell tremendously, for now with the ax he could probe places where he could not see clearly; but to watch George lean out over the slope and tap around with the tip of the ax was anything but reassuring to the other three men on the rope who, standing on slabs covered with powder snow, were trying to safeguard the party. Under these conditions Bell's poise and steady climbing, despite his handicaps, were magnificent. He knew that his own life and ours were at stake, for we were all so near exhaustion that a slip could easily drag all four of us thousands of feet in a fall. And if Bell reached the point where he could not walk, we might be too weak to get him down.

In the back of our minds was the terrible lesson of the fatal storm on Nanga Parbat. We had more food on K2 than the Germans had had, but that wouldn't help if we couldn't reach it. Our feet and hands were numb as we cleared away the snow to find handholds and footholds. In some places the savage wind even helped us, for it had so firmed the snow that we could kick steps down it, but as a rule the powdery coating over the slabs did not adhere well, and climbing on this uncertain surface with such exposure below strained the firmest nerves. The accident of the day before and our miraculous rescue appeared to have developed in most of us a fatalistic attitude about our dangerous position. We had the feeling that matters were beyond our control. We seemed to be puppets pulled by a string, as if things were fated to happen in a certain way, do what we would, and nothing in the world could change them. Under the circumstances this fatalism, caused no doubt by the series of accidents of the past few days, was almost comforting, for we did not lose strength through nervous worry. We were doing our best. If that wasn't good enough, there was nothing else we could do to change things. What would be would be.

I have never had this fatalistic feeling before, but I certainly had it as we moved out onto the exposed col (pass) at the top of the steepest slope. Here, in an utter maelstrom of wind and whirling snow, we had to take off our crampons to climb down the smooth, steeply angled rocks. We were already cold and as we eyed the slabs, which were here too steep for snow to cling, we faced a wind that was eddying furiously up the mountain directly at us. I have seldom been so cold.

With numb fingers we got George Bell's crampons off, pulled off our own, and then Streather climbed over the edge and disappeared. Thank God our fixed ropes there were clear of snow! But despite their help, this steep section of the descent seemed to take hours, and my feet had lost all sensation before the third man on the rope, Molenaar, reached a good belay point and called to me to start down from the col. Like the others, I could not move fast, but the blessed handlines helped, and putting my faith in the pitons that supported them, I stiffly lowered myself off that storm-swept col and onto the steep face. I still had confidence that we would get down that cliff, and on down to Camp VI. I wasn't going to worry, but I was terribly anxious to get all of us under shelter so we could start work to save our feet.

One at a time we moved down across the steep slabs, along the ridge and down another fixed rope on the other side. Here, on loose rocks precariously poised, we had a brief respite from the wind. Our strength was ebbing fast, and Molenaar, who had belayed so well above, was now climbing entirely on reserve strength and hardly able to take care of himself. At 200 feet from camp, Streather, the strongest man on our rope, climbed 20 feet down the wrong place and had to climb back. Reascending cost him frightful effort! Ahead was one more slippery traverse, but no one slipped, and after descending a shallow gully we stepped down almost onto the tents of Camp VI.

The others were already there when we arrived. They had found both tents full of snow, one of them right up to the top, for a couple of small rocks had fallen and made slits in one, and faulty closure of a zipper had provided a tiny opening in the other. Through these small entrances the driving monsoon winds had forced powder snow until the tents were drifted full.

Fortunately for us on the second rope, the others had just finished clearing out the powder snow when we arrived, and they had started a stove. As we climbed into these tents, the most blessed sense of relief came over us. We had come down safely. We had passed the worst part of the route. Here were shelter and food. No matter how exhausted we were now, we had faith that we could get down.

Uncomfortable though we were, the next hours in camp seemed by contrast to be almost luxury. Charlie Houston seemed far more himself. Schoening and Craig reported that he had climbed extraordinarily well for a man in his condition, only occasionally sitting down in the most unexpected places and looking around as if to wonder what he was doing there. All of us looked years older than when we had been here before, but there was a confidence in our voices that had not been there that morning. Nobody made optimistic statements, but morale had improved.

While snow was melting for tea, we blew up the air mattresses which had not been abandoned above, arranged some 1939 sleeping bags we had found there, and took off our boots to work on our feet. My toes had no sensation, but neither did anybody else's, and I was glad to remember that my feet had not hindered my climbing down. Since the tent Houston and I were sharing stood in the lee of the other, and our tent had no holes that let in the wind, we called George Bell to trade places with Bob Craig and move into the warmer tent. Bell's feet were a great worry to us now, for they were in the most dangerous condition of all. George shouted, "Okay," and started to crawl across the space between the tents. As he did so, he saw a little bag about 15 inches long and 8 inches high in the passage between the tents.

"Where did that come from?" he called, and without waiting for an answer he picked it up and pushed it into our tent ahead of him.

"Why, Tony found it about 1,000 feet below Camp VII," I said. "He thinks it's something of Art's. I haven't looked at it yet, but I'm going to take it to his family."

"It isn't Art's," said George huskily. "It's mine. It was in my pack when I lost it in the fall."

Eagerly he pulled at the zipper, drew it open, and began to fumble frantically inside. And now, to our utter amazement, George let out a gasp of joy and pulled forth his spare pair of eyeglasses—unbroken!

What the discovery did for Bell's morale we couldn't tell, but his delight did us all a lot of good. Also in the bag were the expedition accounts, for George was the field treasurer, but at that time we had no interest in such matters. The rest of his pack, however, with camera, exposed film, and diary, like Charlie Houston's, had completely disappeared, and we never saw it again.

All the way down, of course, we had been looking for Art Gilkey's body, but we never found it. We did see, however, a tangle of ropes and a broken ice ax about 1,000 feet below the ice gully where we had last seen him. The wooden shaft of the ax, broken in its fall down the mountain, had jammed between two rocks. Our friend must have had an instant and merciful death, the swift death that is the best kind, before his body was swallowed forever beneath the snows of the Karakoram.

That evening at six o'clock Charlie Houston was so far recovered that he could use the spare walkie-talkie, which was at Camp VI, to call Colonel Ata-Ullah at Base Camp. The emotion and relief in that good man's voice when he learned that we were alive was tremendous. "Thank God," he said, and for a moment or two he said little more. He had listened constantly since we had failed to keep our schedule with him at three o'clock the day before, and by now had practically given us up for dead. Next day he was planning to search the glaciers for us, and then, when weather permitted, climb as high as he could to look for us before accepting the fact that we were lost. He had told his fears to the Hunzas, and together they had had a mournful time.

That night at Camp VI we had a magnificent dinner of tomato soup, canned ham, rice, and cups and cups and cups of tea but darkness overtook us before the cups were cleaned and the sleeping bags arranged. Pushing aside the stove and dishes, Houston and I fell asleep almost before we could pull ourselves into the two parts of my sleeping bag for Houston's bag, of course, had disappeared in the fall. Drugged as I was by exhaustion, my sleep was fitful, however, for Houston was out of his head again and all night long he kept getting out of the inner half of the sleeping bag, which he was using, and crawling about the tent. He was most anxious not to waken me and kept steadily apologizing for the trouble he was causing. "If I can just get out of this warehouse," he would say, "everything will be all right." Then, as best I could in the darkness, I would find the opening to his sleeping bag and try to get him inside. The next thing I knew, I would be awakened again by Houston crawling around the foot of my sleeping bag. "I'm terribly sorry to bother you," he would say. "If I can only get out of this warehouse. . . ."

Next morning the storm had increased in violence and we were apprehensive about starting down to Camp V for fear that George Bell would extend the damage already done to his feet. We were deeply worried about his condition. We feared that he might reach the point where he could not walk, and we hated to think what would happen then, for in our exhausted state and with a storm raging we could not carry anybody, let alone our biggest man, down along the ridges below. Since food and gasoline were short at Camp VI we were anxious to move some men down, and Schoening and Streather took advantage of a lull in the storm to push their way down to the next camp, but the lull ended and the rest of us stayed behind. Supplies of fuel were low and that night we went to bed with a cold supper and the realization that we had to start down again next day. Bell was now the main problem, for Houston was gaining strength and clarity of thought with remarkable rapidity.

August 13 was cold and windy with light snow falling, and much like the day we had moved down to Camp VI. Craig and Molenaar had had a cold night in the torn tent, and after cold meat bars for breakfast, they pulled on their packs and started down. Putting George Bell in the torn tent for shelter, Houston and I began trying to free the bottom of the tent we were in from ice, for it was necessary for us to carry down one tent, and the other one was ripped. Our tent had become iced-in during previous use, and our hands became frightfully cold as we hacked at the ice and pulled at the knots. Meanwhile the wind was getting at the tent Craig and I had emptied, so that by the time we had freed the tent that was to go down, the wind had torn the other one from end to end with Bell in it, and the whole fabric began to shred apart as we huddled in it to try to bring back sensation to our nipped fingers. Then, swinging on heavy packs, we started down to Camp V.

To our delight, Bell climbed steadily and safely. The route from VI to V was normally not particularly difficult, but with fresh snow on the rocks some of the route was dangerously coated with loose snow, especially in one gully. Here Houston did a fine job of anchoring the rope as I went ahead. He seemed almost his old self as we moved down onto a tiny scree slope and around a corner into Camp V. Craig and Molenaar were already there, and they made way for us to move in where Schoening and Streather pumped the stove to a red-hot roar and poured cup after cup of orange juice–flavored tea down our still dehydrated throats. They had battled the storm the day before and had been glad to reach camp safely.

Our descent was going well now and the storm had let up a bit, but there was no indication that another frightful blow wasn't on the way. "If we can only get below House's Chimney," someone said, "it will take mighty bad weather to hold us back after that." We were still going on reserve energy and it was now about two-thirty in the afternoon, but the thought of putting the last major barrier behind us spurred us on. Normally we could climb from Camp V to the top of House's Chimney in five minutes, and from there look down on the tents of Camp IV almost directly beneath.

Now it took over an hour of the hardest work to get to the top of the chimney. Craig and Molenaar, who went ahead, shouted up to watch out for the ice, for everything was glazed over and there was great danger of a slip's pulling a whole rope of men off the mountain. We had heavier loads now, Houston especially, and we concentrated grimly on crossing this dangerously exposed section safely. Even so, Houston and I had a number of unpleasant moments and cut many steps before we climbed to the base of the A-frame and looked down the fixed rope Craig and Molenaar had set up in House's Chimney. And 150 feet below us we could see them working on the tents at Camp IV.

The hour was late enough so that not a moment could be wasted to make the descent before dark. Houston insisted on belaying each man down in turn, and then we began to lower the packs to Schoening, who had climbed up the snow slope across from the foot of the chimney and made himself a platform there. These operations took time, for each pack had to be well secured, and it was almost dark when I climbed down the chimney and, guided by Schoening, crossed the ice steps to the rock outcrop from which we had hoisted loads three weeks earlier. Houston had been first man up the chimney and he wanted to be the last man down it, but it was nearly pitch-black by the time he left the tiny platform where he had been crouching so long and backed off the plunging cliff into space. Such a tangle of old and new ropes hung in the chimney that in the blackness the terrible thought swept over him that he was hanging on the wrong rope! Swinging out over this sheer cliff with the awesome gulf below is an impressive experience at any time, but it was doubly so to Houston, as with numb hands he launched himself out over the blackness, hoping that the rope was the right one and that it would reach the line of steps cut in the snow at the bottom.

The rope held, and Schoening was soon helping to guide Houston across the slope. A few minutes later we were all at the tent platforms of Camp IV, too tired to do more than swallow some tea, eat a cold meat bar for energy, and climb into our sleeping bags. Having House's Chimney behind us was a boost to our determination to get the whole party down safely. That night Molenaar, Houston, and I shared one tent, and I remember rubbing and rubbing to try to get feeling back into my toes. They didn't hurt and they weren't swollen, but try as I would, I couldn't bring back any sensation to some of my toes. Still, the chimney, which had been long in our thoughts, was now behind us and we lay down scarcely conscious of the dampness of the half sleeping bag each of us was using.

When another gray dawn broke on August 14, gaunt, hollow-eyed men began to stumble out onto the slippery scree to collect pieces of ice to melt. Craig's feet were very painful but George Bell was an even greater worry, for he was obviously now going on nerve alone. This morning his feet were so swollen that he couldn't get his boots on no matter how hard he struggled, and at last he was forced to slit the boots with a knife in order to pull them on. These openings wouldn't increase his protection against further cold damage, but at least they would permit him to climb down with something on his feet.

This time Streather and I started down ahead to find and improve the route if possible. We found powder snow masking loose rocks and making part of our upward route unusable. Worse still, most of our fixed ropes were completely buried and we had to hack and hack to cut steps in smooth ice that covered slopes we had descended with ease before. Cutting steps straight down is arduous work, and both Streather and I were feeling the strain of the past few days. A couple of hundred yards above Camp III, we checked a slip before it got started, and then Schoening took over the lead to give us a rest and began cutting the last of the steps needed to get to camp.

How rich the air seemed! We had descended the equivalent of five Eiffel Towers, or ten Washington Monuments, below Camp VIII, and that part of the mountain already seemed impossibly remote. New York and home by contrast now seemed almost around the corner. But we were not down by any means. Storm clouds shrouded the slopes above us, and we knew that if the ice we had met just above Camp III plastered the route to Camp II, the next part of the descent would be especially dangerous, for the continuous strain was having its effect on all of us.

Camp III was well stocked with food, and since the wind had dropped, we made a solid lunch there. Like starving men, we gulped down date bars with almonds in them, chunks of Gruyère cheese, dried apricots, biscuits, and chocolate. We mixed a can of concentrated orange juice with snow, beat the icy mixture with a spoon until it grew mushy, and then took turns gulping great spoonfuls. Our bodies sorely needed replenishing with hot food and sleep, but Camp II was calling to us, for we knew that our faithful Hunzas would be there. Also, it was imperative that Bell waste no time in getting as low as possible, for we realized that before long, no matter how much nerve he had, he would be unable to walk on his frozen feet.

Ice over the rocks would make the route below Camp III very dangerous, and while we were pondering whether to descend or wait until the next day, Schoening moved down to the traverse across the first gully and found not ice but firm snow. We were much impressed, for we had expected more of the ice we had found just above. Morale soared. We even added to our packs a few items that had been left in duffel bags at Camp III, and then continued the descent.

This time Houston, Bell, and Schoening went first on one rope; Streather and I followed; and Craig and Molenaar brought up the rear. More than ever we were determined not to slip, and despite the need for one delicate maneuver after another, no one fell. Luckily the ice was not so bad as we had feared, and we gained confidence as we climbed down. The mountain took one parting shot at us, however, for just before Schoening, Bell, and Houston turned off the main slope into the shelter of a safe gully, a rock plummeting with great speed and noise from high on the mountain whizzed within a few feet of their heads.

Streather had the walkie-talkie, and exactly at six o'clock he tried to call Ata-Ullah. There was no flat place near us. Actually at exactly six I was standing on one foot traversing a steep rock wall, and didn't dare to move for fear of dislodging Streather, who was in an only slightly more secure position with one hand on the walkie-talkie. We hoped to tell Ata-Ullah to send porters next day to the glacier near Camp I to help Bell down, but Ata couldn't hear us and Streather finally folded in the radio aerial and went on.

As we started down the last couloir (gully) toward Camp II, we could hear the Hunzas shouting, and as we stepped onto the last snow slope, Ghulam, Vilyati, and Hidayat, roped together with what looked like string, swarmed out onto the steep slope and embraced us with tears rolling down their cheeks. It was an overwhelming welcome and almost too much for us in more ways than one, for we were clinging to small holds and standing at the top of a steep couloir which fell away 1,500 feet to the glacier below. Such a position is not suited to an uninhibited heart-to-heart embrace!

Our packs were taken from us and these hardy frontiersmen, with tears streaking their cheeks, handed us down from rock to rock as if afraid that at the last moment we would collapse. As each one of us reached Camp II, where sleeping bags had been laid out in the rocks for us to sit on, each Hunza in turn with great emotion embraced each one of us. The storm had ebbed away, the wind had dropped, and the first stars we had seen for weeks were glittering in the night sky as Craig and Molenaar climbed down the last rock pitch above camp.

Our feeling of relief and luxury at that moment is too great to describe. The ship had been saved; the lost, found. Every man who had started down from the dreadful bivouac at Camp VII had reached the safety of Camp II and the protection of our Hunzas. That evening was one of the sweetest any of us will ever spend, for a sense of supreme peacefulness enveloped us. Yet we were sad, too. We talked about Art Gilkey, and the Hunzas cried and prayed in unison for him. They wanted to know what had happened and how we had forced our way down through the storm.

And slowly as we lay there on sleeping bags with our boots off in the warm, rich air, with a stove roaring cheerily *in the open* at our feet, we began to return to life. First the Hunzas fed us rice cooked in milk; then, with three stoves burning, we started on tea. Fuel and fire were plentiful here, and we made the most of it. Stacks of the flat pancakes called *chupattis* were cooked and pot after pot of tea and milk was brought over to us as we lay talking, relaxing, rubbing our feet, too emotionally stirred to go to bed. And all this while, kindly Hunza hands were kneading our tired muscles as only Asiatics can, bringing us back to life. At that heartwarming moment differences of race and language meant nothing. We and the Hunzas by the light of a flickering flare shared a great emotional experience as we talked and talked. Those who also have faced hardship and danger can appreciate our emotions and the bond between us all as we lay there. Then, after hours of delicious rest, we hoisted ourselves to our feet, staggered to our tents, and crawled gratefully into our sleeping bags. We had done it.

The K2 Mystery
by David Roberts

Writer and climber David Roberts has called Fritz Wiessner "the century's greatest mountaineer." The claim rests largely upon Wiessner's astonishingly strong climbing as leader of the 1939 American K2 expedition. But the outcome of the expedition, which ended with four deaths, clouded the German-born climber's reputation for decades. Roberts attempted to sort out—and helped rekindle—the controversy in a 1984 article for Outside *magazine.*

I t was July 19, 1939. At nine o'clock that morning, Fritz Wiessner and Sherpa Pasang Lama had left Camp IX at 26,000 feet on K2, the second-highest mountain in the world. All day long they had moved upward on slopes of snow, ice, and rock that had never before been climbed. Neither man used oxygen.

Throughout the day, Wiessner had stayed in the lead. At age thirty-nine, he was in the best shape of his life. And at that moment in history, there was no better mountaineer anywhere in the world.

Some of the climbing had been extraordinarily difficult, considering the altitude. With his crampons, ice axe, and handful of pitons, Wiessner had mastered, in succession, a couloir of black ice, a short overhang of iced-up rock, and two rope lengths of broken rock covered with a treacherous skin of ice called verglas. The air was still, however, and Wiessner had been able to take off his gloves and do the hardest moves bare-handed.

Now he made a short traverse to the left, then climbed twenty-five feet up a very demanding wall of rock. At the top of this section, he hammered in two pitons for security. With growing elation, he surveyed the terrain above. The wall continued for another twenty-five feet that, while difficult, lay back at a lower angle than the rock he had just climbed. He knew he could get up this obstacle without much trouble. Above the rock, there was an apparently easy snow slope leading to the summit. It was late afternoon. The two men had reached an altitude of more than 27,500 feet. At the very most, the top of K2 stood only 750 feet higher.

In that moment, Fritz Wiessner stood on the threshold of a deed that, had he accomplished it, might today be regarded as the single most outstanding triumph in the long history of mountaineering. By 1939, none of the highest peaks in the world had been climbed. Only the year before, the seventh major expedition to Everest had been defeated some 2000 feet below the summit, and a strong American effort on K2 had turned back at 26,000 feet. Many experts had begun to doubt that the highest mountains would ever be conquered without oxygen. There are fourteen peaks in the Himalaya that exceed 8000 meters in height. Success on an "eight-thousander" was to become the four-minute mile of climbing. Not until 1950, with the French on Annapurna, was the feat accomplished. Everest was not to be climbed until 1953; K2, not until the year after.

But that July day in 1939, Wiessner and Pasang Lama had K2 in their grasp. It would mean coming down in the night, but the weather was holding splendidly, and the moon would be out, and the two men were in superb condition. Wiessner had no qualms about descending the easy ridge from the summit during the night, if necessary.

He began to move up the last twenty-five feet of the wall. There was a tug at his waist as the rope came tight. Turning to look at his partner, Wiessner saw Pasang smile almost apologetically. As a Buddhist Lama, Pasang believed that angry spirits lurked about the summit at night. "No, sahib, tomorrow," said the Sherpa.

When he saw that his companion's resolve could not be shaken, Wiessner thought for a moment about unroping and going for the summit alone. In 1939, however, the ethics of climbing prevented a leader from leaving his partner. But there were twelve days' worth of food and fuel at Camp IX, and the good weather looked as though it would stay forever. He gave in and agreed to descend. The next day would surely bring success.

Never again would Wiessner reach such a height on K2. Instead of claiming a great triumph, he would find himself embroiled for the rest of his life in one of the bitterest controversies in mountaineering history. For reasons that remain unclear today, the camps that had been so carefully supplied as the team moved up the mountain had been systematically stripped—the sleeping bags were removed and much of the food thrown out in the snow. As an indirect result of this catastrophe, four members of the 1939 expedition perished on K2. Wiessner returned to the United States not to be laureled for his heroic attempt on the great mountain, but to be plunged into the unjust opprobrium of his peers.

Fritz Wiessner turned 84 this February. He still rock climbs regularly at a creditable standard. His long career has been crowned with achievement, both in and out of the mountains, and with deep happiness. Toward other climbers, Wiessner has always maintained a generous and magnanimous stance. For several generations of mountaineers all over the world, he has become a hero.

But K2 remains the great disappointment of his life, and when he talks about it his voice shakes with the sense of betrayal that has lingered in his memory of that expedition for the last forty-five years.

PART I: THE MOUNTAIN AND THE CLIMBER

K2 stands at the head of the Baltoro Glacier in the Karakoram of Pakistan, some 900 miles northwest of Everest. Seen from a distance, it is a striking, pyramidal peak, more beautiful than Everest, just as it is the harder ascent. The mountain was first attempted in 1902 by a small party that included the redoubtable Oscar Eckenstein, and again in

1909 by an Italian team led by the brilliant explorer Luigi Amedeo, Duke of the Abruzzi. Both parties had to turn back a little above 21,000 feet, nowhere near the 28,250-foot summit; but for such an early era, both expeditions were remarkable efforts.

The mountain was not attempted again until 1938, when a small but strong American party of four made a late but bold assault on the Abruzzi Ridge, the line first tried by the Italians. Paul Petzoldt, a cowboy from Wyoming, and Charles Houston, a Harvard-educated medical student, pushed up to 26,000 feet before having to quit. This expedition, too, had been an exceptional feat. Wiessner's attempt would be next.

His credentials were superb: born in Dresden in 1900, he had done his first climbs as a teenager in the Elbsteingebirge, the cluster of intimidating sandstone pinnacles near the banks of the river Elbe. In the second decade of this century, probably the hardest pure rock climbs in the world were done on these towers by Wiessner and his cronies, a fact not broadly recognized until the 1960s, thanks to the subsequent isolation of East Germany from the mainstream of climbing culture.

After World War I Wiessner moved on to the Alps, where he made some of the finest first ascents of the 1920s. Two of his most memorable were the southeast wall of the Fleischbank, which a German commentator later called "the great problem of its time," and the oft-attempted north wall of the Furchetta. In 1932 Wiessner went on his first Himalayan expedition, a pioneering effort on Nanga Parbat, where he reached 23,000 feet.

By 1929 Wiessner had emigrated to the United States, where he ran a very successful chemical business. He began climbing with American friends, in effect teaching them what European alpinism was all about. As Wiessner's latter-day friend Richard Goldstone puts it, "He probably went down a little bit in standard from what he had done in Germany when he came to the U.S. But he was so far ahead of the people here, they didn't understand what he was doing."

One of Wiessner's finest American accomplishments was the first ascent of Devils Tower in Wyoming in 1937, on which he led all the hard pitches. (Goldstone: "Fritz took along his standard three pitons.

He basically soloed it.") Another was the first ascent of Mount Waddington in British Columbia's Coast Range, certainly the hardest climb yet completed in North America.

It was Wiessner, in 1937, who first won official permission for an American expedition to K2, but business commitments prevented his going to Pakistan the next summer. Charles Houston took over the leadership of the 1938 expedition, while Wiessner retained permission for 1939, should Houston's party not reach the summit.

As he began planning for the 1939 expedition, Wiessner was disappointed that none of the four veterans from the previous year's attempt could go again. By spring he had recruited two other first-rank mountaineers, one of whom had led the second ascent of Mount McKinley. Only four weeks before the team's departure, however, both had to back out.

The remaining party was so weak that Wiessner pondered postponing the attempt for another year. But the American Alpine Club urged him to persevere, and so the team sailed for Europe in late spring. Two of the members, Chappell Cranmer and George Sheldon, were twenty-one-year-old Dartmouth students. Eaton Cromwell had made many climbs in the Alps and Canada, but none of great difficulty; he was now forty-two years old. Dudley Wolfe, at forty-four, was a strong skier and alpinist but had little technical experience. After the team had embarked, an AAC mentor persuaded twenty-eight-year-old Jack Durrance, a Teton guide and one of the country's best climbers, to join the expedition. To Wiessner's great surprise, Durrance showed up in Genoa with an explanatory letter from the well-meaning AAC executive.

"I was a little worried then," says Wiessner today. "I knew Jack as a great sportsman, and I knew he was strong. He had done some climbing in Munich when he lived there, and he had good climbs in the Tetons. But I also knew he was very competitive, which might cause troubles. Actually, at that time I liked Durrance, and hoped he could do well."

Wiessner lives in retirement on an idyllic country estate in Stowe, Vermont. He is a short man, perhaps five feet five. He looks extremely fit, and the barrel chest and strong arms of his best days are still in evidence. His bald pate and great-browed forehead dominate his expressive face: as he talks, strong wrinkles delineate his forehead, and his eyebrows arch with meaning. He speaks in a clear, emphatic voice, still heavy with a German accent. His manners and bearing breathe old-world civility; his smile could conquer a drawing room. But he is equally captivating when he conjures up the troubles of the past. And the troubles in 1939 began when Wiessner and Durrance met.

"After we had reached base camp," Wiessner says, "and were on our first trip up the glacier, I wanted to check a little bit on safety and roping. We had two ropes. Soon Jack's rope started to put up speed, trying to go faster than the others. Cromwell and Wolfe said to me, 'What's up? Do we have to do this running?' When we got back to base camp, I gave a long talk. I said, 'Look, fellows, I can tell you right now, we will never climb this mountain if there's competition between the members. Get it out of your head. We have to work really hard and work together.' Jack didn't say anything, but seemed to agree."

Nevertheless, during the first five weeks above base camp the expedition went much as planned. The 1939 party had the advantage of knowing where the 1938 camps had been placed and, in some of them, benefited from rock platforms that had been built the previous year. Slowly a logistical ladder of supplies was constructed up the mountain. The Sherpas were tremendously useful in stocking the camps. Each camp was equipped with three sleeping bags, air mattresses, stoves, and gasoline. "I believed," says Wiessner, "that if you climb a mountain like this, you want to be sure, if something goes wrong or somebody gets ill, you can hold out for at least two weeks in any camp. If a man had to come down in very bad weather, he ought to be able to just fall into a tent, and everything would be there."

But in other respects, Wiessner insisted on a spartan, lightweight style. Oxygen was standard on Everest, but Wiessner refused even to bring it to base camp on K2. "My ideal has always been free climbing," he explains. "I hated mechanical means. I didn't even want walkie-talkies on the mountain."

Even as the chain of supplies was being built up, some of the climbers were having trouble. Because of his late inclusion in the party, Durrance had to wait for his high-altitude boots, specially made in Munich, to arrive. Cranmer almost immediately came down with a serious illness, probably pulmonary or cerebral edema. At base camp, Durrance, who was a medical student, nursed him back to health. According to Wiessner, Cromwell had the idea that being up high for very long was unhealthy, and soon he too wanted to go down. Wiessner suspects that these worries, continually expressed, made Durrance apprehensive. Sheldon got chilblains on his toes and went no higher than Camp IV. Among the sahibs, only Dudley Wolfe kept up fully with the high-altitude work of Wiessner and the best Sherpas.

Once Durrance's boots had arrived, he started eagerly up the route with Wiessner and Wolfe. Carrying loads to Camp VI, however, he began to move very slowly. On July 12, after five days of storm, Wiessner, Wolfe, and Durrance, with seven Sherpas, prepared to ferry supplies from VI to VII. Says Wiessner, "A very short distance above VI, Jack told me, 'Fritz, something is wrong with me. I am ill. Maybe I am not well-enough adjusted to the altitude. I will go back to VI and come up tomorrow or the next day.'" Durrance turned around and descended to Camp VI.

Wiessner, Wolfe, and three Sherpas stayed at VII. The others returned with Durrance to VI, planning to bring more supplies the next day. But on July 14, instead of coming up with loads, Durrance retreated down the mountain. Even more unfortunately, from Wiessner's perspective, Durrance took two Sherpas with him, including the most experienced, Pasang Kikuli, who had been earmarked for a summit attempt but was suffering from frostbite. Wiessner's purist refusal to use walkie-talkie radios meant that he now had no way of communicating with Durrance, who did not stop until he was all the way down to Camp II.

The advance guard pushed on and established Camp VIII at 25,300 feet. From there, Wiessner sent two Sherpas down to VII to meet up with the anticipated contingent of Durrance and several Sherpas. Left at VIII were Wolfe, Pasang Lama, and Wiessner. After two days of storm, this trio set out upward again, but immediately got bogged down in extremely deep, loose snow. Wiessner literally had to swim through the drifts. Wolfe, the heaviest of the three, exhausted himself trying to flounder up a trough Wiessner had plowed in the drifts. He decided to return to camp and make another attempt the next day with the others. (Loose, new-fallen snow often compacts after a day of sun.)

Wiessner and Pasang Lama pushed on and established Camp IX. For security, they built a rock wall completely around the tent. The next day, July 19, they made their first attempt on the summit. It ended when Pasang, afraid of the coming night, refused to let out any more rope. "No, sahib, tomorrow!" he pleaded, and Wiessner gave in.

On the way down, as Pasang rappelled over a cliff, the rope got entangled in the crampons on the back of his pack—he was carrying both men's pairs. With a furious effort, the Sherpa got the rope loose, but the crampons came loose too. Wiessner watched with a sinking heart as they bounced away into the void. The descent grew more difficult, and only at 2:30 a.m. did the men regain Camp IX. To Wiessner's consternation, no one had arrived from below.

Nevertheless, the camp was well stocked and the weather continued to be perfect. Wiessner had decided on an easier alternative for the second attempt. It was a route up a gully that he had planned originally, but had given up when avalanches from an immense ice cliff near the summit had roared over it. On July 18, on their climb up to Camp IX, Wiessner and Pasang Lama had crossed the one-hundred-foot-wide track of such an avalanche, and this had led Wiessner to choose the more difficult rock-and-ice route of the first attempt. In the middle of that attempt, however, he had had a good view of the alternative route, and could see that no more avalanches were likely to come down for some time, and so the gully route was now safe.

The men rested the whole next day. It was so warm in the thin air that Wiessner sunbathed naked! At 6 a.m. on July 21—three hours earlier than their previous attempt—the two men left Camp IX to go for the summit. The alternative route lay over hard snow that had turned, in the sun, to ice. The loss of the crampons came home with a vengeance. In the crucial gully, as Wiessner later wrote, "With crampons, we could have practically run up it, but as it was we would have had to cut 300 or 400 steps. At these heights that would have taken more than a day." Once again the two men descended to Camp IX.

Wiessner was still quite confident of making the summit, however. The team members coming up in support would undoubtedly have crampons, as well as more provisions. Thinking his teammates were probably ensconced at Camp VIII, Wiessner decided to go down on July 22 to pick up Wolfe, more food and gas, and the all-important crampons. Pasang carried his sleeping bag down, but Wiessner, certain he would return, left his in the tent at Camp IX.

Without crampons, the descent was tricky, especially since the Tricouni nails (which climbers used on the soles of their boots in the days before Vibrams) had been worn dull on both men's footgear. "Pasang was behind me," recalls Wiessner. "I should have had him in front, but then I would have had to explain to him how to cut steps. I had just got my axe ready to make a few scrapes, when suddenly he fell off. I noticed immediately, because he made a funny little noise. I put myself in position, dug in as much as possible, and held him on the rope. If I hadn't been in good shape, hadn't climbed all those 4000-meter peaks in the Alps, I wouldn't have had the technique to hold him." Wiessner makes such a belay sound routine, but it was a difficult feat.

At VIII, Wiessner had expected to find Durrance and the other Sherpas with their precious loads. Instead, Dudley Wolfe was there alone. He was overjoyed to see Wiessner, but furious that no one had come up from below. He had run out of matches two days before and had been able to drink only a little meltwater that had run off a ground cloth.

By now Wiessner was utterly perplexed by the absence of reinforcement from below. At Camp VII, however, he knew the bulk of the reserve food had already been cached. With a quick trip down to VII for supplies, the three men could still probably climb K2 without any help from below. Wiessner could use Wolfe's pair of crampons to lead the ice.

So on July 23 the trio started down to VII. Wolfe, not the most graceful of climbers even on his good days, was tied in to the middle of the rope. Pasang Lama was ten or fifteen feet in front, Wiessner the same distance in the rear. Once again the snow got icy, and Wiessner had to go first to cut steps. As he leaned over in a precarious position, Wolfe accidentally stepped on the rope. The jolt pulled Wiessner off.

"I immediately called back, 'Check me! Check me!'" Wiessner remembers. "Nothing happened. Then the rope came tight to Dudley, and he was pulled off. The rope tightened to Pasang behind, and he too came off. We were all three sliding down, and I got going very fast and somersaulted.

"I had no fear. All I was thinking was, how stupid this has to happen like this. Here we are, we can still do the mountain, and we have to lose out in this silly way and get killed forever. I didn't think about family, and of course I was never a believer in Dear Old God.

"But getting pulled around by the somersault and being first on the rope, it gave me a little time. I still had my ice axe—I always keep a sling around my wrist—and just in that moment the snow got a little softer. I had my axe ready and worked very hard with it. With my left hand I got hold of the rope, and eventually I got a stance, kicked in quickly, and leaned against the axe. Then, bang! A fantastic pull came. I was holding it well, but it tore me down. But at that time I was a fantastically strong man—if I had a third of it today I would be very happy. I stood there and I wanted to stop that thing. I must have done everything right, and the luck was there, too. "

Wiessner's belay has become the stuff of legend. Very few men in all of mountaineering history have performed the like: having already been pulled off a slope, to recover, gain a stance, and, with only the pick of an ice axe for purchase, to stop the otherwise fatal falls of three men roped together.

The men made their way on down to Camp VII at 24,700 feet. There they received an incomprehensible shock. Not only was there no one in camp: The tents had been left with the doors open. One was full of snow, the other half-collapsed. The provisions that had been so carefully carried up nine days before lay wantonly strewn about in the snow. Most of the food was missing, as were all the sleeping bags.

Utterly dismayed and confounded, the three men cleaned out one tent and repitched it. It was too late to go farther down. With one sleeping bag and no air mattresses, they huddled through a bitterly cold night. In the morning the weather was raw and windy. Wolfe decided to stay with the one bag at Camp VII while Wiessner and Pasang went down to VI. Despite all their setbacks, the trio was still of a mind to push upward. Surely there would be sleeping bags and food still at VI, and there ought to be at least six Sherpas there as well.

On July 23 the two men headed down. At VI they found only a dump of two unpitched tents and some provisions: again the sleeping bags and air mattresses were gone. Grimly Wiessner and Pasang continued the descent. Camp V, IV, III . . . still no sleeping bags. At nightfall, the men reached Camp II, supposedly the best-provisioned camp on the mountain. No sleeping bags! Utterly worn out, Wiessner and Pasang took down one tent and wrapped themselves up in it while they tried to sleep in the other. Their fingers and toes froze, and they got no sleep.

By the time the two men reached the level glacier the next day, they were dragging themselves along, often falling. Wiessner recalls the effort: "We were so exhausted. We would go 100 or 200 meters, then sit down a little. Suddenly we look, and there comes a party up the glacier. It was Cromwell with some Sherpas. My throat had gotten very sore, and I could hardly speak, but I was mad enough. I asked him, 'What is the idea?'

"He told me they had given us up for dead. He was just out looking to see if he could find any sign of anything on the glacier. I said, 'This is really an outrage. Wolfe will sue you for your neglect.' We went on to base camp. The cook and the liaison officer came out and embraced me and took me to my tent. Pasang Kikuli and all the Sherpas came and embraced me. But Durrance didn't come for about half an hour.

"When he did, I said immediately, 'What happened to our supplies? Who took all the sleeping bags down? And why were they taken down?' Durrance said, 'Well, the Sherpas . . .' It was blamed on the Sherpas."

It is a measure of Wiessner's intense commitment to K2 that even after such a colossal setback, he still had hopes of making another attempt on the summit. All that was needed to rebuild the logistical ladder, he reasoned, was to get the sleeping bags back into the camps and to bolster the food supplies above. Also, Dudley Wolfe was waiting alone at Camp VII. On July 26, Durrance and three Sherpas set out, hoping to climb all the way up to VII. Wiessner planned to follow in two days, after recuperating from his ordeal.

Durrance, however, could go only as far as Camp IV before altitude sickness forced him down again on the third day. He left two Sherpas at IV, with instructions to go up to VII and explain matters to Wolfe. Meanwhile, Wiessner had not recovered from his debilitating descent, and Pasang Lama was in even worse shape. When Durrance reappeared, Wiessner realized that at last all hope of climbing K2 had to be abandoned. It remained only to bring Wolfe down.

Despite his exhausted state, Wiessner wanted to try to climb up to VII himself, but Pasang Kikuli dissuaded him, saying he himself would go up to get Wolfe and bring him down. Instead, on July 29, Kikuli and another Sherpa went all the way from base camp to VI—a gain of 6800 feet—in a single day. This feat of fortitude remains virtually unmatched in Himalayan history. On the way, Kikuli picked up the two Sherpas who had been left by Durrance at Camp IV.

The next day, this rescue team of four found Wolfe in a bad state. He had lost, it seemed, the will to live. Again he had run out of matches, and he had lain apathetically in his bag without eating. He had grown so lethargic, in fact, that he had not left the tent to defecate. The Sherpas tried to rouse him, but he declared that he needed another day of rest before he could make the descent. Without sleeping bags, the Sherpas could not stay at VII, so they went down to VI, determined to try to prod Wolfe into descending the next day. A storm intervened, and it was not until the day after, July 31, that Pasang Kikuli, Pinsoo, and Kitar started out again to climb up to VII. They left Tsering alone in VI with orders to have tea ready.

At base camp, little could be known of the doings high on the mountain. Through binoculars Durrance had seen three figures cross the snow just below Camp VII. Finally, on August 2, a terrified Tsering returned to base alone. On July 31 he had brewed tea and waited. No one had come the rest of the day, nor all of the next day. After that, he could wait no longer.

Wiessner made one more attempt to go up the route. He left on August 3, with two Sherpas, and it took him two days to "drag" himself, in his own phrase, to Camp II. On August 5 a full-scale storm broke, dumping twelve inches of snow and ending any further hopes of rescue. On August 7 the expedition turned its back on K2.

The fate of Dudley Wolfe, Pasang Kikuli, Pinsoo, and Kitar has never been determined. It may be that the Sherpas reached Wolfe, and all four men perished in an avalanche or in a roped fall like the one Wiessner had barely managed to stop. No trace of any of the four has ever been found.

PART II: AFTERMATH

During Wiessner's absence in the middle of July, the mood at base camp had worsened. Sheldon, Cranmer, and Cromwell wanted nothing more than to head for home. In the end Cranmer and Cromwell left early, leaving Wiessner and Durrance to bring up the rear as the expedition left the Baltoro Glacier for good.

"We were together every day," says Wiessner. "Durrance looked after me as if I were a baby. He made pancakes for me. And every day we talked. I just couldn't comprehend what had happened on the mountain. 'I don't understand it, Jack,' I told him, 'why those sleeping bags were taken out after all our agreements.' He kept answering, 'It was a matter of those Sherpas.'

"I kept asking him. Finally, he stood there and shouted, 'Ah, Fritz! Stop it! Stop it! We have talked about it long enough!'"

Once the men reached civilization, they parted. World War II had broken out. Wiessner traveled from Karachi to Port Said, then took a liner back to the United States. Durrance traveled in the other direction, across the Pacific. The two men would not set eyes on each other again until thirty-nine years had passed.

Upon his return, Wiessner went into a hospital in New York City. His many nights out on K2 had caused severe arthritic problems in his knees. He was bedridden for six weeks. Durrance came to New York City, stayed in a hotel, and sent some belongings to Wiessner in the hospital. He never paid a visit.

In his bed, Wiessner brooded about the stripped camps. He had talked not only to Durrance but to the Sherpas. They tended to blame Tendrup, one of their younger men. Gradually Wiessner deduced that, after he had parted with Durrance on July 14, something like the following chain of events must have unfolded.

Durrance had immediately descended to Camp II, taking with him Pasang Kikuli and another Sherpa. This left two Sherpas at Camp VI, who were soon joined by the two sent down by Wiessner. Kikuli had appointed Tendrup the leader of this group of four. Their orders were to carry loads to Camps VII and VIII in support of the summit effort.

Tendrup, however, came down with Kitar from a ferry to Camp VII, claiming that he was sure the three men in the lead had been killed in an avalanche and urging all the Sherpas to descend at once. The other two Sherpas refused to go along with the story and stayed put in Camp VI. Tendrup and Kitar descended to IV, where they ran into Pasang Kikuli, who angrily ordered them back up the mountain. So the pair made another foray up to VII. There they yelled up toward VIII, but got no answer. The silence added credibility to Tendrup's avalanche story, and the four Sherpas broke open Camp VII, scattering the supplies on the snow—exactly why remains problematic—before heading down the mountain with the sleeping bags from VI and VII. At base camp, the other Sherpas called Tendrup a devil who wanted to wreck the expedition. Wiessner concluded, however, that Tendrup was not so much malevolent as lazy—that he had invented the avalanche story to get out of carrying loads. Even so, this explained only the missing bags at VI and VII. Why had the lower camps also been stripped? Wiessner puzzled over this point for days. Then, he says, among his personal papers from the expedition, he came across a note he had earlier overlooked. It had been left for him by Durrance at Camp II on July 19.

According to Wiessner, the note congratulated him and Wolfe for making the summit, then explained that the day before (July 18, on the eve of Wiessner and Pasang Lama's first summit attempt) he had ordered the bags from the higher camps and from Camps IV and II—thirteen bags in all—taken down to base, in anticipation of the expedition's departure and to save valuable equipment. The implication was that Durrance assumed Wiessner, Wolfe, and Pasang Lama would be bringing their own bags down all the way from Camp IX. When Wiessner had found this note at Camp II, he had been too exhausted and emotionally overwrought to make sense of it. Now, in the hospital, it supplied the missing piece to the puzzle.

Wiessner says today, "As I told others, I had no ill feelings against Durrance, but I thought a man should be honest. If only he had come to me and said, 'I'm sorry, Fritz, I made a mistake. I meant the best. I wanted to save the sleeping bags,' I would have accepted this without hard feelings." But Durrance never communicated with Wiessner.

According to Wiessner, he deposited the all-important note in the files of the American Alpine Club. When he later tried to locate it, it was gone. Assuming Wiessner's interpretation is correct, what could have possessed Durrance to pull out support so flagrantly behind the summit trio? The defeatist mood of base camp must have contributed to a shared impatience to go home. Moreover, the sleeping bags were the most valuable gear on the expedition. If indeed Wiessner, Wolfe, and Pasang Lama had made the summit and descended without mishap, they would probably have brought their own sleepings bags with them, obviating the need for the bags in the intermediate camps. Sitting at base camp day after day with no news from above is a vexing business: the mind all too easily begins to invent theories about the maneuvers out of sight above. More than one Himalayan leader has felt the urge to pull out and go home while the advance guard was still high on the mountain. But another suggestion with respect to K2 is that everyone at base camp had given Wiessner's party up for dead and the survivors were retrieving the equipment. Cromwell had virtually admitted this when he had found Wiessner and Pasang Lama staggering across the glacier.

What was done was done. The loss of four men on K2 was a deep tragedy, but Wiessner's extraordinary feat in reaching 27,500 feet without oxygen, with no strong teammates except the Sherpas, ought to have been widely hailed for its excellence. Instead, one of the sorriest chapters in American climbing politics was about to unfold.

The American Alpine Club launched an investigation of the expedition, headed by some of the most distinguished men in American mountaineering. Ostensibly, their purpose was to "point the way towards a greater control of the risks undertaken in climbing great mountains." But the investigation report made some patronizing conclusions. It claimed that the expedition's "human administration seems to have been weak"; that there was "no clear understanding" of plans between Durrance and Wiessner when they parted; that it was an "error in judgment" to leave Sherpas alone in the middle camps; and that an ill climber (presumably Wolfe, who was not in fact ill) should not have been left alone to make his own decisions. The brunt of all these criticisms fell on Wiessner. Correspondingly, the committee gave Durrance's actions an implicit but total whitewash. The club sent a letter to members summarizing the report and ended by congratulating itself for the investigation, with its "valuable contribution" in the way of guidance "if Himalayan expeditions are undertaken again."

There were two significant calls of dissent. One came from Al Lindley, the strong mountaineer who had had to back out of K2 shortly before the party left for Pakistan. Lindley argued cogently that Wiessner was being dealt a serious injustice by the report, for the simple reason that "the action of the Sherpas and Durrance in evacuating these camps was so much the major cause of the accident that the others are insignificant." The other came from Robert Underhill, who as much as any American had brought the techniques of the Alps to this country. Underhill's long rebuttal came to this eloquent conclusion:

> What impresses me most is the fact that thruout all the bad
> weather, the killing labor and the grievous disappointments,
> [Wiessner] still kept up his fighting spirit. Except Wolfe, the

rest of the party were excusably enough, finished and thru—
quite downed by the circumstances; toward the end they
wanted only to get out and go home. Wiessner, with Wolfe
behind him, was the only one who still wanted to climb the
mountain. Far be it from me to blame the others; I know well
that if I had been there myself I should have come to feel
exactly the same way, and probably much sooner. But this
leads me to appreciate Wiessner the more. He had the guts—
and there is no single thing finer in a climber, or in a man.

These wise appeals, however, fell on deaf ears. In November 1941,
Wiessner resigned from the American Alpine Club.

To understand the harshness of the American reaction, one must
reflect on the climate of the 1930s. The British, who had invented
alpinism a century before, were becoming increasingly conservative as
climbers. The best routes in the Alps were being done by Germans,
Austrians, and Italians. As political tensions between Britain and
Germany escalated in the 1930s, British rock climbers began to dero-
gate their German counterparts as suicidal risk-takers. There was no
more dangerous prewar climbing arena than the north face of the
Eiger, where the best alpinists in Europe competed for the first ascent,
at the cost of a number of lives. When four Germans succeeded in
1938, Hitler awarded them medals. These likable young men were
thoroughly apolitical; nevertheless, a sour-grapes reaction dismissed
them and their brethren as Nazi fanatics, throwing their lives away on
Nordwände for the glory of *Führer* and *Vaterland*.

In this nasty debate, American climbers, who were technically
decades behind the Europeans, tended to sympathize with the British.
Fritz Wiessner, though he had come to America in 1929, long before
Hitler had risen to power, was a German; he was a far better climber
than anyone in this country; and he seemed willing to take greater risks
than American climbers. The AAC reaction to K2, then, amounted to
institutional conservatism tinged with the chauvinistic passions of the
onset of the war.

The drama reached its nadir a few months after Wiessner was released from the hospital. "One day my secretary in my New York office told me that two men from the FBI had come by," Wiessner recalls. "I went down to the FBI office and met two very nice young chaps—they were both Yale graduates. We sat down and talked. They wanted to know my whole history, and they had the funniest questions. Such as, 'You go skiing often in Stowe in the winter, do you not? That's very near Canada, isn't it? Can you get easily over the border?' I said, 'Yes. It's quite a distance to walk, but I am in Canada very often anyway because I have a business in Toronto.' And they laughed.

"I wasn't very keen on Roosevelt then. And so they said, 'You don't like the president? You made some remarks about him.' I said, 'Well, I wasn't the only one. There are very many people who feel that way!' They laughed again.

"They asked about some of my friends. We sat there half an hour, then we just talked pleasantly. On the way out I said, 'Now look, fellows, I was pretty open to you. I have my definite suspicions. Would you tell me the names of the men who put you up to this?' They said, 'Naturally we can't do that.' So I said, 'Let me ask this question: Was it some climbers from the AAC?' They nodded. They said, 'Don't worry about it. You know who we had here yesterday? We had Ezio Pinza, the famous opera singer. It was the same thing, a little jealousy from his competitors. They complained that he was a Mussolini follower.'"

Wiessner can joke about the episode today, but it must have been a chilling encounter.

The 1939 K2 expedition began to recede into the past. In 1956, in the journal *Appalachia*, Wiessner published a brief, restrained narrative of the climb from his point of view. The editor invited any readers with dissenting versions to speak up. None did.

Sadly, the expedition itself settled into a somewhat ambiguous place in climbing history. At its worst, the second-guessing British analysis prevailed; thus a book like Kenneth Mason's *Abode of Snow*, summarizing an utterly garbled version of the events on K2, could sermonize, "It is difficult to record in temperate language the folly of this enterprise."

Wiessner for the most part put the controversy behind him. In 1945 he married Muriel Schoonmaker, an American woman, with whom he has climbed and traveled extensively for almost forty years. Their daughter, Polly, is a research anthropologist; their son, Andrew, an adviser to Representative John Seiberling.

Most climbers tail off drastically after the age of forty or quit altogether. Wiessner has climbed steadily now for seventy years. In the United States he pioneered routes on local cliffs all over the country. As Richard Goldstone says, "There are these crags in the woods that people come upon and think they've discovered. Then they find a rusty old piton high on some route. Fritz was there in the 1940s."

Well into his seventies, Wiessner could still lead 5.9 climbs comfortably. Even today, at the age of eighty-four—hobbled by the arthritis that has plagued his joints since 1939, the survivor of a heart attack on a climb in France in 1969—Wiessner can second some 5.9s, and he regularly goes to the Shawangunks of New York State and solos both up and down easy routes that he "put in" forty years ago. There is no other example in mountaineering history of a climber keeping up such standards at that age.

In 1966 a number of AAC members, led by Bill Putnam, Andy Kauffman, and Lawrence Coveney, persuaded Wiessner to rejoin the club. In an act that went some way toward expiating the wrong that had been done him years before, the club soon afterward made him an honorary member for life.

In December 1978, the annual AAC banquet meeting was held in Estes Park, Colorado. The previous summer, four Americans had finally reached the top of K2. The slide shows to be presented at the meeting were accordingly focused on K2, and Jack Durrance, who lives nearby in Denver, was invited to talk. Wiessner got word of this development and flew back from a meeting in Europe in order to be present. This writer, who was present, vividly remembers the events that ensued.

All day in Estes Park the rumors flew that the long-delayed confrontation was about to take place. Durrance was finally going to tell "his side" of the story. Meanwhile, a veteran of the 1953 K2 expedition managed to talk Wiessner and Durrance into saying hello to each other. It was the first time they had met since parting in India in 1939. The meeting was curt in the extreme.

A number of AAC old-timers took Durrance aside. They managed to talk him out of making any inflammatory remarks. Their belief was that whatever dirty laundry remained from 1939, this meeting to celebrate American success on K2 was not the place or time to air it. Durrance gave in. His slide show carried the expedition up to base camp, then closed abruptly with a photo of himself in "retirement" in a cabin near the Tetons.

Later, at the banquet, Wiessner was given a special toast in recognition of his years of service to mountaineering. The crowd's reaction was deeply emotional, and the whole assemblage rose to its feet, applauding wildly—except for Durrance, who remained seated, his face fixed in a scowl.

In the course of researching this article, I asked Jack Durrance for his version of the events. Though he has never publicly told his side of the story, Durrance consented to an interview, during which that version emerged. On later reflection, however, Durrance decided against allowing his remarks to be published.

For more than forty years, the 1939 K2 expedition has lain under a cloud of criticism and rumor. Yet younger climbers the world over have come to an appreciation of it that is relatively free of the biases that animated the 1930s. And their response has been one of almost unilateral reverence and awe.

Wiessner was far ahead of his time. His refusal to rely either on oxygen or radio, criticized as cranky in his day, has come to seem an uncompromisingly high-minded example of "clean climbing." The logistical organization of the assault was utterly brilliant. Good weather helped the expedition get as high as it got, but the solid buildup of camps with tents, food, and gas amounted to the kind of textbook execution no other expedition had yet pulled off in the Himalaya.

The most astounding facet of this accomplishment is that Wiessner performed it with only one able-bodied American teammate and a group of dedicated Sherpas. The other four sahibs were of only marginal help low on the mountain. Equally astonishing is the fact that Wiessner led every bit of the route himself. On contemporary expeditions to Everest, the route had been put in only by the laborious leapfrogging of separate teams. On K2 in 1939, one man "in the shape of my life" broke every step of virgin ground himself.

Then, at his highest point, he was ready to climb through the night to reach the summit—a feat that had never been attempted in the Himalaya. There were only, at most, 750 feet to go; as subsequent parties found, those last 750 feet were mostly easy walking on a snow ridge. It is possible that even Wiessner might have lacked the strength to cover that last bit, but it seems more likely that he would have made it.

Forty-five years from his decision late that afternoon of July 19, Wiessner wonders whether he made a mistake. He considers what he might do, given another chance, at the moment when Pasang Lama balked and held the rope tight. "If I were in wonderful condition like I was then," he says, "if the place where my man stood was safe, if the weather was good, if I had a night coming on like that one, with the moon and the calm air, if I could see what was ahead as I did then . . . then I probably would unrope and go on alone." Wiessner pauses, his thoughts wrapped in the past. "But I can get pretty weak, if I feel that my man will suffer. He was so afraid, and I liked the fellow. He was a comrade to me, and he had done so well."

g l o s s a r y

abseil. A method of descending a slope or cliff using rope with a friction device to slow the descent. (see *rappel*).

alpine-style. A method of climbing that calls for fast, light-weight, small-scale assaults. In recent years this style has become routine even on peaks and routes once attempted only by expeditions employing multiple camps, fixed ropes and large teams of porters.

anchor. Natural features or manmade devices that hold climbers and gear on a mountain slope or cliff.

arête. A steep narrow ridge.

belay. A method of using a rope and friction device to soften the potential consequences of a climber's fall.

bergschrund. The gap or crevasse between a glacier and the upper part of a climb.

bivouac. An impromptu or sketchy overnight camp consisting of light-weight, minimal shelter at best—a snowhole or "bivvy sack," for example.

carabiner (also *karabiner*). A metal snap-link used for purposes such as attaching climbers to anchors.

chimney. A crack in the rock or ice wide enough to enter and climb from inside.

col. A pass or dip in a ridge.

cornice. A mass of snow projecting over the edge of a ridge or cliff. Climbers have been known to step through cornices.

couloir. An open gully.

crevasse. A crack created by movement in a glacier. Crevasses are especially dangerous when snow covers them.

cwm. A rounded hollow at the head or side of a valley.

fixed ropes. Ropes left in place during a climb to protect or assist team members as they move up and down a long mountain route.

jumar. Friction device to help climbers ascend fixed ropes on steep terrain.

moraine. Gravel, rocks, sand, and the like carried by glacial movement.

pitch. A stretch of climbing between two belay stances.

piton. A metal peg hammered into a rock crack to serve as an anchor or protection.

protection. Pitons, natural features or other devices used to make a pitch safer to lead. A lead climber who is ahead of a belayer can safeguard himself or herself by placing protection in the rock, ice or snow, then letting his or her rope run through a carabiner attached to the protection.

rappel. A method of descending a slope or cliff using rope with a friction device to slow the descent. (see *abseil*).

serac. A large block, pinnacle or tower of ice.

spindrift. Powder snow carried by wind or small avalanches.

verglas. A thin layer of ice.

a c k n o w l e d g m e n t s

Many people made this anthology.

At Thunder's Mouth Press and Avalon Publishing Group:
Neil Ortenberg and Susan Reich offered vital support and expertise.
Dan, Ghadah, and Jeri were also indispensable.

At Balliett & Fitzgerald Inc.:
Sue Canavan designed the book, found the artwork to illustrate each
selection and labored mightily to put the thing to bed; her good
nature is as impressive as her eye. Tom Dyja and f-stop Fitzgerald gen-
erously shared their time and contacts to land permissions for some
selections. Maria Fernandez smoothly managed production, despite
many other pressing demands upon her time. Mike Walters and Aram
Song kept things moving.

At the Thomas Memorial Library in Cape Elizabeth, Maine:
The librarians helped us to find many, many books. Karla Sigel
deserves special thanks.

At the Writing Company:
Meghan Murphy gathered books, permissions and facts. Mark Klimek
helped run things and, with Nate Hardcastle and Shawneric Hachey,
gracefully took up slack on various projects while I read books.

At various publishing companies and literary agencies:
Many people supported this project. Nick Lyons and Mary Metz
deserve special mention.

Among friends and family:
Ellen Brodkey helped expedite permissions for some important selections. Thanks also for friendship, support and counsel to John
Climaco, Mike Jewell, Anne McFarlain, Judy Mello, Jay Schwamm,
and my brother Perry Willis. My sons, Abner Willis and Harper Willis,
make my day, daily. Jennifer Willis worked harder on this book than
anyone: gathering materials, helping to choose selections, tracking
rights, negotiating permissions, issuing contracts and doing everything else that had to be done. I would be astonished at such generosity, but she's like that all the time.

This book was worth doing just for the pleasure of working with Will
Balliett. He's always right, and I always agree with him.

Finally, I am grateful to the writers whose work appears on these
pages.

b i b l i o g r a p h y

The excerpts used in this anthology were taken from the editions listed below. In some cases, other editions may be easier to find. Two sources worth trying are The Adventurous Traveler Bookstore in Williston, Vermont (800/282-3963) and Chessler Books in Evergreen, Colorado (800/654-8502). Internet sources also may be able to locate these titles.

Bonatti, Walter. *On the Heights*. London: Rupert Hart-Davis, 1964.

Bonington, Chris. *Everest the Hard Way*. New York: Random House, 1976.

Bonington, Chris and Clarke, Charles. *Everest: The Unclimbed Ridge*. New York: Random House, 1984.

Burgess, Alan and Palmer, Jim. *Everest Canada: The Ultimate Challenge*. Toronto: Stoddart, 1983.

Coffey, Maria. *Fragile Edge*. London: Chatto & Windus, 1989.

Dickinson, Matt. *The Other Side of Everest*. New York: Times Books, 1999.*

Haberl, Jim. *K2: Dreams and Reality*. Vancouver: Tantalus Publishing Ltd., 1994.

Houston, Charles S. and Bates, Robert H. *Five Miles High*. New York: Dodd, Mead and Company, 1939.

Houston, Charles S. and Bates, Robert H. *K2: The Savage Mountain*. New York: McGraw- Hill , 1954.

Krakauer, Jon. *Eiger Dreams: Ventures Among Men and Mountains*. New York: The Lyons Press, 1990.

Ridgeway, Rick. *The Last Step*. Seattle: The Mountaineers, 1980.

Roberts, David. *Moments of Doubt and Other Mountaineering Writing*. Seattle: The Mountaineers, 1986.

Rowell, Galen. *In the Throne Room of the Mountain Gods*. San Francisco: Sierra Club Books , 1986.

Smythe, F. S. *Camp Six: An Account of the 1933 Everest Expedition*. London: Hodder and Stoughton, 1934.

Stokes, Brummie. *Soldiers and Sherpas: A Taste for Adventure*. London: Michael Joseph, 1988.

Webster, Ed. *Snow in the Kingdom: My Storm Years on Everest*. Eldorado Springs, Colorado: Mountain Imagery, 1998.

* This book was previously published in 1997 by Hutchinson, as *The Death Zone* .

adrenaline ™

Read these other exciting titles from
Adrenaline Books

EPIC: Stories of Survival from the World's Highest Peaks

A collection of 15 memorable accounts of legend-making
expeditions to the world's most famous mountains, including
selections by Jon Krakauer, Greg Child, David Roberts
and Maurice Herzog.
$16.95 ($25.50 Canada), 336 pages

ROUGH WATER: Stories of Survival from the Sea

A unique collection of 16 pieces of great writing about storms,
shipwrecks and human resourcefulness. Includes work by
Patrick O'Brian, John McPhee, and Herman Wouk, as well as a
story previously unpublished in book form by Sebastian Junger.
$16. 95 ($25.50 Canada), 368 pages

All Adrenaline Books are available at your
neighborhood bookstore, or directly from the publisher.

Send your check or money order to:
Publishers Group West
Attention: Order Department
1700 Fourth St
Berkley, CA 94710.

Please indicate the title or titles you wish to purchase,
and the number of titles; include $4 shipping and
handling for the first book ($5 international),
and $.75 for each additional book ($1 international).

Please allow 4 to 6 weeks for delivery.